HELLO

Olá

SCHÖN DICH
ZU TREFFEN

MEET
YOU
AGAIN

+

こんにちは

Visual greetings on business cards,
greeting cards and invitations

WIE
GEHT

BONJOUR
BONJOUR
BONJOUR

*

CIAO

HOLA

好久
不見

만나서
반가워

viction:ary

NICE TO MEET YOU AGAIN

Visual greetings on business cards, greeting cards and invitations

First published and distributed by viction workshop ltd

viction:ary

viction workshop ltd
Unit C, 7/F, Seabright Plaza, 9-23 Shell Street,
North Point, Hong Kong
Url: www.victionary.com
Email: we@victionary.com
www.facebook.com/victionworkshop
www.twitter.com/victionary_
www.weibo.com/victionary

Edited and produced by viction:ary

Concept & art direction by Victor Cheung
Book design by viction workshop ltd

ISBN 978-988-13203-4-6
Printed and bound in China

NICE TO MEET YOU AGAIN
Visual greetings on business cards, greeting cards and invitations
Published and edited by
viction:ary

Quality will be recognised and a generous gesture will be remembered.

Andreas Friberg Lundgren
Co-founder and Art Director, Lundgren+Lindqvist

FOREWORD

In a not so distant future, I imagine my future self explaining the term 'business card' to a twenty-something, stepping off his hover board to pick up the card that I have just mistakenly dropped on the pavement. A stuttering "Back when I was young..." is met with a reluctant glance from the polite youngster. In a world where most information is available just a few taps away, even manually typing someone's name and number into your smartphone's address book can be a strain.

Let's face it — the business card may no longer be the matter of course that it once was, proudly residing in the briefcase of each business man and woman. However, this does not necessarily mean that the card has lost its status. On the contrary, as business cards are rapidly transcending into exception rather than rule, presenting somebody with a well-considered, physical item rather than a v-card will surely make a lasting impression.

When done right, a business card will do much more than simply bearing somebody's contact details — it will instigate a dialogue and mark the starting point of a relationship. Gone are the days when just any, low quality, flappy card could do the job. Today, the business card will have to motivate its existence through capitalising on the few but significant advantages it still holds over its digital counterparts. A carefully selected paper stock will remind the holder of the subtle beauty of materials. An embossed detail; of the exquisite craftsmanship of the experienced printer, working under the wing of his trusted Heidelberg press. Feel the card's weight in your hand and slowly stroke its surface, allowing your fingertips to register every grain in the paper. To some, the experience is almost sexually charged. Although not all of us will share the interest in stationery displayed by the humorously vain men in that famous scene in American Psycho (2000) — quality will be recognised and a generous gesture will be remembered.

Our conversion into living and communicating increasingly through computers, smartphones and tablets, has surely accelerated an evolution in which the business card will have to adapt and evolve in order to continue to exist as something more than an item of nostalgia. This has led designers to think of business cards as multi-functional objects, capable of doing more than just telling its recipient what number to dial. Suddenly, a business card is also a bookmark, a ruler or even a bottle opener. The really efficient solutions are the ones that build upon the nature of their owners' business, rather than those which equip cards with unnecessary functionality, just for the sake of entertainment.

In tandem with this development, the interest in visual culture and graphic design is bigger than ever before, and business cards are not an exception — as manifested by the many vibrant books on the subject. On Pinterest, a search for 'business card' will generate uncountable results. While PDFs and encrypted email systems are steadily pushing printed letterheads and invoices closer to the brink of extinction, the business card seem to scent the morning air.

The business card is dead, long live the business card.

FOREWORD

First impression counts as we were taught in school—the same applies to the art of branding. Depending on the nature of business in question, more often than less, one of the first collateral a person would interact with in a brand would be the business card.

Business cards are exchanged during formal introductions as a convenient memory aid. They help businesses establish professional presence during such meetings by serving as a remote, tangible marketing tool. They can also be free for grasp at the countertop as patrons enter a shop. The business card would eventually be that one collateral that can be taken away. While carrier bags or folders may have a subsequent functional use, many business cards may not see the light of day again once they are set aside in a drawer, hence the need for it to be memorable in its short interaction time with people.

While a brand can be physically or emotionally experienced in different ways as a whole, business cards are meant to stand on its own. Like movie trailers which attempt to introduce a film's plot within a short duration, business cards seek to do the same by displaying key brand information using visual elements such as colours, typefaces, patterns, images, shapes, and graphics—all within a palm-sized space.

In a day and age where the digital frontier is becoming more prevalent in brands with the rise of apps and elaborate interactive web experiences, the business card remains one of the essential brand identity items for its ability to express tactility. Paper choice and thickness suggests the business' regard for quality and its willingness to spend.

Good business cards should not only look good, but serve a particular purpose. With a goal to leave a lasting impression, some businesses would opt for special production techniques, unconventional materials, or fancy printing effects and thoughtful designs to enhance interactivity with the holder. Others keep the design simple and communicate through a clever choice of graphics, catchy lines and meaningful quotes. The choice of which depends directly on the intended brand persona—be it clever, witty, bold, dynamic, exciting, muted, rustic, futuristic, classy or modern.

Sometimes, brands like to produce a series instead of a standard design throughout. They can vary elements such as colours, brand patterns, work examples or even handmade elements such as stamped graphics. These variations could also form a larger picture, or to have that 'collect-all-4' effect.

Being 'over the top' and experimental should only be done if they help express an idea or mirrors what the business does. The truly interesting ones can form part of a memorabilia collection. But when going down this route, some solutions might border at being highly impractical to produce or carry around.

At ACRE, we address problems with a pragmatic approach. As when business cards ought to stimulate and smooth the way for conversations, we planned it in such a way that our names are set prominently on one side of our cards, and contact details, company website and location on the other. Besides our portfolio of works, we feel we are best represented by the very people behind us—our team members. As such, it introduces the team member upfront; the conversations that follow will do the rest.

The role of the business card will stay relevant in future. Although its primary role of information exchange is more often replaced by digital mediums, its other role of communicating brand visuals and professionalism over a tactile medium remains. Print is far from dead.

Like movie trailers which attempt to introduce a film's plot within a short duration, business cards seek to do the same by displaying key brand information.

T Y Zheng
Co-founder and Creative Director, ACRE

Key to symbols

Size | Materials | Colour | Printing & finishing

Index of initials

AD	Art direction
AG	Agent
CD	Creative direction
CL	Client
CP	Copywriting
CR	Special credits
DE	Design
IL	Illustration
PD	Production
PH	Photography
PP	Paper
PT	Printing

TABLE OF CONTENTS

The third of the Nice To Meet You series, Nice To Meet You Again presents 130 recent visual greetings that span business card, greeting card and invitation designs created for diverse sectors. Get ready to flip the pages and make contact with more than 100 creative units from around the globe!

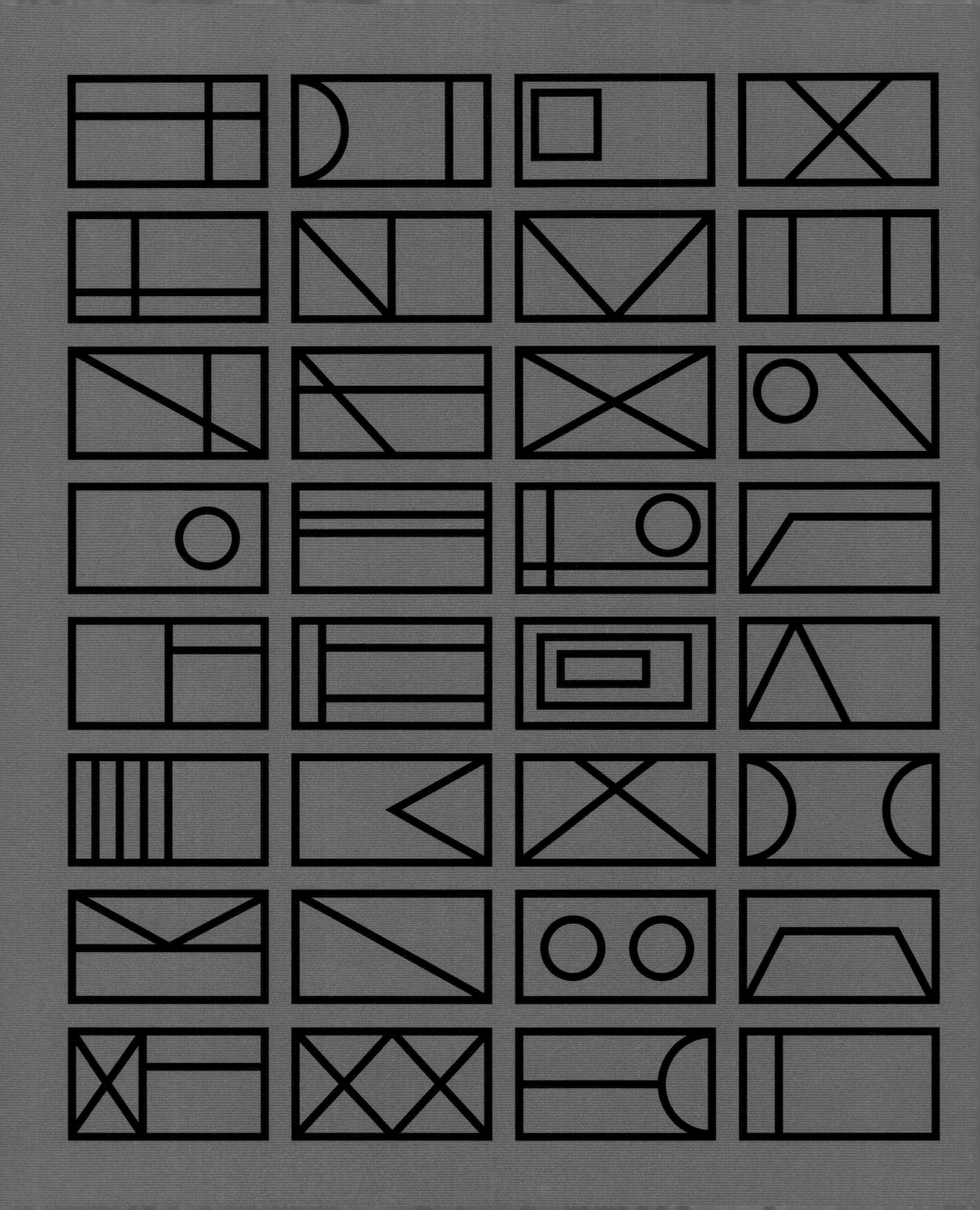

Business cards

Be it the whole or a part of a brand's identity, these business cards epitomise how brand stories can be detailed in a tiny surface just about the size of a palm. Strategically arranged into a clean layout, cleverly designed logos, monograms and lettering solidify brand vision to memorable graphics, humour and words. Fine paper, unconventional materials and finishing touches further convey a brand's attitude and commitment to quality.

A1000X BETTER

A1000XBETTER is an eclectic interior design studio. Its Californian style and casual yet elegant sensibility were visualised in the studio's business cards, a type-based design hand-printed with an antique letterpress. All cards were made from a cotton paper and hand-torn to attain unique deckled edges, complemented by a blend of clean and graceful types.

DE Julia Kostreva Studio **CL** A1000XBETTER **CR** Blackbird Letterpress (PT)

50.8 x 88.9mm
Cotton Paper Ecru 110lb
Letterpress printing

ARGO

ARGO is committed to bringing unseen art to public attention. Combining artwork provided by ARGO with a simple palette and clean layout, Anagrama created a modern museum-like space for the appreciation of art across the consultancy's brand communications. An emblem, depicting a stylised compass, highlights ARGO's mission to discover art as they compare themselves to the Greek legend of Jason and his ship, ARGO.

DE Anagrama **CL** ARGO **CR** Caroga (PH)

50 x 90mm

Fabriano Rusticus Neve 200gsm

CMYK, spot colour

Hot stamping

Carlotta

A traditional Mexican style bakery's passion is matched with "El Porfiriato" era's graphic styles, a time when Mexico was governed by Porfirio Diaz, an admirer of French architecture and art. An illustrated all-over floral motif responds to the brand's delicacy and elegance, completed with typographic redesign referencing official documents from the time. A black frame settles the movements within it and thus preserves the brand's delicate personality.

DE Anagrama **CL** Carlotta **CR** Caroga (PH)

50 x 90mm
Neenah Classic Crest Avalanche White 216gsm
CMYK, spot colour
CARLOTTA
MENU
PANADERIA
PASTELES
TAMALES
CARLOTTA
CARLOTTA
CARLOTTA
CONTACTO
RIO DE LA PLATA 302
CARLOTTA
MENU
PANADERIA
PASTELES
TAMALES
BEBIDAS

Cora Hillebrand

An art photographer at heart, Cora Hillebrand extends her talents working with everything from video installations to portraits and still life. Often carrying heavy equipments, Hillebrand wanted something light that she could leave behind to her clients. The solution was a combined business card and mini portfolio housed in a sturdy envelope, in the shape of a Polaroid picture, with an open front. The portfolio is highly customisable with Hillebrand's work printed on cardboard and perforated for easy detachment.

DE Lundgren+Lindqvist **CL & PH** Cora Hillebrand **CR** Göteborgstryckeriet (PT)

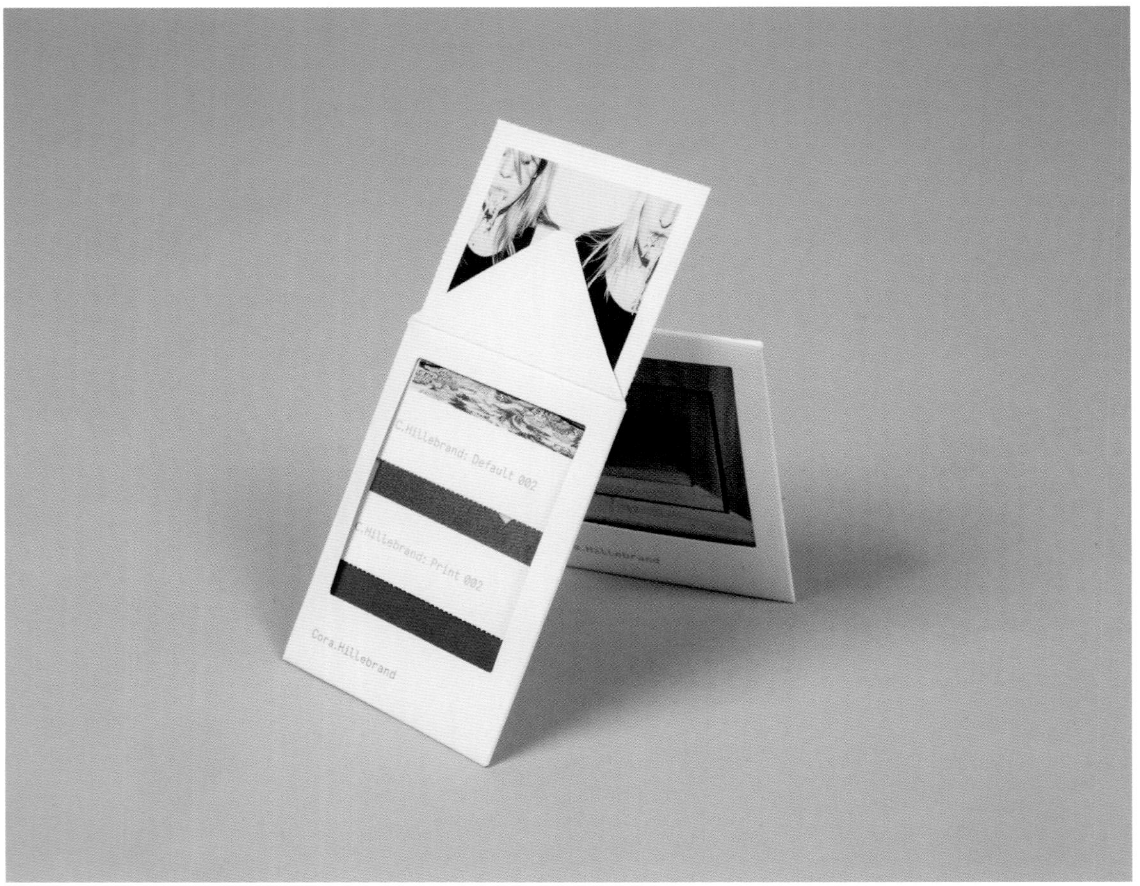

87 x 68mm
Rives Design Bright White 250gsm, Invercote Albato 290gsm
CMYK, spot colour
Die cutting, perforation

loft
loft

Cora.Hillebrand
Cora.Hillebrand
Cora.Hillebrand
Cora.Hillebrand
Cora.Hillebrand

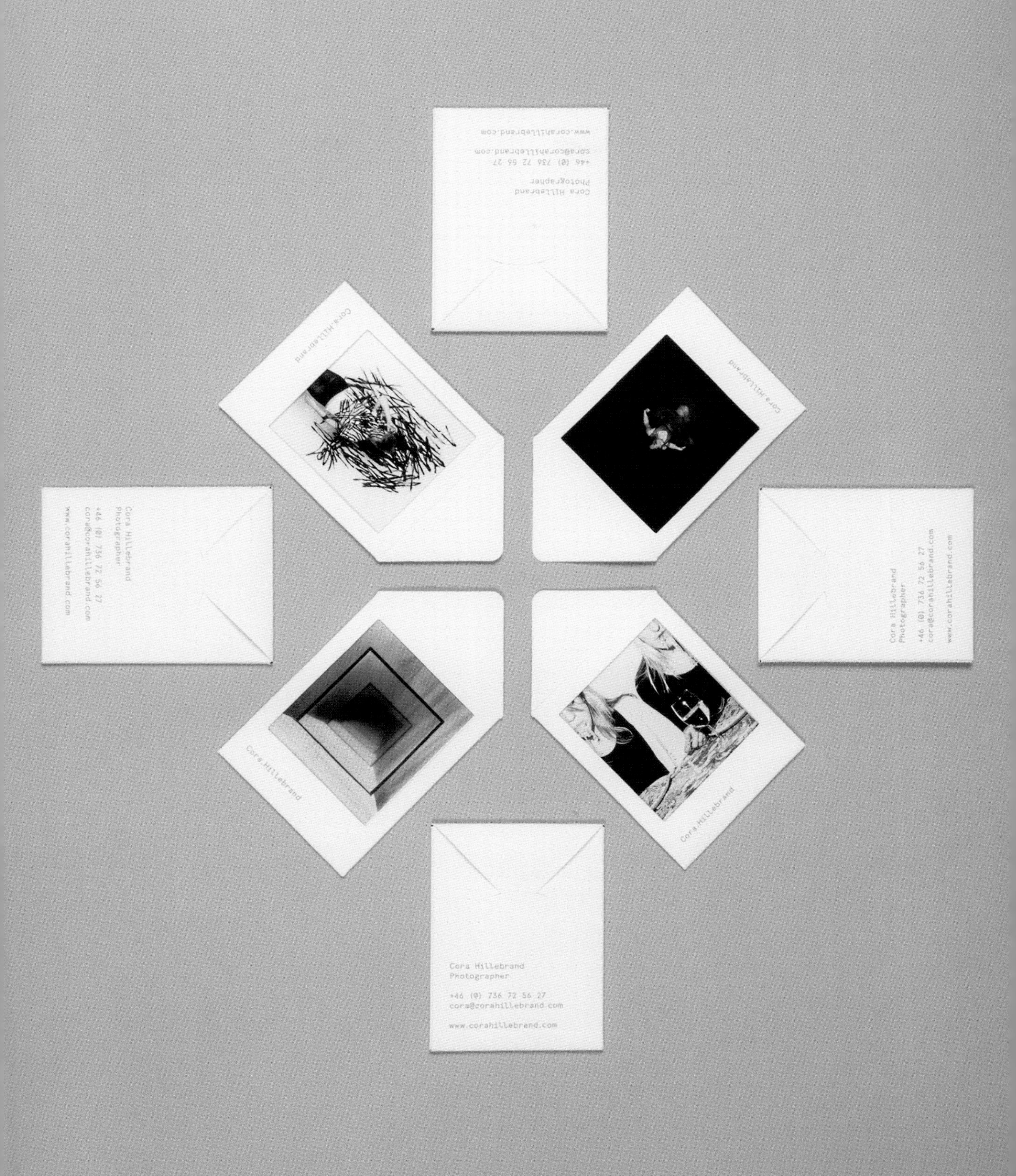
Cora Hillebrand
Photographer
+46 (0) 736 72 56 27
cora@corahillebrand.com
www.corahillebrand.com
Cora.Hillebrand

Ascui & Co. Architects

Anchored in the concept of 'Process and Possibility' the flexible identity system created for the newly renamed Ascui & Co. Architects celebrates the creative and progressive nature of the practice. A morphing grey-tone visual language sequence along with a suite of 'temperature'-based palettes were developed to encourage on-going evolution of the brand through the client's own creative contribution and experimentation.

DE Grosz Co.Lab **CL** Ascui & Co. Architects **CR** G.F Smith (PP), Taylor'D Press (PT)

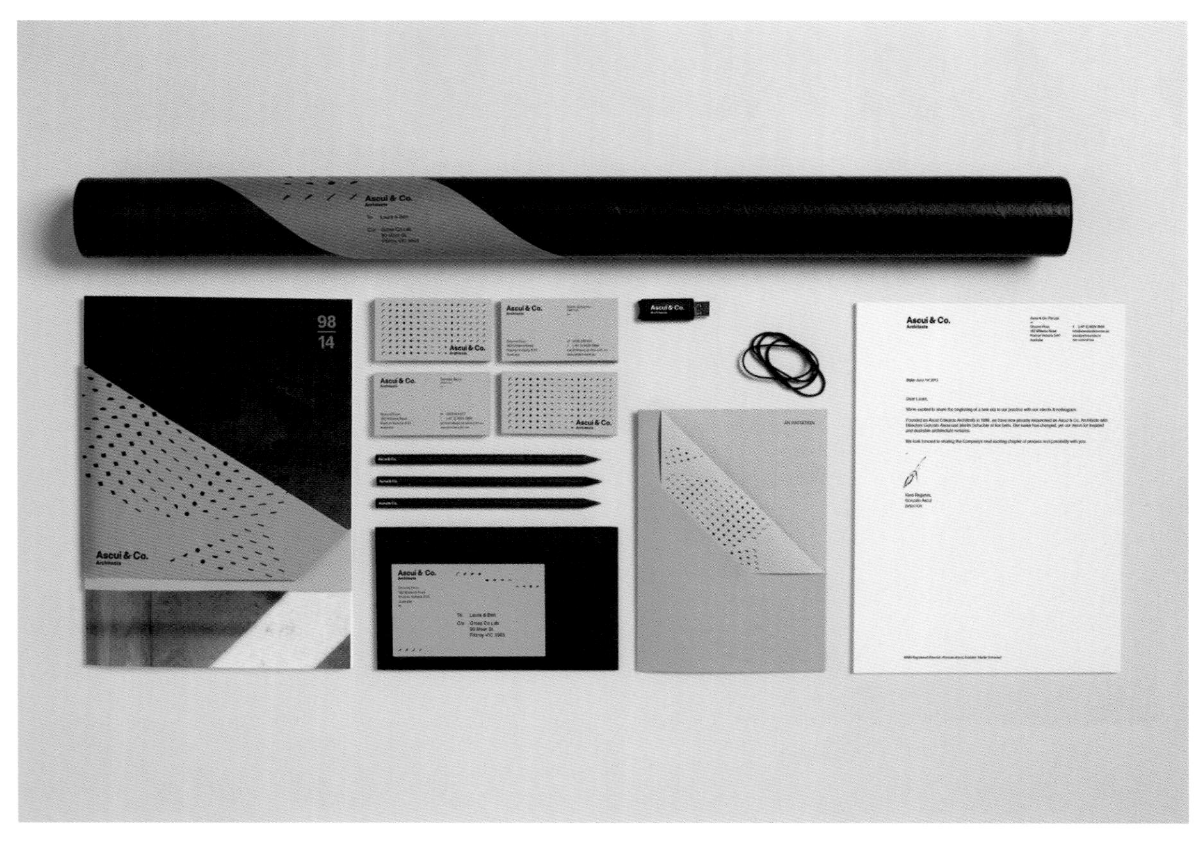

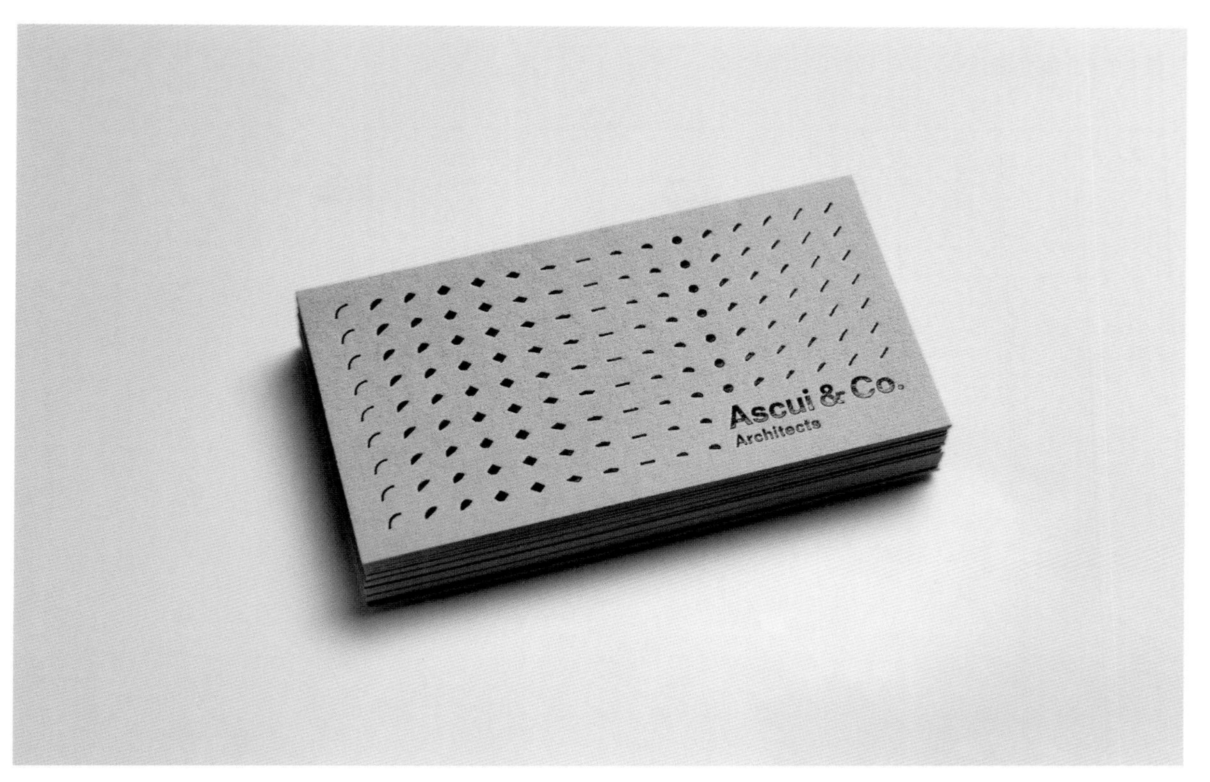

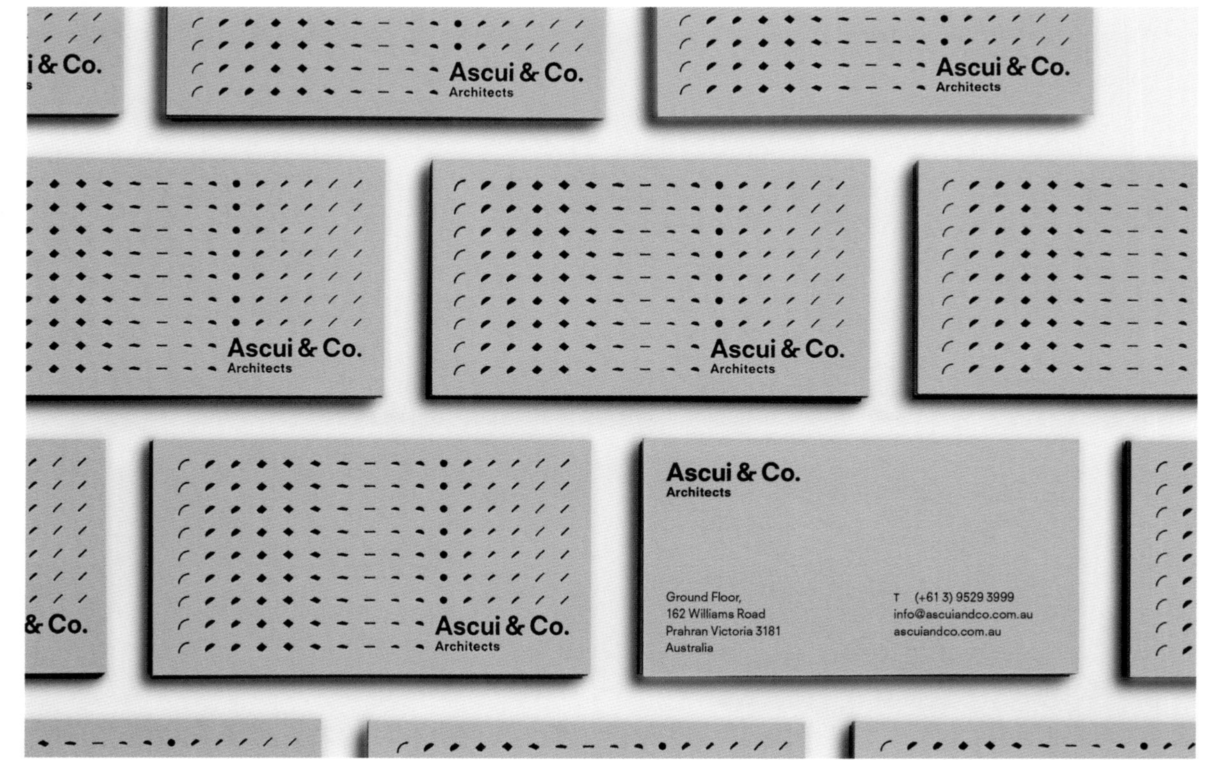

50 x 90mm
G.F Smith Colorplan Real Grey 270gsm
Spot colour
Duplex, hot stamping

Neurotrend

Neurotrend brings about marketing and creative strategies based on human behaviour research. Integrating apparatus-inspired lines as the key graphic elements, though in a much orderly fashion, Neurotrend's identity establishes a strong connection between its services and expertise in research. Embossed shapes introduce a subtle sense of dimensionality in their communications as they bend the lines.

AD & DE Vladimir Shlygin **CL** Neurotrend Research Centre
CR Olga Papsuy (DE), Maxim Pantsyrev (CP)

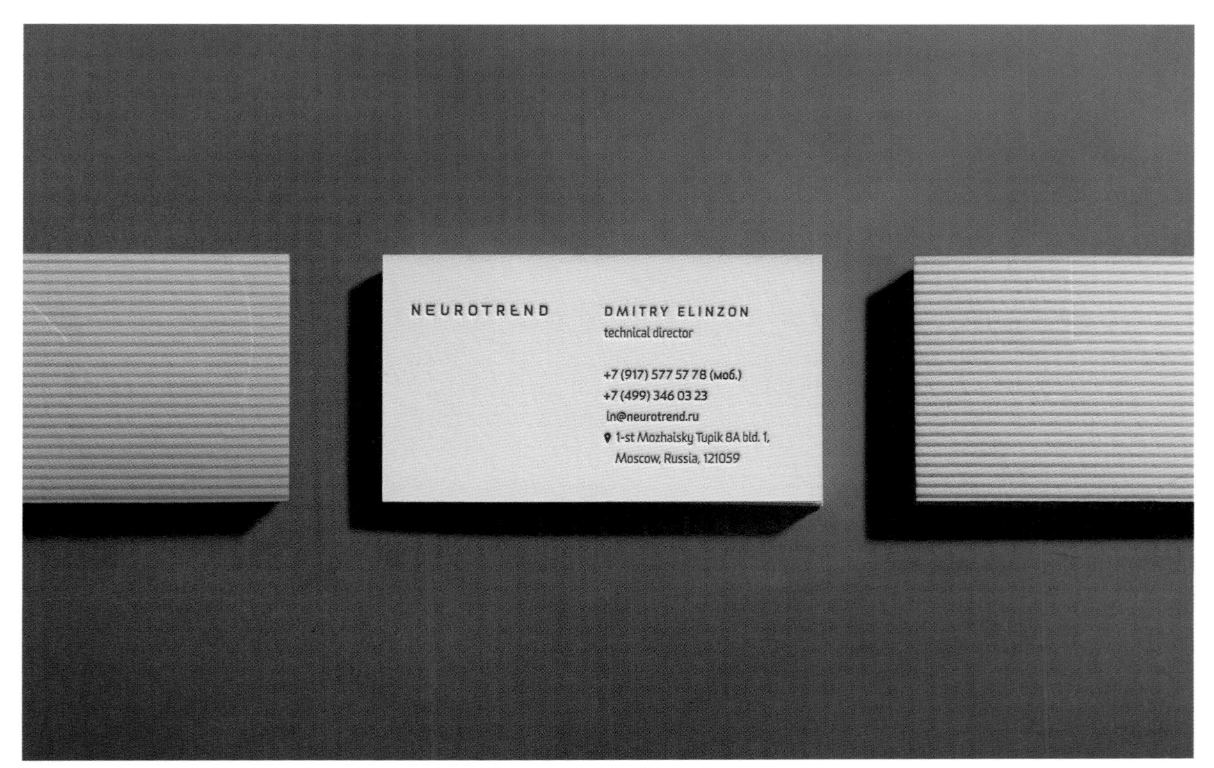
NEUROTREND
DMITRY ELINZON
technical director
+7 (917) 577 57 78 (моб.)
+7 (499) 346 03 23
in@neurotrend.ru
1-st Mozhaisky Tupik 8A bld. 1,
Moscow, Russia, 121059

55 x 80mm
Crane's Lettra 220lb
CMYK, Spot colour
Embossing, hot stamping, letterpress printing

Doug Liddle Guitar Instruction

Start your guitar lesson and learn to play the first basic tunes with guitar instructor Doug Liddle's business cards. Featuring shapes of various major-chords over a standard chord diagram, these business cards demonstrate how easy it is to get the basic chords right within moments of holding them. Raised thermographic spots function as a tactile indicator that facilitates finger placement without even looking at the card.

DE Saint Bernadine Mission Communications Inc. **CL** Doug Liddle Guitar Instruction

88.9 x 50.8mm
Mohawk Black Vellum Cover 80lb
Spot colour
Thermographic printing

VOLTA

Porto-based design studio VOLTA's dedication to create successful brands is reinforced in their own graphic identity. Placing the studio's logotype and information in four corners and directions, their business card integrates their name, meaning "turn" in English, their all-round creative approach, and the ever-changing nature of brands into the design. The colour variations also epitomise the varied perspectives they adopted to analyse brands.

DE VOLTA Branding & Digital Studio **CR** Luís Espinheira (PH)

55 x 85mm   Keaykolour Sandy Beige, Jet Black, Navy Blue, Holy Green 300gsm   Spot colour

Eskimo 2015

The pairing of pristine white and wood in Eskimo's new identity manifests the studio's creed about minimalistic design, with subtle reference to eskimo's meaning as 'ice-cream on a stick' in Russian culture. The studio's emphases on the richness of simplicity is reflected in its careful choices of materials and printing techniques for its stationery. Where wood suggests manual work, white implies "openness" which is amplified to the max with a white-on-white approach to the business cards.

DE Eskimo design studio **CR** Anatoly Vasiliev (PH)

50 x 90mm · Arjowiggins Curious Touch Texture Natural 400gsm · Duplex, hot stamping

CORPORATE IDENTITY PROPOSAL
1. IDENTITY PACK
2. TIME AND WORK ORDER
3. PAYMENT TERMS

ДЛЯ ПРЕССЫ

Joanna Borromeo

Joanna Borromeo, the independent jazz musician and songwriter herself, is the focus of this business card design. Capitalised and stamped in copper metallic foil over a pure white duplexed card, Borromeo's name stands out in a confident, classy manner and offers a common ground for the artist's music that seamlessly threading elements of R&B, jazz and hip hop.

DE Julia Kostreva Studio **CL** Joanna Borromeo
CR Madelene Farin, Julia Kostreva (PH), Mama's Sauce (PT)

50.8 x 88.9mm French Construction Pure White 100C Duplex, hot stamping

KANICA Weaving art.

Laura Vargas Llanas is the creative force behind KANICA, a brand of handcrafted and limited edition weavings. Devised as a bare hint of the brand's offering, KANICA's business cards were modelled into looms, with notches to hold tiny threads like a real one. An earthy palette, clean design and recycled paper, accented by a metallic copper colour, combine to propose Laura's artistic background and use of natural yarns.

DE STIT™ Creative studio. **CL** Laura Vargas Llanas (KANICA Weaving art.)
CR Vasilis Kouroupis (PH)

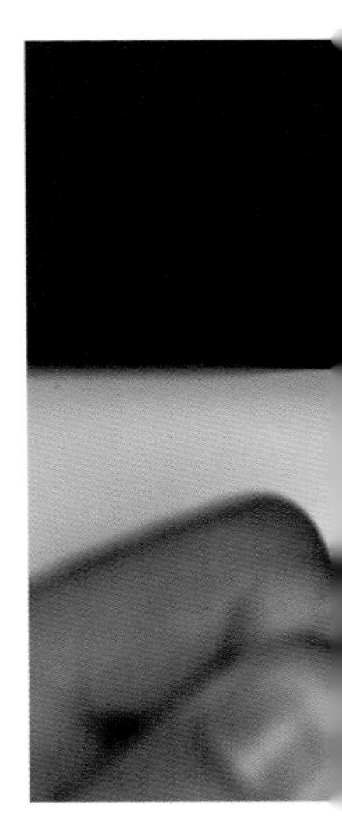

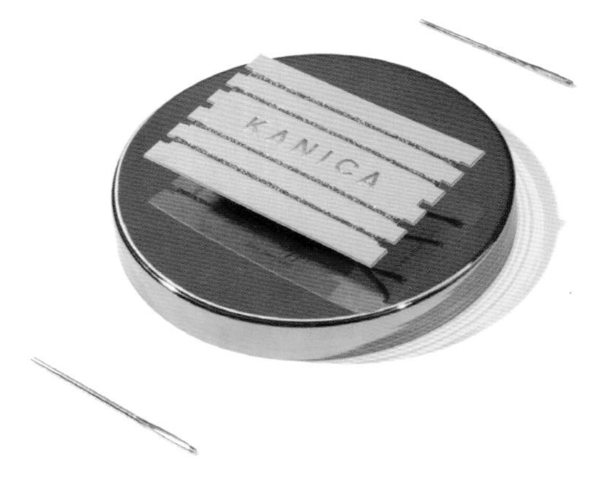

55 x 85mm Arjowiggins Creative Papers Curious Matter Andina Grey, Goya 380gsm Spot colour Die Cutting, duplex, hot stamping

Tamarindo

Tamarindo is a kitchen and tapas bar in Spain city, Ourense, with two distinct moods and spaces. This duality is reflected across the restaurant's visual identity, neatly united by simple aesthetics as the architects and husband-and-wife owners have instilled into Tamarindo's interior. Blocks of pastel colours, suggestive of relaxing afternoons and warm vibrant evenings, were punctuated by varied materials that correspond the space, featuring light wood ceilings, adobe walls and steel furniture pieces.

DE & PH La Tortillería
CL Ruben Gil D., Gretta R. Valdés

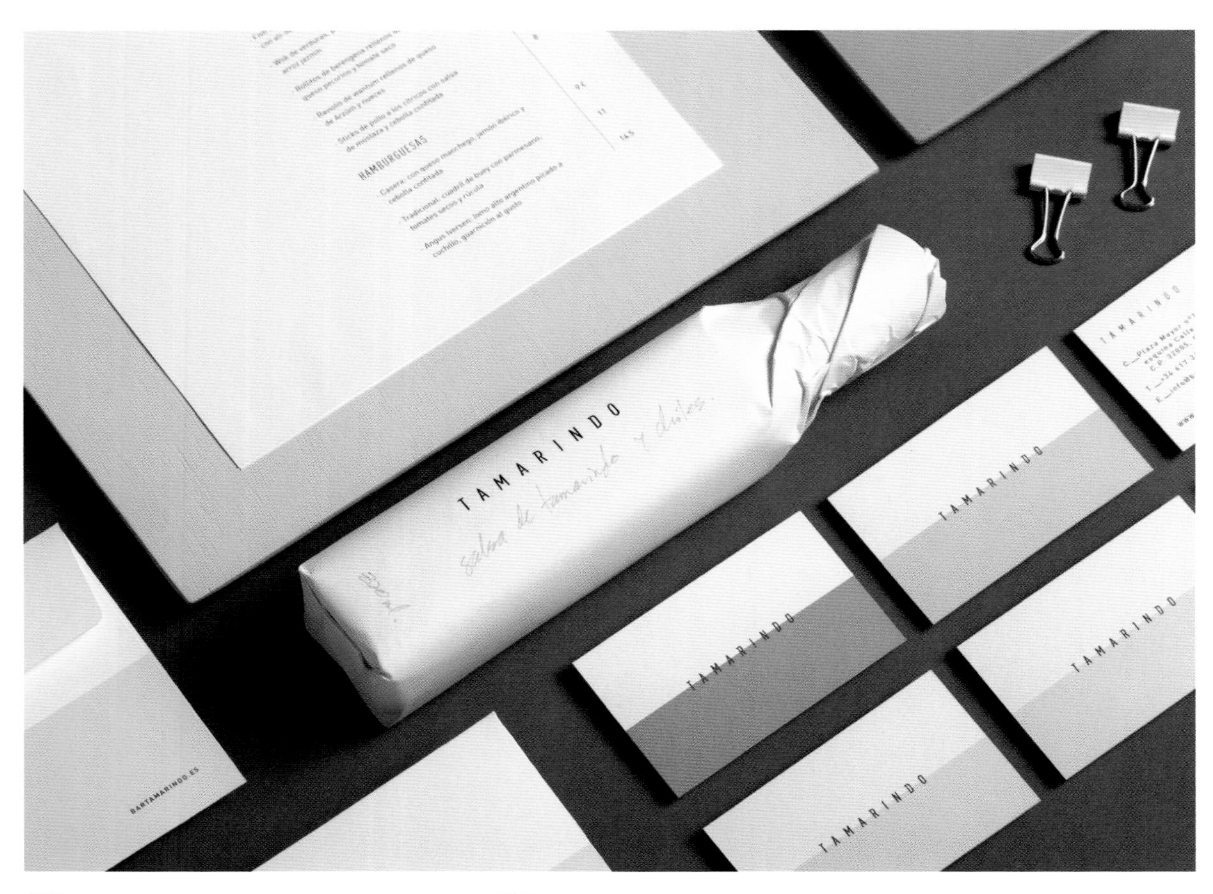

55 x 90mm · Classic Crest 400gsm · Spot colour

Business Cards

Léa Munsch

Parisian creative manager and editor Léa Munsch's professional identity is simultaneously bold and sweet. Munsch links management strategies with culture and arts, and work closely with creatives on a regular basis. With three colour editions, these business cards makes for a delightful conversation starter with common opening lines bronze foiled along with Munsch's contact details and online profile.

DE Hey **CL** Léa Munsch **CR** Roc Canals (PH)

55 x 85mm · Pop Set & Torres Paper Mint, Violet, Salmon 320gsm · Hot stamping

Poesis

Poesis supports organisations and their team by boosting their energy levels in terms of consciousness, transformation and healing capabilities. Inspired by Greek figure Strophalos or the Hecate wheel, Savvy developed a logo that symbolically represents the flame of life, knowledge and fulfilment, wrapped by a labyrinth that hinted at the learning process. The foil finish and gray substrates give the card a mystical look, much alike Poesis' work appears to be.

DE Savvy Studio **CL** Poesis **CR** Nydia Lilian (PH)

90 x 55mm
Bristol Paper 300gsm
Spot colour
Hot stamping

Bain

Nicolas Kovac and Cindy Defort were entirely in charge of the brand's direction and business card design. Largely grounded in the duo's love for the 1970s attitude, the French swimwear brand breathes a vintage spirit and the idea of freedom and spontaneity to the core. Depicting two bathers swimming in circle and side by side, the logos represent the communion between human and nature, rejoicing themselves in front of the dramatic skies of endless summer.

DE Cindy Defort, Nicolas Kovac **CL** Bain **CR** Tind (PT)

85 x 55mm
Conqueror Connoisseur 100% Cotton 300gsm
Spot colour
Screenprinting

Floralpunk

Floralpunk is an online fashion and accessories boutique from Germany, recently relocated to Vietnam. A brand update follows the relocation, which blends the beauty of Floralpunk women with casual effortless chic. The air of modern elegance further extends to its contrasting typefaces and palette, where roman meets modern types, and delicate floral colours underlay underlies the classy black.

DE Oddds **CL** Julia Doan

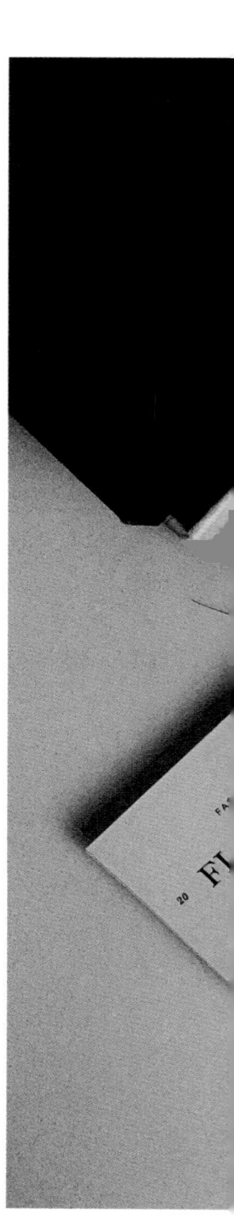

57 x 93 mm Keaycolour Original Snow White 450gsm CMYK, spot colour Hot stamping, letterpress printing

KOIKI EATERY

Located in Jakarta, KOIKI serves Japanese food in a casual setting. The mood is captured and projected across KOIKI's brand items, featuring recognisable Japanese cultural icons as photographs or illustrations in varied styles. Layout arrangement creates a sense of ease as a random mix of imagery floats freely across the business cards, resulting in 10 editions for grasp.

DE Brownfox Studio **CL** KOIKI EATERY

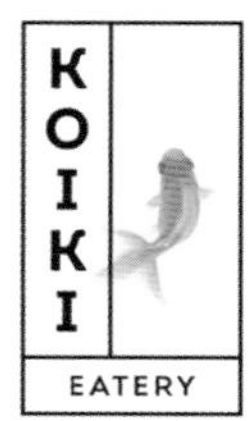

90 x 50mm
Finch Fine BW 270gsm
CMYK

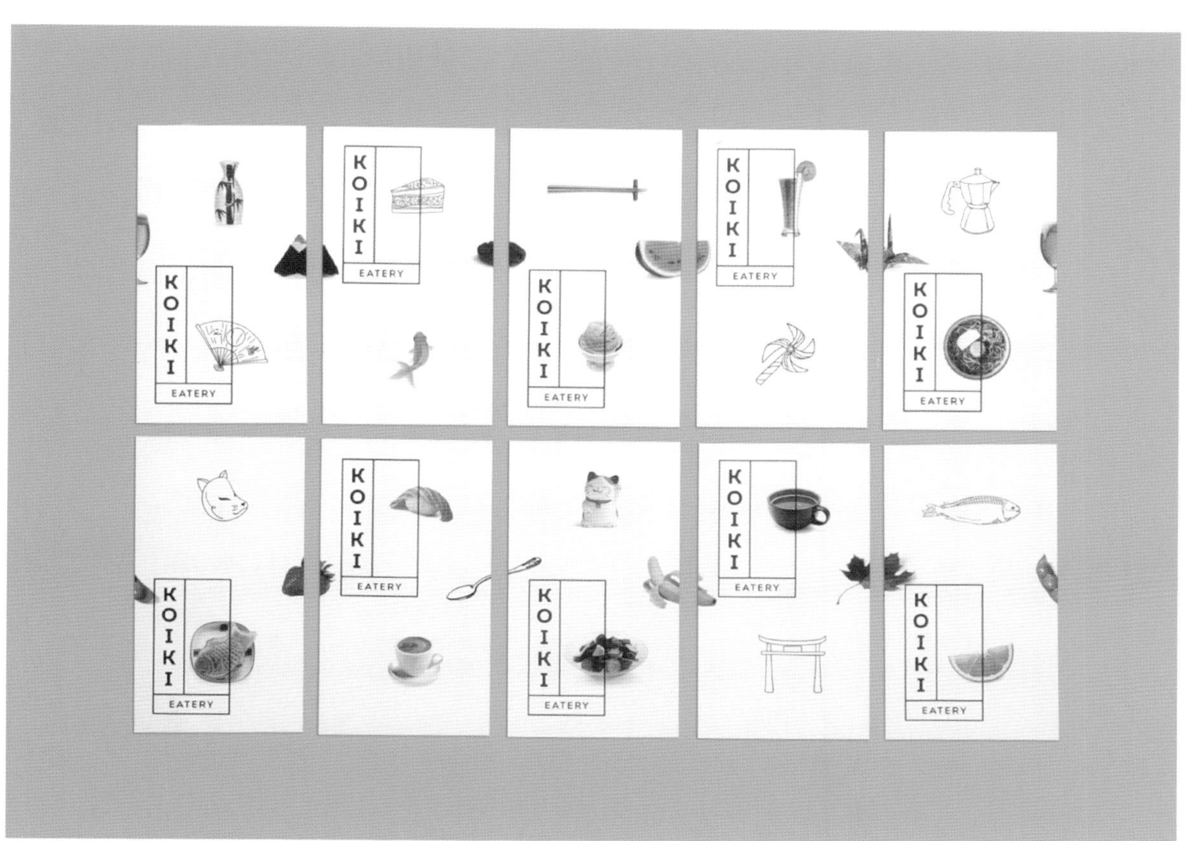

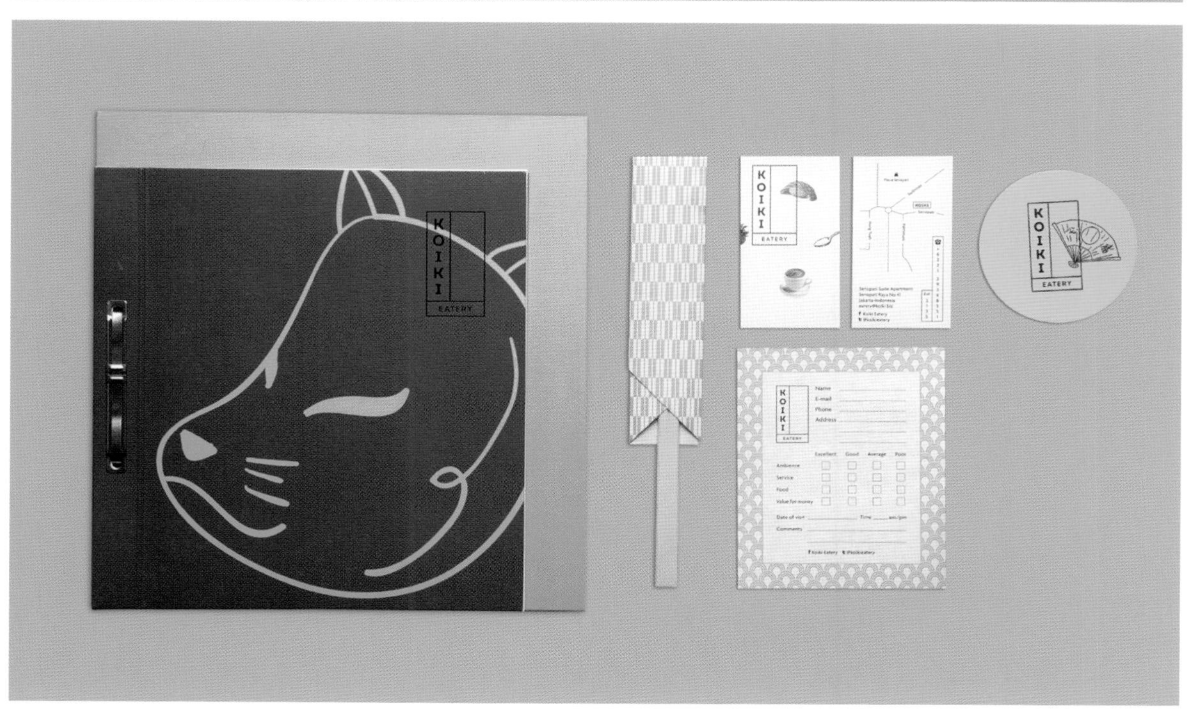

The Chain Reaction Project

The Chain Reaction Project is a Singapore-based non-profit striving to improve the lives of people in the least developed nations. With an objective to promote public participation, the identity directs viewer's focus to 'man' as the constituent element of the initiative's success, with a range of logotypes derived from the Chinese character of 'people'. The business cards are produced in a slightly larger-than-standard format and perforated to enable easy distribution as one receives and cuts up the card.

DE Bravo **CL** The Chain Reaction Project

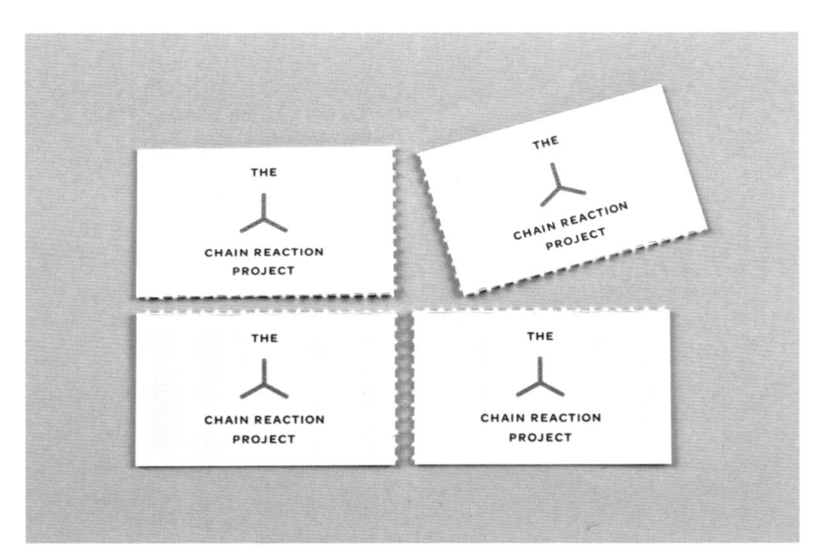

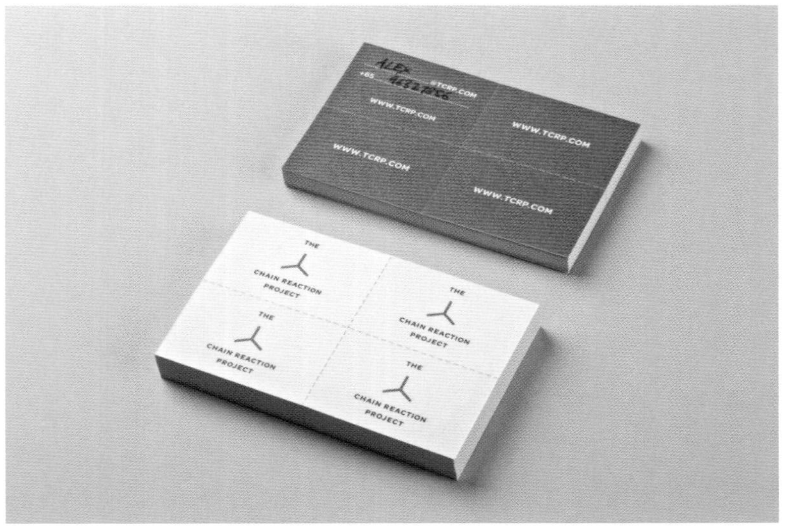

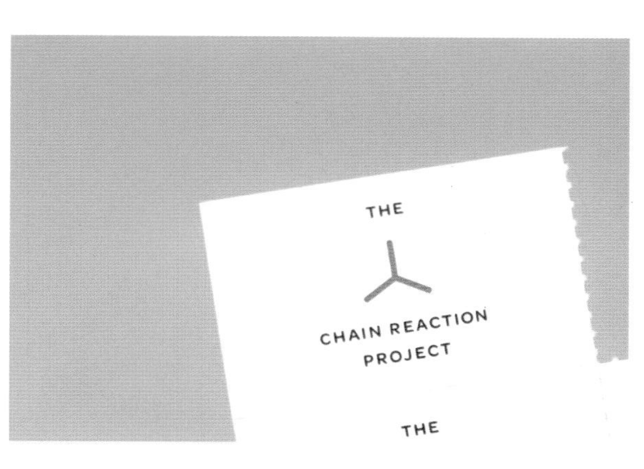

54 x 86mm
Maple White 300gsm
CMYK, spot colour
Perforation

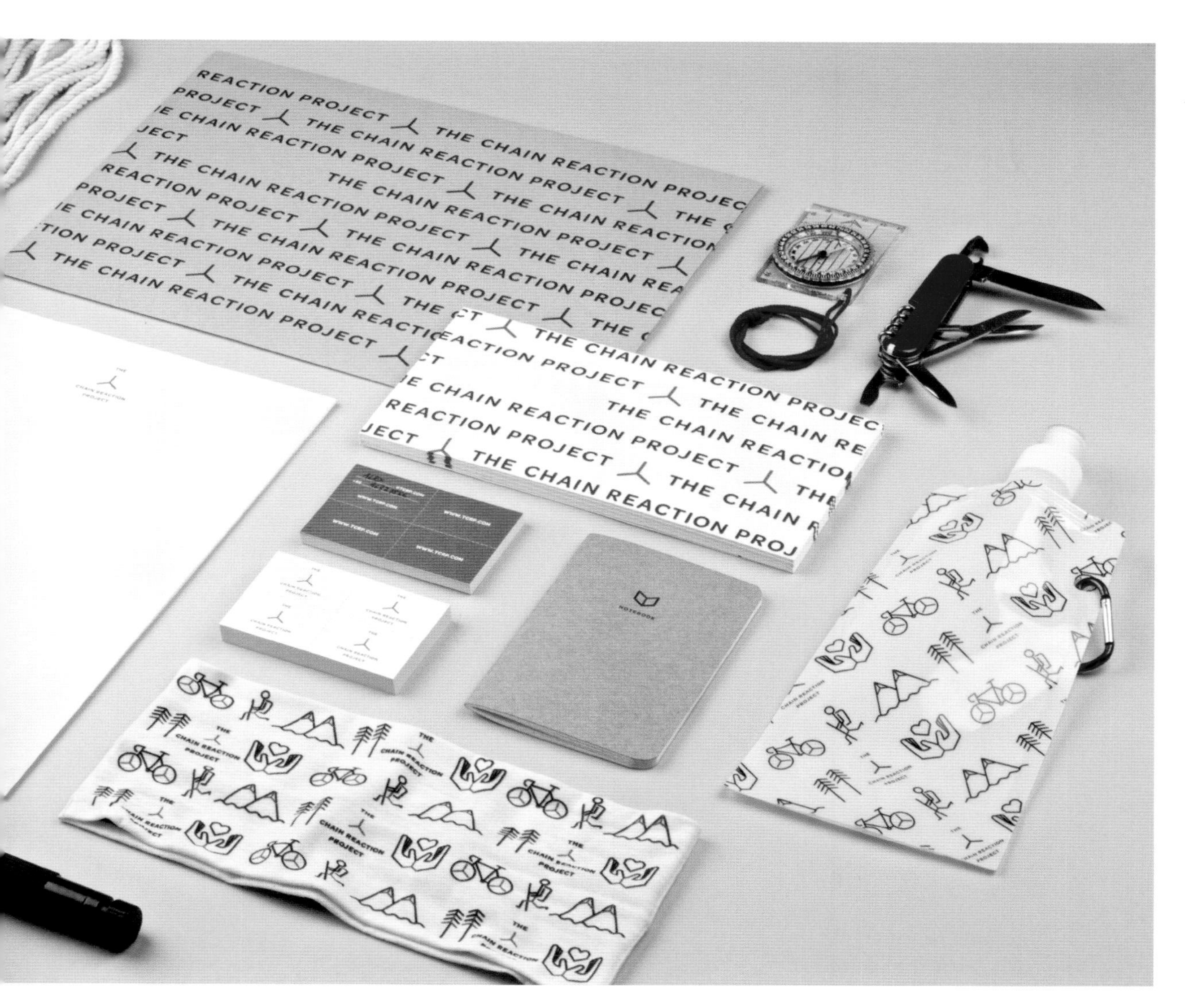

Paulina Aranda

Paulina Aranda is an independent translator from Mexico, with a great passion for travelling and a poetic eye for other languages and mindsets. Factoring in the young professional's enthusiasm for foreign culture and a master's degree obtained in Melbourne, Menta. draws on passport aesthetics to create this business cards, completed with a slender Art Deco lettering as a subtle hint of her classy-chic personality and global footprint.

DE Menta. **CL** Paulina Aranda

50 x 90mm
Corolla Damasco 240gsm
CMYK
Rubber stamping

Passport 2014

Independent Leeds-based brand identity and print design studio, Passport, has refreshed their studio stationery and website to coincide with the two year mark. Both founders now have two business card designs printed on Colorplan with textured embossing, featuring white foil on Royal Blue and gold foil on Vellum White. New travel-themed mailing stamps were also designed to create personalised communications and packages.

DE Passport

PASSPORT.

55 x 85mm | G.F Smith Colorplan Royal Blue, Vellum White 540gsm with Morocco Embossing | Hot stamping

Lana Dansky Handmade Toys

Lana Dansky represents a world where the strange and beautiful happens. Patterning the cards with debossed toy making supplies and tools, the tactile set of business card delivers the toy brand's strive for craftsmanship that gives memorable touches. A button-inspired logo with a tagline "Handmade Toy" once again brings to mind clearly what Lana Dansky offers, with a sweet pastel palette to underline the love and care they put into their craft.

DE Alexey Malina Studio **CL** Lana Dansky

54 x 85mm

Colorplan Azure Blue, Candy Pink, Park Green, Natural White 135gsm

Duplex, hot stamping

Mirror Shine Valets

Mirror Shine Valets had wanted a brand item that can be left in their customers' vehicles in the wake of car cleaning. Capitalising on the expandable nature of a dry compressed sponge, Michael O'Shea created a business card that encapsulates their expertise and services in every aspect. With a simple one-liner, the card intrigues Mirror Shine's clients to find out what happens after they "just add water".

DE Michael O'Shea **CL** Mirror Shine Valets **CR** Tayburn

*Just add water.
MIRROR SHINE VALETS
Matt Smith
Gifford House, Main Street, West Linton EH46 7EE
T. 07515 874 955 E. msvalets@yahoo.co.uk
www.mirrorshinevalets.co.uk
55 x 85mm
Dry sponge
Screenprinting

Meat & Bakery TAVERN

Made explicit in the name and its logotype, Meat & Bakery TAVERN is a Brooklyn-themed restaurant in Nakameguro, Tokyo known for prime meat dishes and homemade bread. Cast and letterpressed to simulate thick, fresh steak cuts, the business card set materialises the tavern's emphases on serving only quality meats and their classic setting for the enjoyment of good food. The cards come in an edition of six designs, featuring cuts from different parts of a cow.

AD & DE Ren Takaya **CL** Conception Co.,Ltd. **CR** AD&D (AG), Shunryo Yamanaka (DE), Mao Nishida (IL), Keibunsha Co., Ltd. (PD), Shinichi Adachi (PT)

BAKERY CHIEF
AZUSA MOGAMI
最上 梓
〒一五三-〇〇五一
東京都目黒区上目黒 一-五-七
代官山関ビル一階
1-5-7, Daikanyama Seki Bldg. 1F,
Kamimeguro, Meguro TYO. 153-0051 JP
T. 03-6412-7644
U. www.conception-gp.com

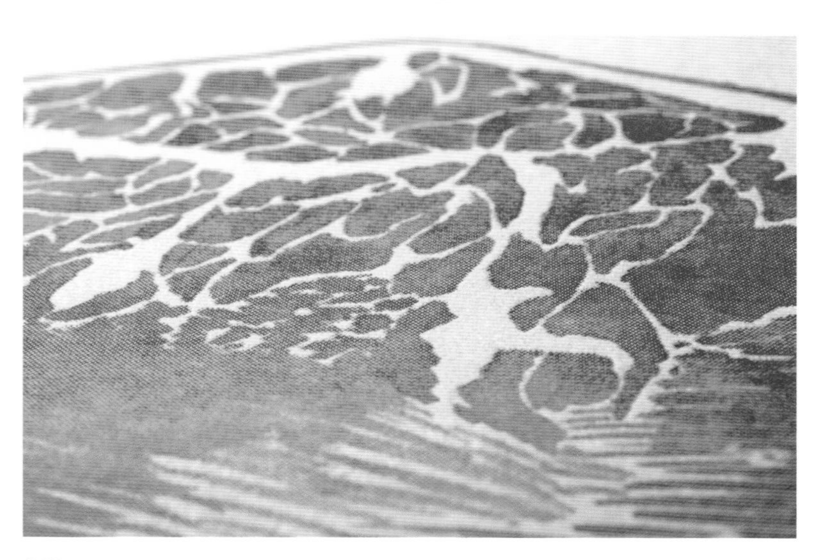

55 x 70mm
Cushion Paper 0.5 mm
Spot colour
Letterpress printing

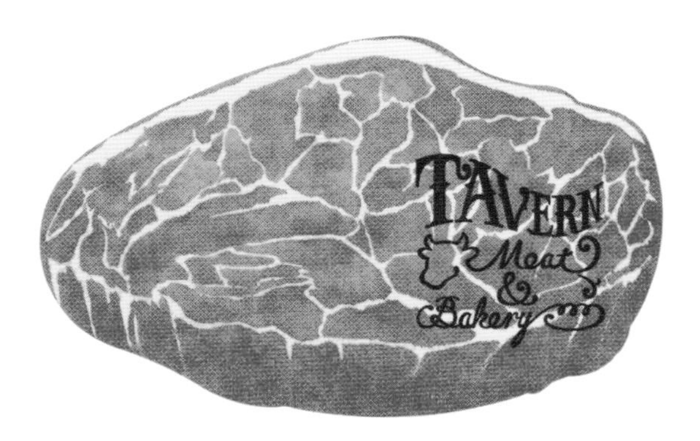

Katsuya Ishida

Katsuya Ishida's work explores the communicative capacity of visuals and sound within space. Taking "light" and "time" as the component elements of visual data transmission, COMMUNE condensed Ishida's work into a fluorescent plane on his business card. The section can metaphorically "store" light and convey "a persistence of vision" that linger on even in the absence of light.

DE COMMUNE **CL** Katsuya Ishida **CR** Kei Furuse (PH), Manami Sato (PT)

90 x 55mm

Clark Kent 310gsm

CMYK

Phosphorescent ink

ITO salon de the

ITO is a tearoom in Kyoto, the town of Japanese tea. Named "ITO", which translates into "thread" in English, the salon stands for the owner's wish to offer a place where people connect. The idea was illustrated by ITO's business cards which are rendered like bobbins with finely drawn threads neatly wound around the spindle.

AD & DE Kimiko Sekido **CL** ITO salon de the

67 x 55mm

Vent Nouveau

CMYK, spot colour

Die cutting

Absorb

Graphic designer Tsai Chia-hao created a business card for himself on the theme of learning. Featuring a black and natural ombré gradient shift, Tsai's business card visualises the cause of imbibing knowledge, in the way that paper absorbs ink. The idea becomes a functional design when the card was die-cut and turned into a bookmark clip.

DE Tsai Chia-hao

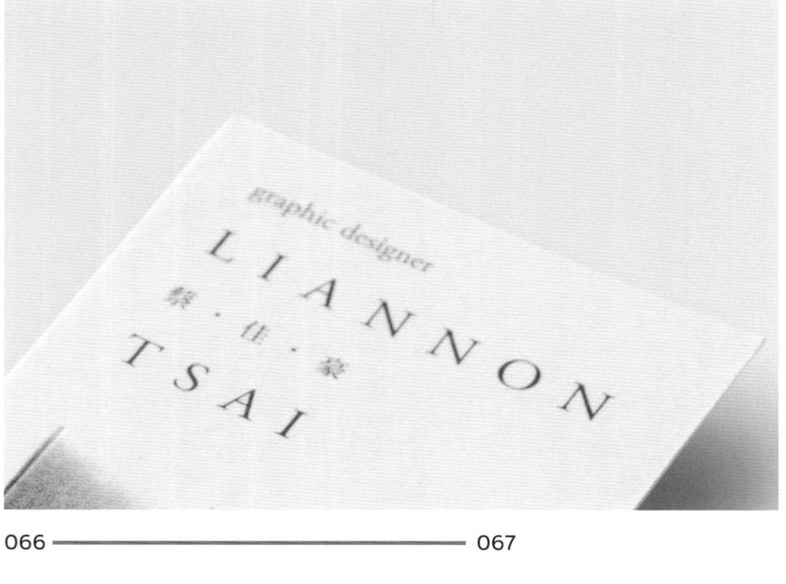

95 x 48mm
Kai-li yin-he 400gsm
Spot colour
Die cutting

HAPPY TREE & CO. LTD

HAPPY TREE is a merry enterprise dedicated to apparel recycling and leather repair. Their philosophy was well illustrated on their die-cut business card, with a 'tree of happiness' popping in the front. Full-length portraits of individual staff lift the Happy Tree spirit further at the card's back. The rippled edge of the tree extends to the card's bottom, adding a jolly touch.

DE COMMUNE
CL HAPPY TREE & CO. LTD
CR Kei Furuse (PH), Atsuhiro Kondo, Manami Sato (PT)

55 x 90mm

GA Bagasse Sugar 210gsm

CMYK

Die cutting

NECKTIE

NECKTIE design office is designer Takeo Chiboshi's new platform to manifest his ability to create memorable brands. Starting with an interesting name to jog potential clients' memory, Chiboshi strengthens NECKTIE's identity further with a collection of stylishly attired business cards. Each card is manually finished by the designer, from joining up the die-cut collars to laminating the "shirts" for extra strength. Each piece also serves as a tactile display of the designer's varied production skills.

DE NECKTIE design office **CR** Cosmotech Co., Ltd (PD), HEIWAPAPER Co., Ltd (PP)

81 x 55mm
Cotton Life Snow White 112gsm, 146gsm
Die cutting, duplex, hot stamping, letterpress printing

Kokoro Piano Studio

Kokoro Piano Studio is not only dedicated to perfecting student's technical piano skills, but also inspiring a deep love for music so that they can enjoy it and play it from the heart. Since the school adopts a flexible teaching style and curriculum, their brand identity embraces the idea through the use of a pliable stock. Soft colours and a motif made out of simple lines and curves were added to reflect the playful and relaxing aspect of learning at this school.

DE The Folks Studio **CL** Kokoro Piano Studio

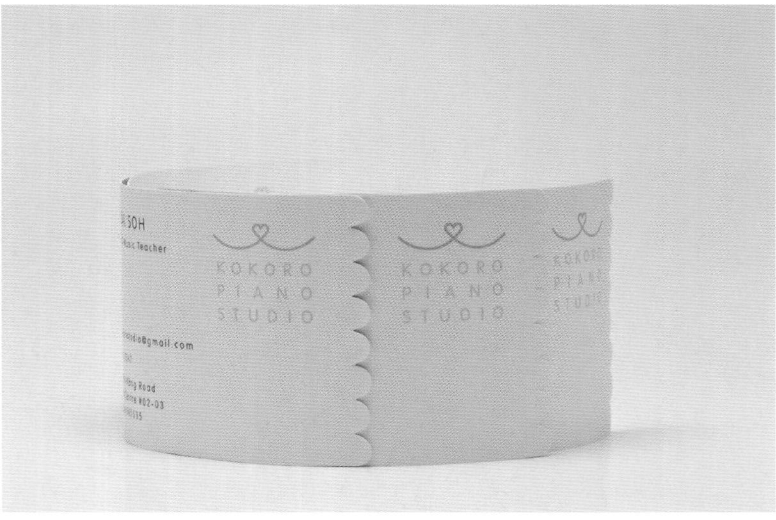

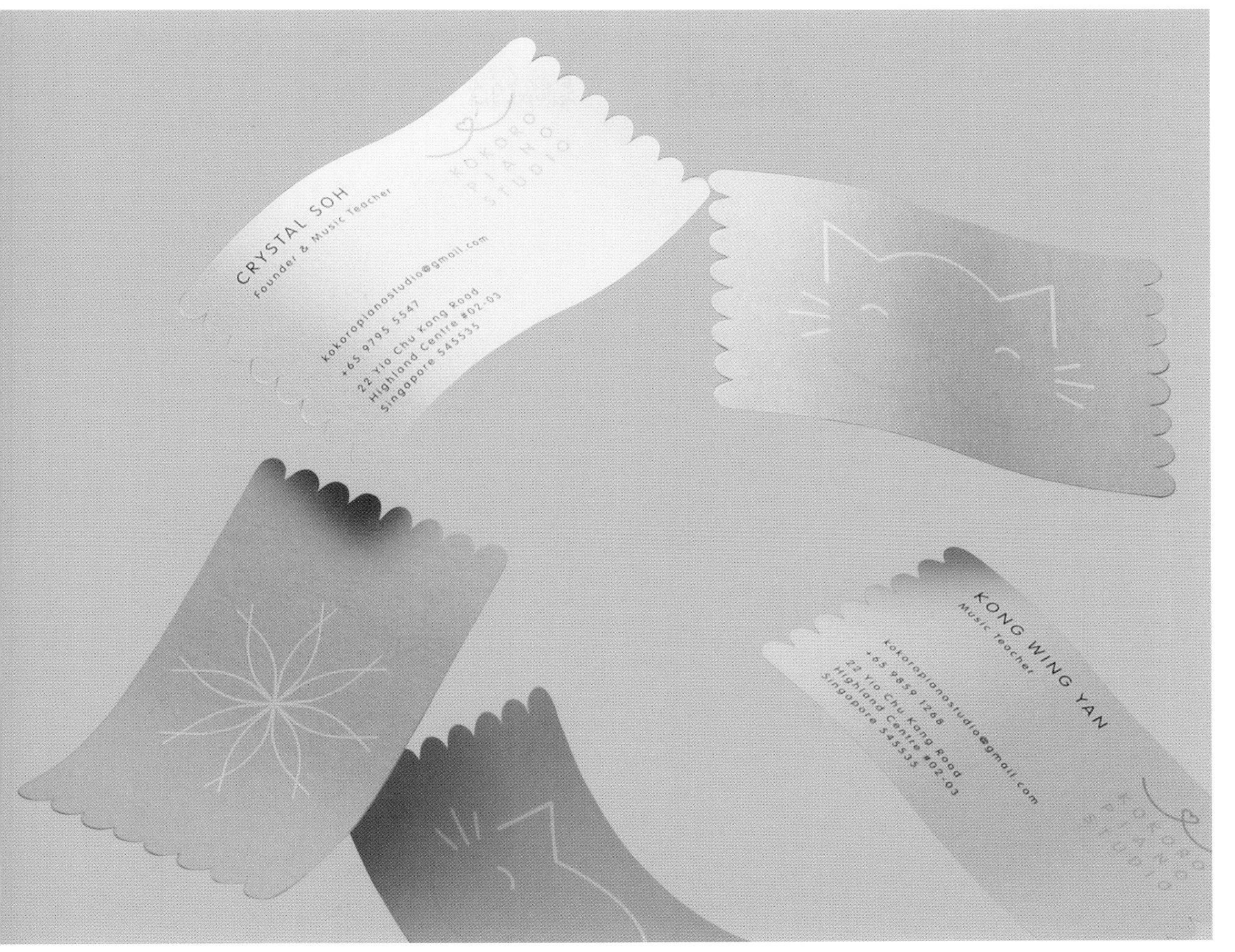

55 x 90mm
RJ Maple Bright 250gsm
CMYK
Die cutting

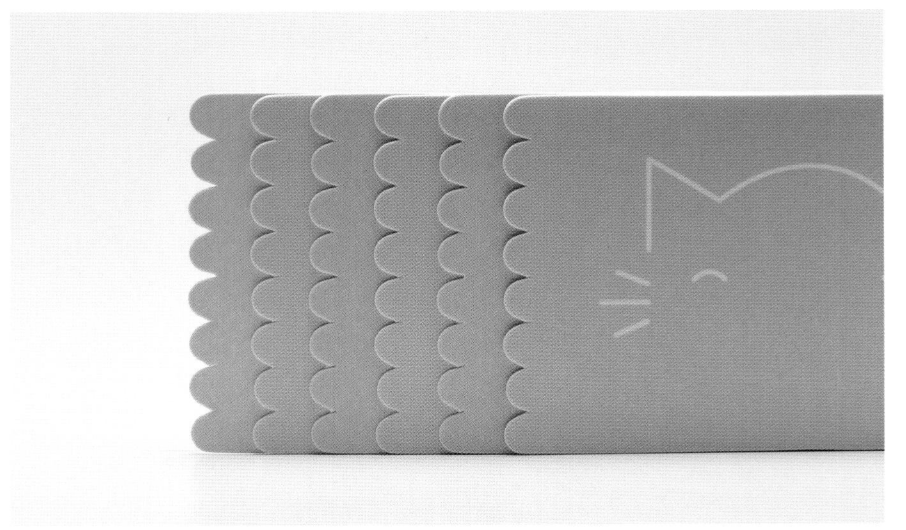

teakha

teakha is a concept tea café and zakka that promotes a simple, sustainable lifestyle. To coincide with the café's expansion plan in 2015 and in keeping with the distinctive taste and tea culture it has brewed in Hong Kong since its inception, gardens&co. refreshed teakha's identity and celebrated the café's progressive nature through a morphing pattern made of tiny flecks and strokes. The colour adds a pleasant grassy note to the brand.

DE gardens&co. **CL** teakha

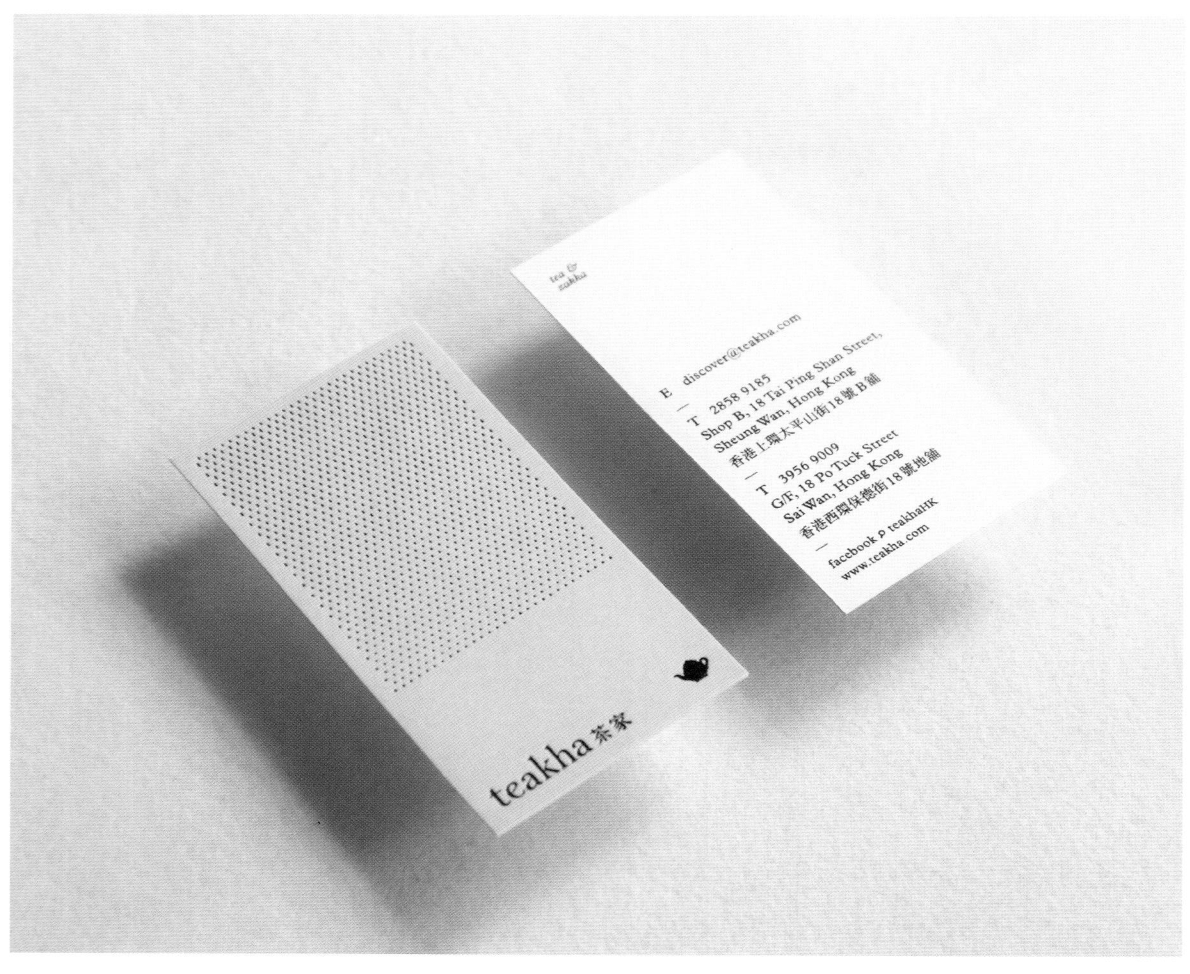

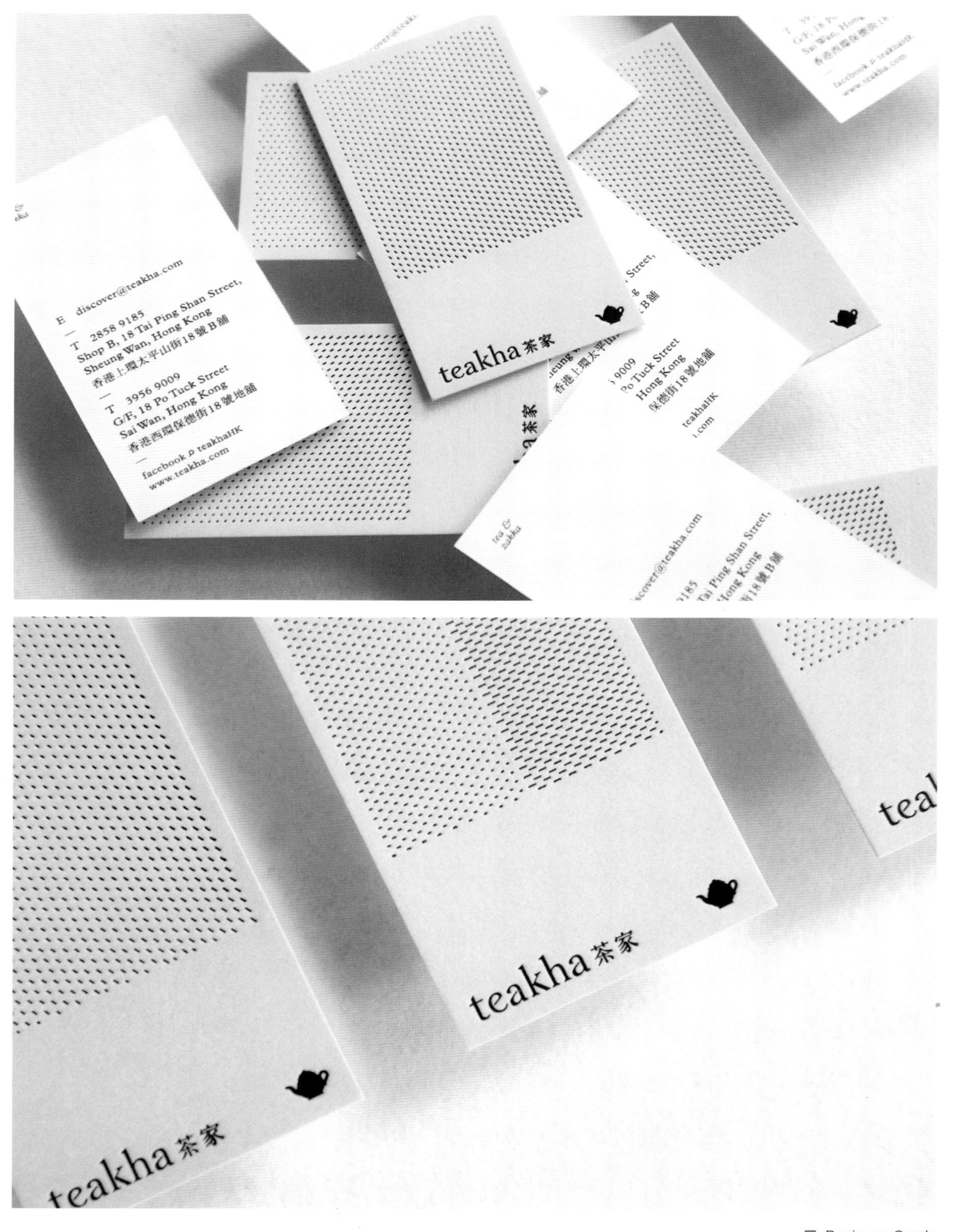

90 x 55mm · Keaykolour Original Snow White 215gsm · CMYK · Debossing, hot stamping

Tomohiro Nagasawa

Tomohiro Nagasawa is an artisan who manages and makes leather shoes under the brand Eterna. A tribute to Nagasawa's craftsmanship, business cards for this shoemaker were cast in the shape of soles, the fundamental part of footwear, completed with a fine leather-textured ivory paper. With its logo on one side and Tomohiro Nagasawa's contact details on the other, the cards can easily form a perfect pair for the left and right foot.

DE AURUM INC. **CL** Eterna **CR** Kei Tanaka (PH)

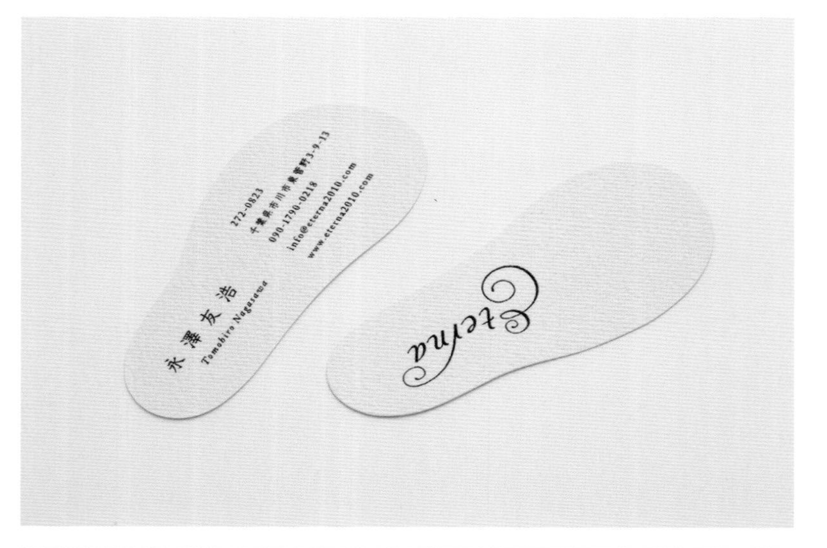

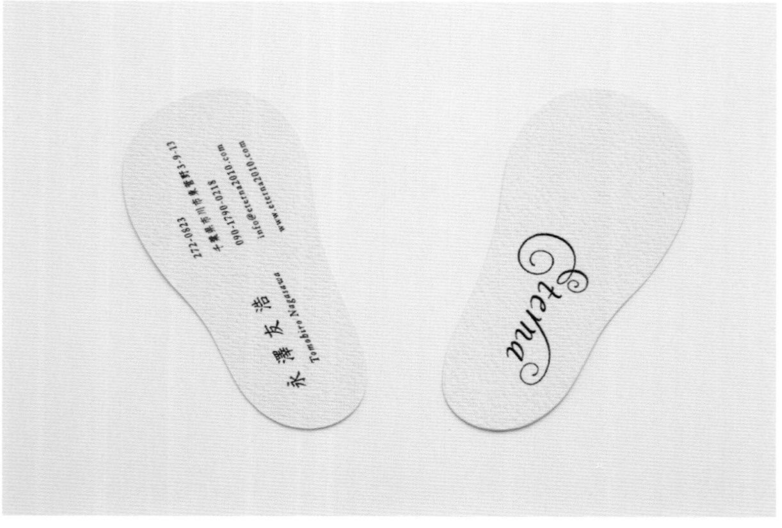

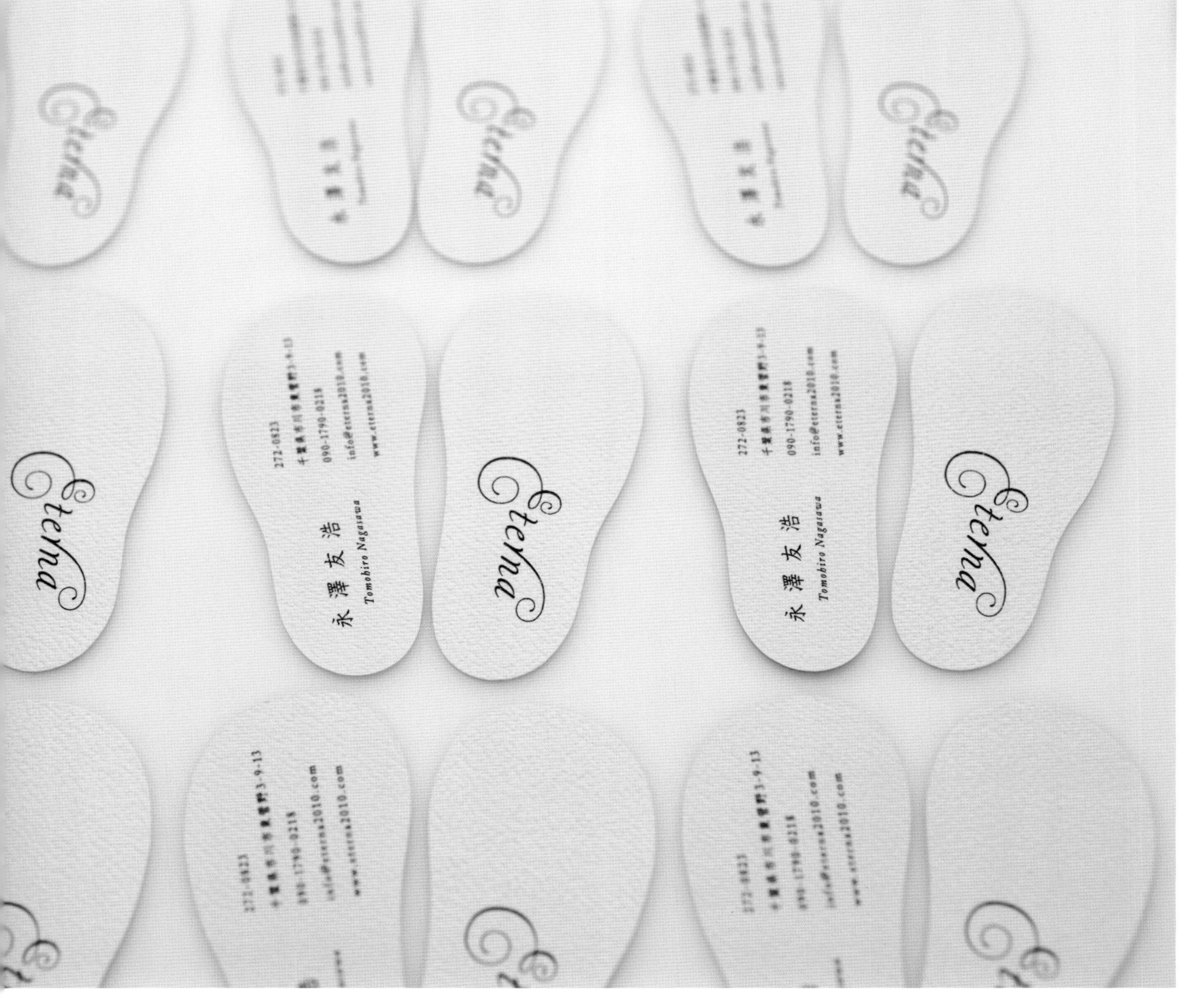

91 x 40mm
Alezan Ivory 204gsm
CMYK
Die cutting

Ascreen

Brand identity for multimedia agency aims to foster a new understanding of interactive media: rather than just abstract visuals and novel technology, they are a fun, uncomplicated applications accessible to clients and audiences in wide-arranging sectors and context. Striping away colours, Ascreen's brand stationery exhibits the young specialists' creative attitude and holistic service in bold icons and patterns, extracted from the language of the digital communication realm.

DE Masha Portnova

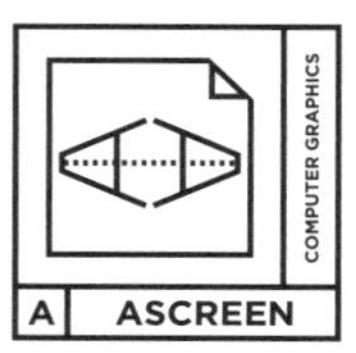

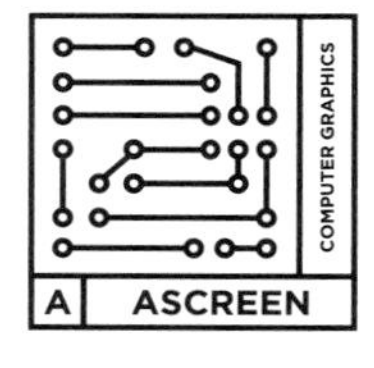

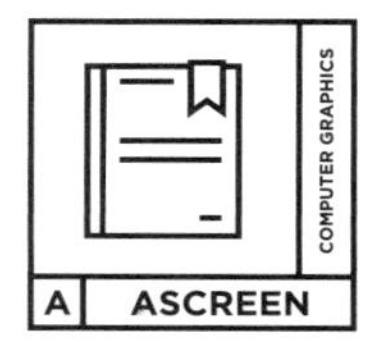

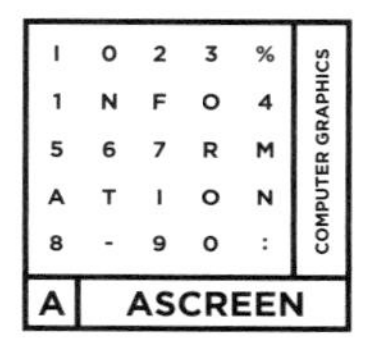

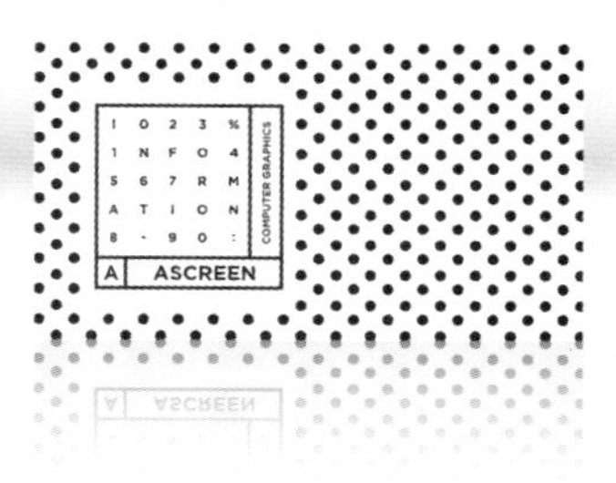

Николаичев Борис

Директор | Санкт-Петербург | ул. М. Новикова, д. 41

mail@ ascreen.ru | ascreen.ru

+ 7 (812) 456 70 34 / + 7 (904) 333 7 999

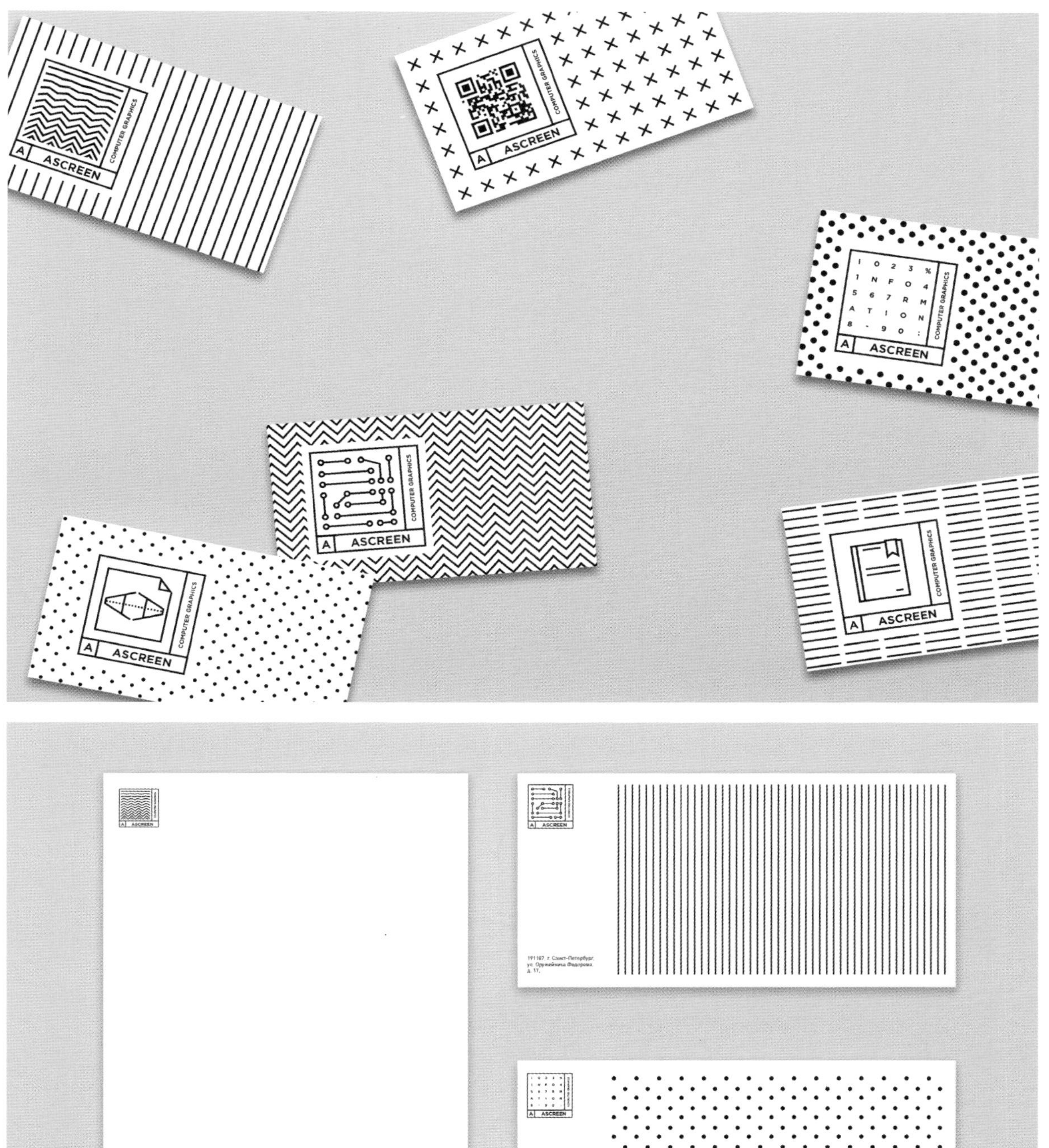

50 x 90 mm
Coated paper 350gsm
CMYK

Spilt Milk Interior Design

Confetti has developed a set of interchangeable logos for Melbourne based interior design studio, Spilt Milk. The variations capture the unpredictable nature of dancing fluids with the letter 'I' and 'L' twisting in different ways, which stretch into an infinite looping pattern pressed on to the card's back. On the cards' faces are two compact logo designs, also with a spontaneous appeal. The use of drink coaster card was a possibly conscious choice to conclude the concept.

DE Confetti Studio **CL** Spilt Milk Interior Design

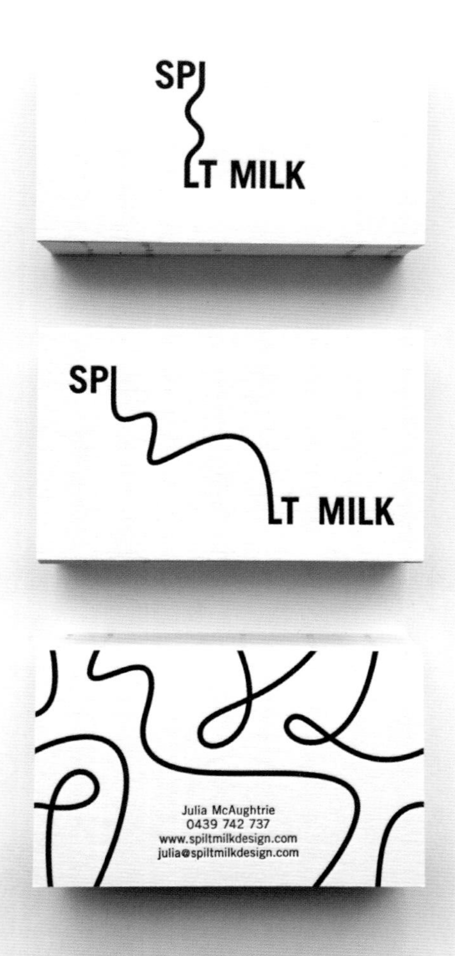

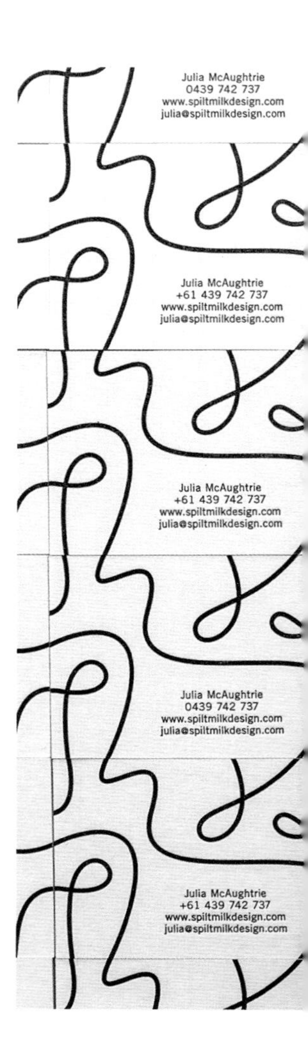

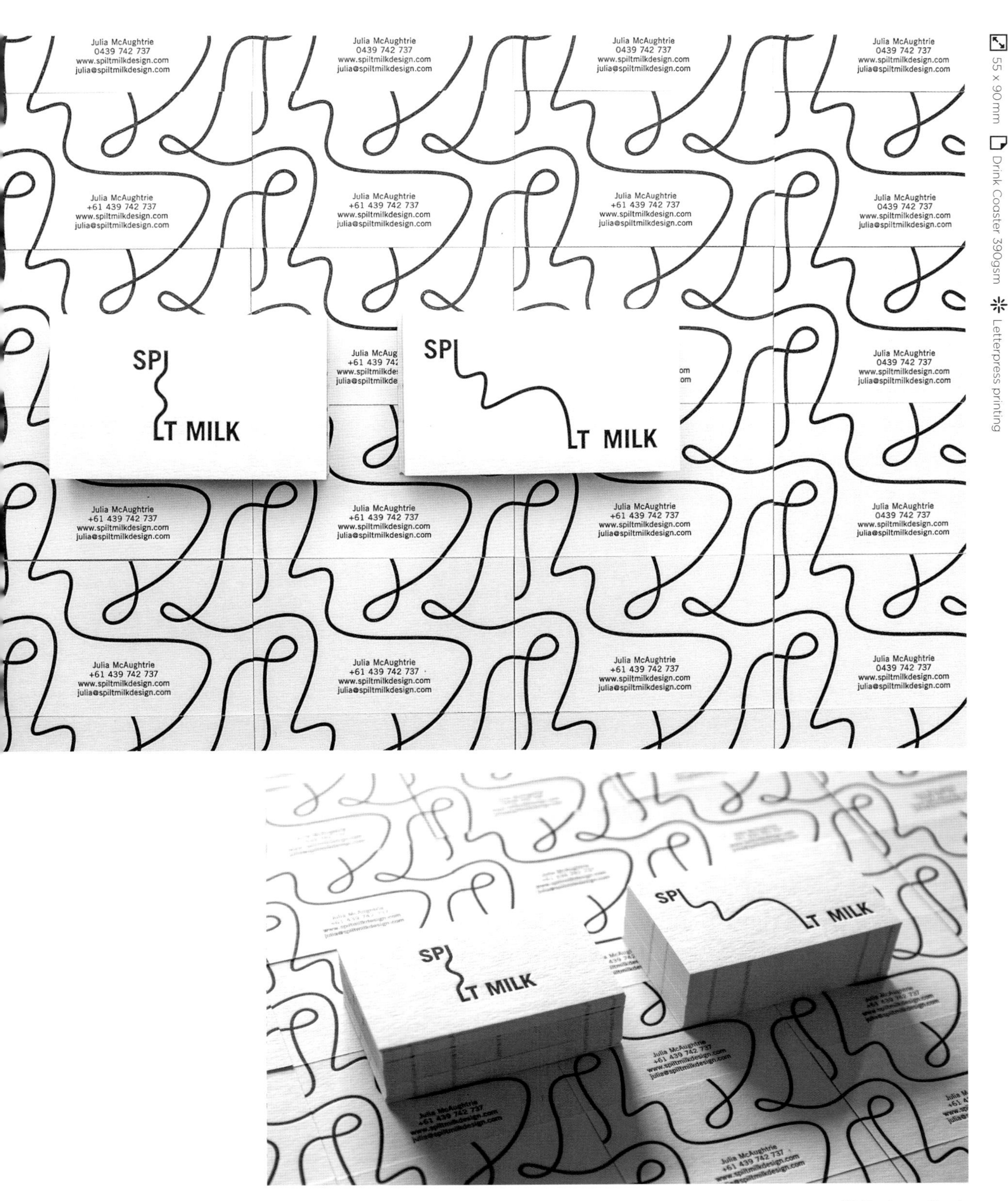

55 x 90mm

Drink Coaster 390gsm

Letterpress printing

Giuseppe Giussani

Giuseppe Giussani's brand identity speaks of the inseparable connections between the bespoke wood flooring craftsmen and wood. Since everything related to Giussani starts with wood, tree growth rings naturally become a poetical synonym for the artisan, his mastery and his work. A letter 'G' was subtly incorporated into the ring pattern to imply "Giussani's fate is written in wood" in a literal sense.

DE 45gradi **CL** Giuseppe Giussani

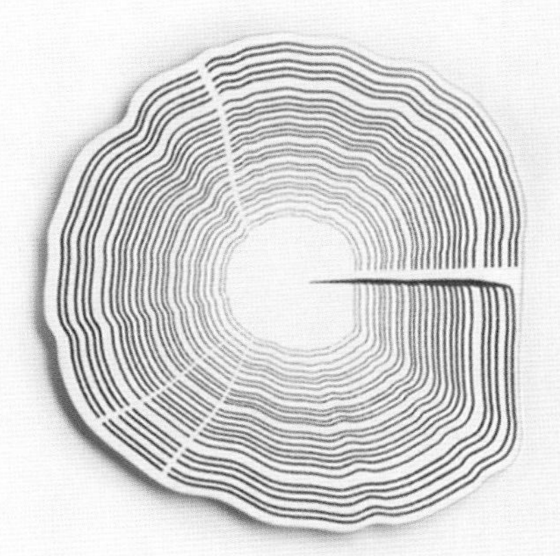

58 x 55mm
Old Mill White 250gsm
CMYK
Die cutting, edge dipping

Husler & Rose

Husler & Rose is an online boutique that sells furniture and lifestyle goods personally sourced and restored by the owners. Inspired by Herbert Bayer's Bauhaus posters and old Jazz record sleeves, overlaid blocks of colour and stripe pattern adorn the shop's stationery with a timeless appeal. Blank spaces were left on their business cards where the owners can customise messages, a detail that responds to the shop's personalised sourcing service and emphasis on personal care.

DE POST— **CL** Husler & Rose

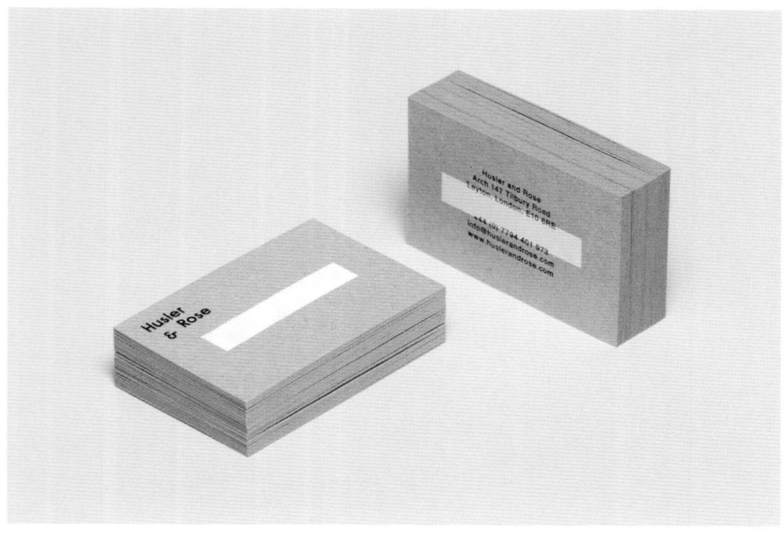

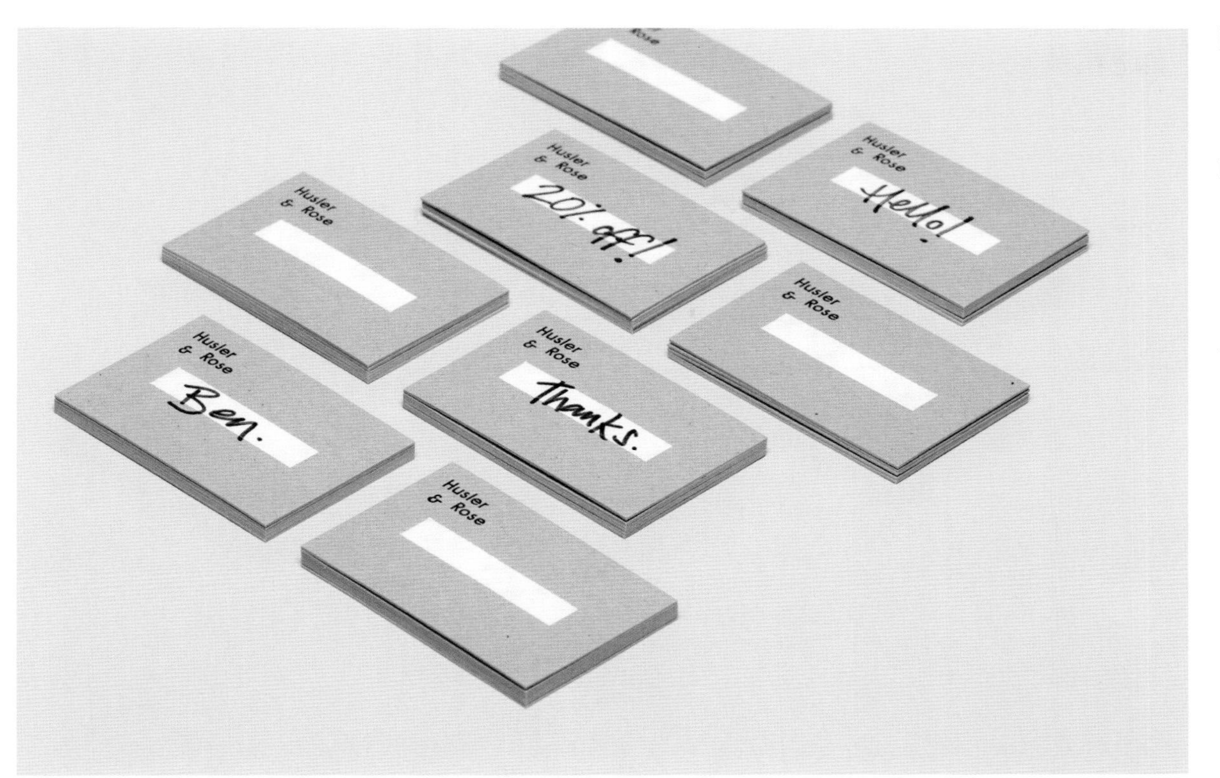

55 x 85mm
Eco Kraft 430gsm
Hot stamping

Fat Cow

Fat Cow is a specialist beef restaurant employing the Japanese way of picking, cooking and serving beef. To establish a Japanese cultural tie within the Singaporean steakhouse, traits of wabi-sabi aesthetic that finds beauty in simplicity, economy, austerity and the integrity of natural objects are visible across its communications and menus which use grained veneer as the base. The mark and the searing on the wood are also reminiscent of the branding of cattle.

DE Foreign Policy Design Group **CL** Fat Cow, Singapore

40 x 90mm · Wood Veneer · Laser cutting, searing

Noocity

Comprising "Noo" for "collective consciousness" and "city" for the urban world everyone lives in, Noocity stands for a passion for bringing food production to homes, made possible with efficient and affordable equipments. Another Collective proposed a visual identity that pulls together planting tools and crops as sketches in one big white space, alongside a logo that unifies urban dwelling with a sturdy green leave. Only the logo was accepted at the end.

DE Another Collective **CL** Noocity

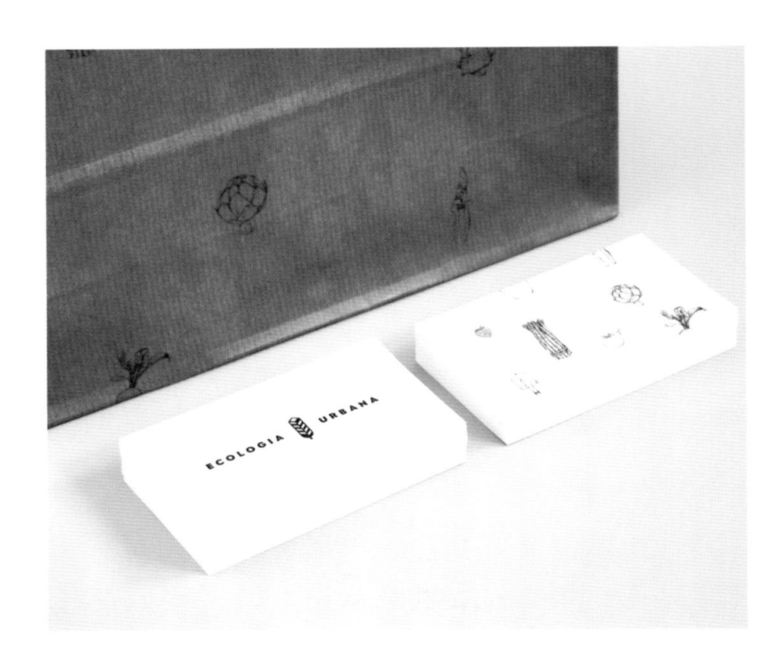

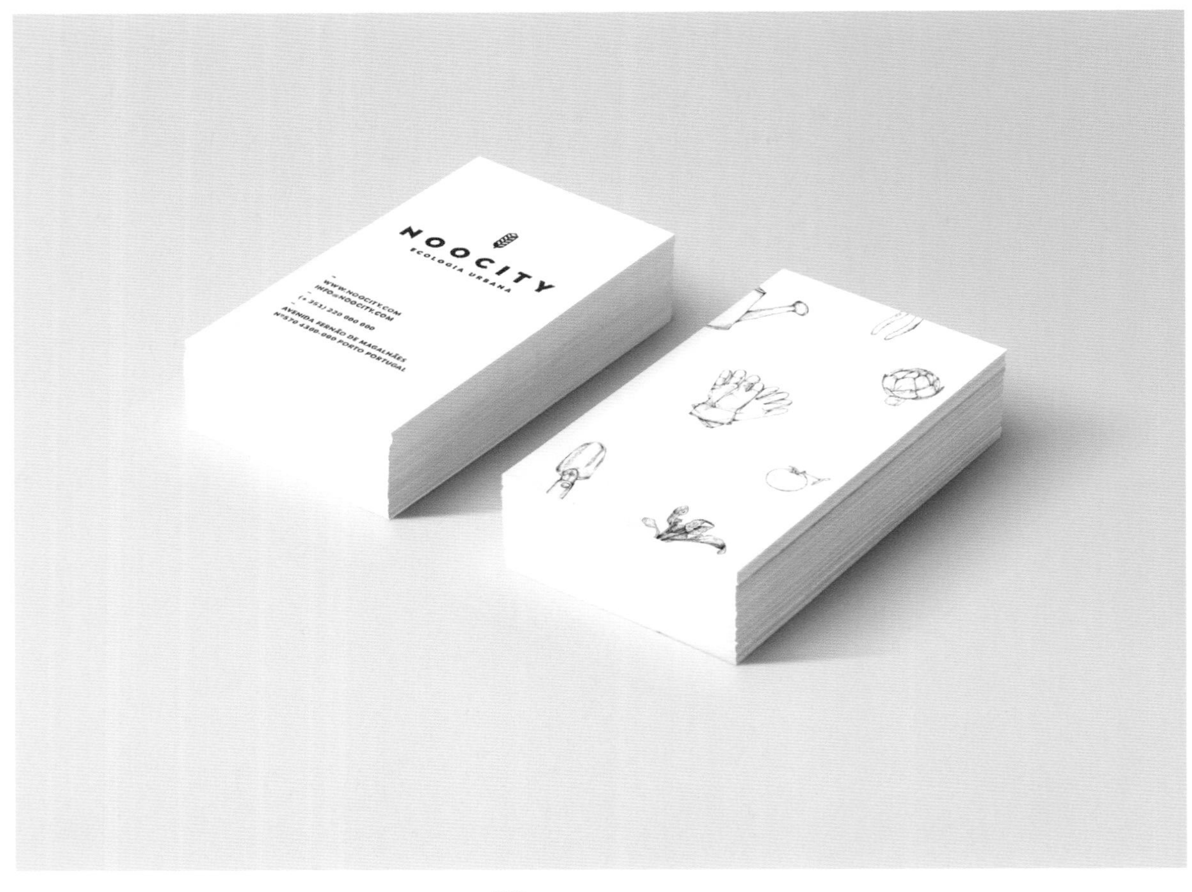

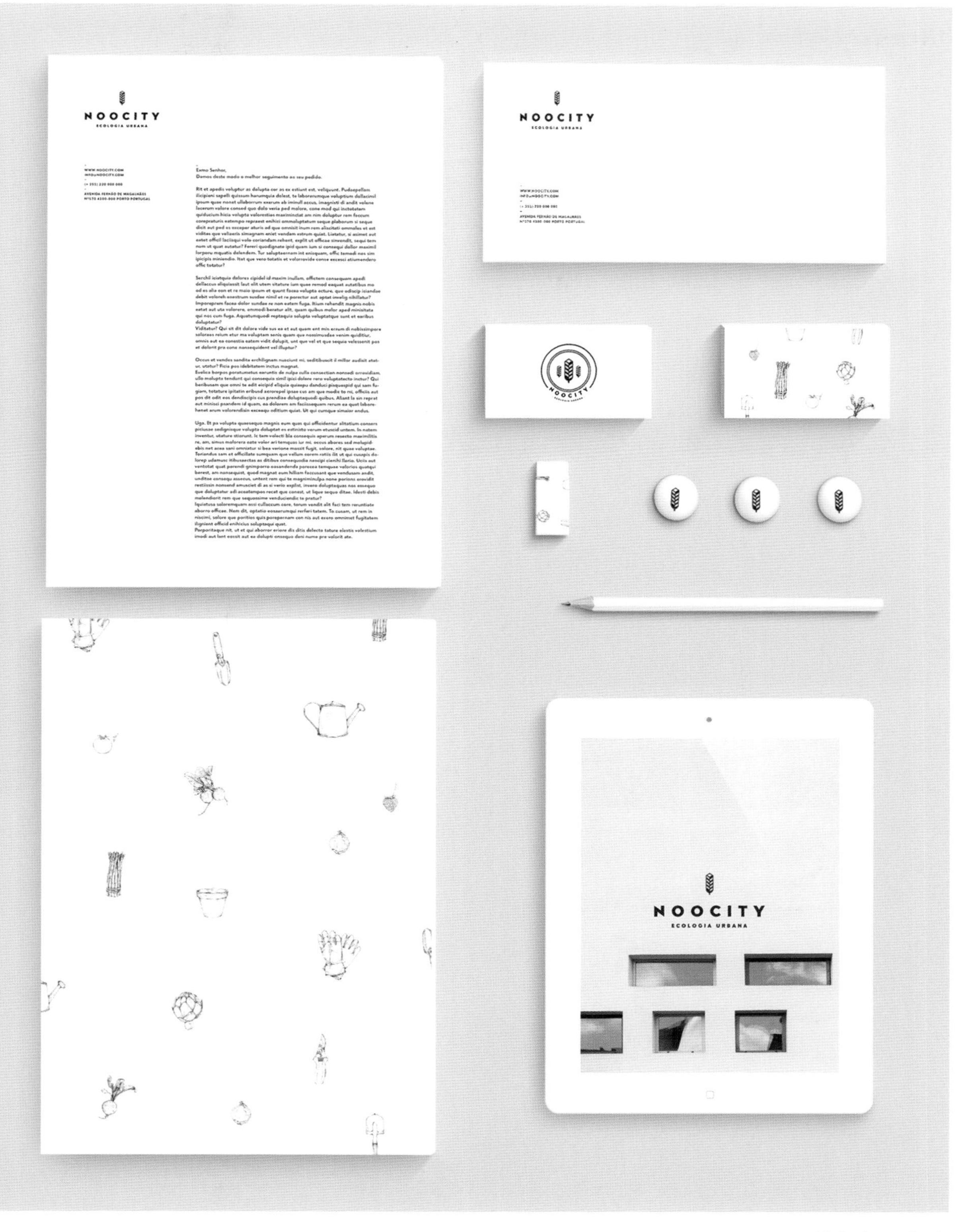
NOOCITY
ECOLOGIA URBANA

Pin-to Livros

A Cantonese expression for "where" and a Portuguese word for "books" together bring about Pin-to Livros, an upstair bookshop in Macau stuffed with art books, literature and publications from local independent publishers. Its unconventional positioning is generally reckoned as "rebellious" when compared with the mainstream bookshops. The idea was integrated into Pin-to Livros' logo and business card design as a tear-off page and a torn edge.

DE Pinmo Design Studio **CL** Pin-to Livros

90 x 55mm
Beautone Fancy Paper Cotton Fibre Paper 216gsm
Spot colour
Die cutting, letterpress printing

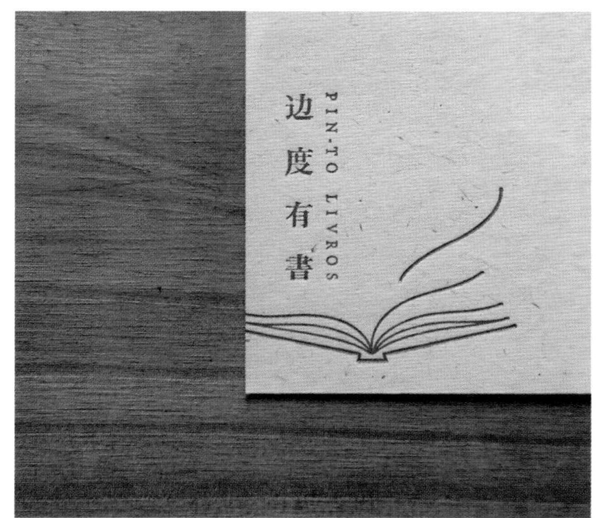

Nicholas Farnworth

Designer Nicholas Farnworth has updated his professional identity in an effort to kickstart his career and start out as a freelance graphic designer. A logo made of Farnworth's initials is central to his new identity. The bold contemporary ligature juxtaposes with the geometric characters of the logotype and robust black and white structural choices to pronounce the creator an honest, skilled person. A bold black frame concludes the design and holds the separate info lines together.

DE Nicholas Farnworth

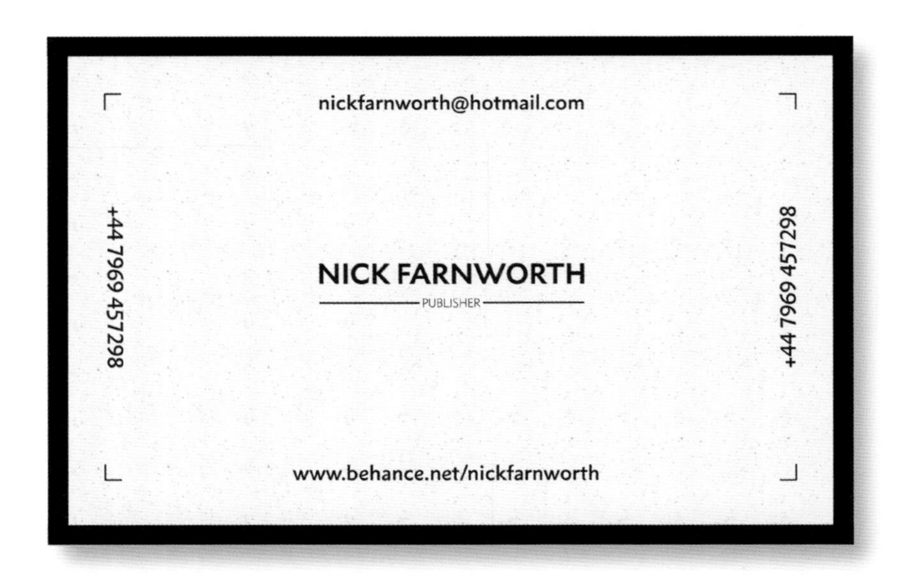

55 x 85mm
Gmund Bier Weizen 250gsm
CMYK
Screenprinting

Jolien Brands

Graphic designer Jolien Brands has conceived a logo and stationery set to define her design approach. The result is a bold yet feminine identity that conveys a sense of personal responsibility, consistency and rationality through a geometric, single-weight monogram, effective infographics and a tall, rounded functional sans serif typeface ideal for letterpress printing. Letterpress printing adds tactility to Brands' business cards and faithfully translates her enthusiasm for print-based design.

DE Jolien Brands **CR** Studio Esteban (PT)

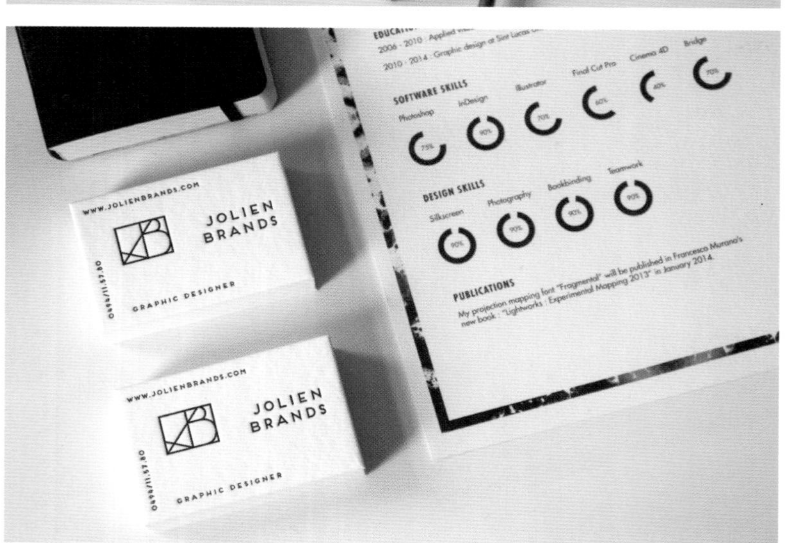

55 x 85mm

WILD Cotton Paper 850gsm

Letterpress printing

Mitsuori Architects

Mitsuori is a Melbourne based boutique architecture studio. Translated as 'threefold' in Japanese, their name inspired a set of business card and compliment card designs with a simple 45 degree crease on each end. When bent correctly, the paper stationery will be able to stand independently and convey an aesthetic architectural form that takes in mathematical calculations, structure and shade. A dark grey uncoated stock was used, with six passes of white ink to provide a unique matte finish.

DE Thomas Williams & Co.
CL Mitsuori Architects

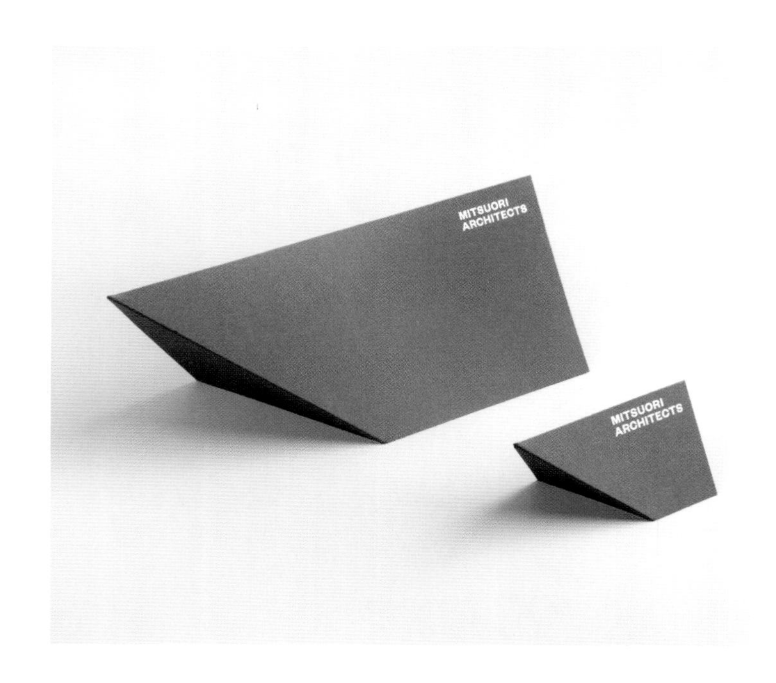

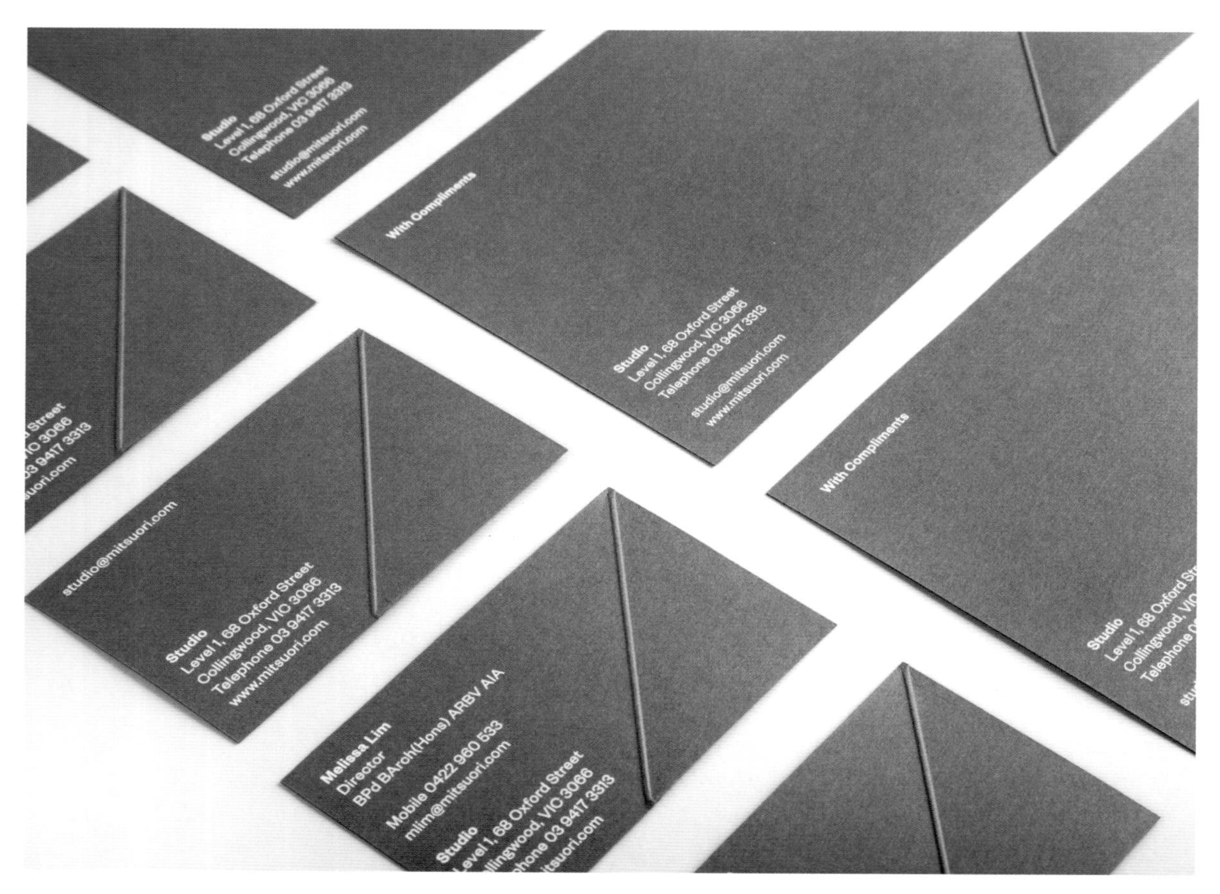

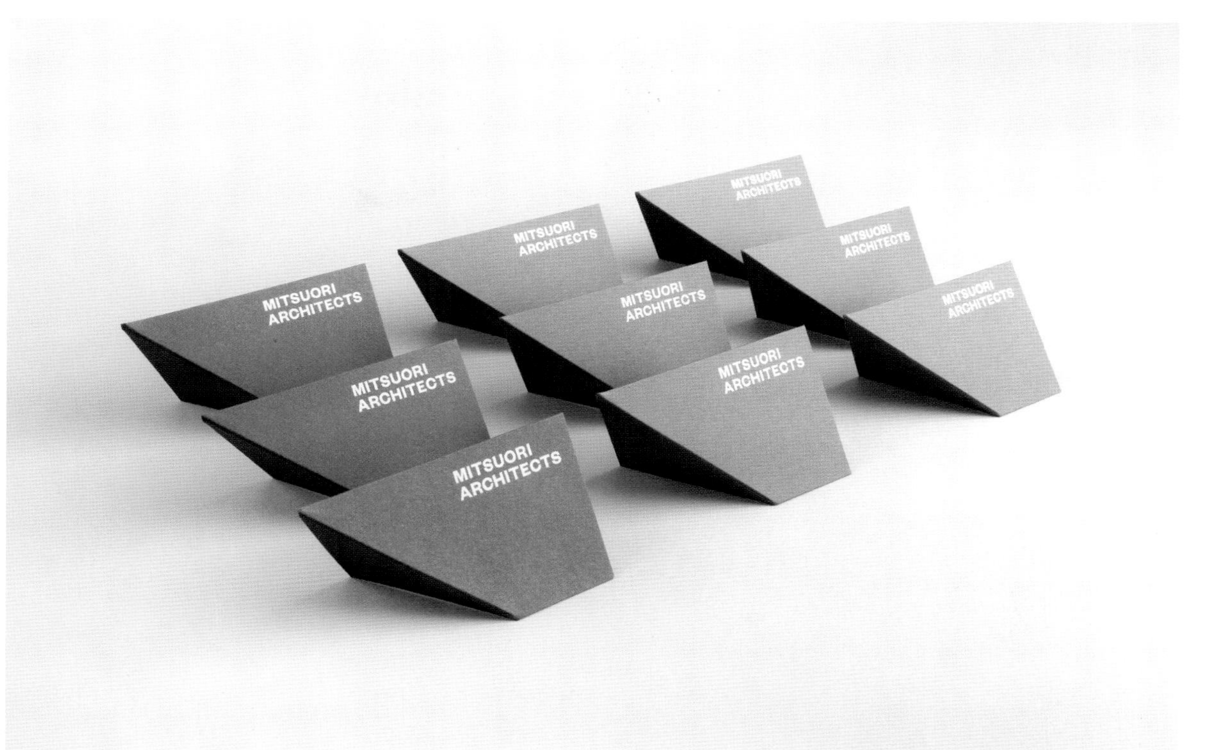
MITSUORI ARCHITECTS

MITSUORI ARCHITECTS

55 x 89mm
Keaykolour Vellum Sombre Grey 300gsm
Spot colour
Embossing

JUSTA

Ukrainian JUSTA legal group's visual identity was informed by their motto "Flexibility Within the Law" that responds to the country's adaptable judicial practices and a clientele with little trust in the system. Without a logo as the main element, multidirectional folds create understated decorative patterns across JUSTA's printed collateral and form a literal interpretation of Ukraine's fluid judicial system in the absence of marketing graphics.

DE Graphic design studio by Yurko Gutsulyak **CL** JUSTA legal group

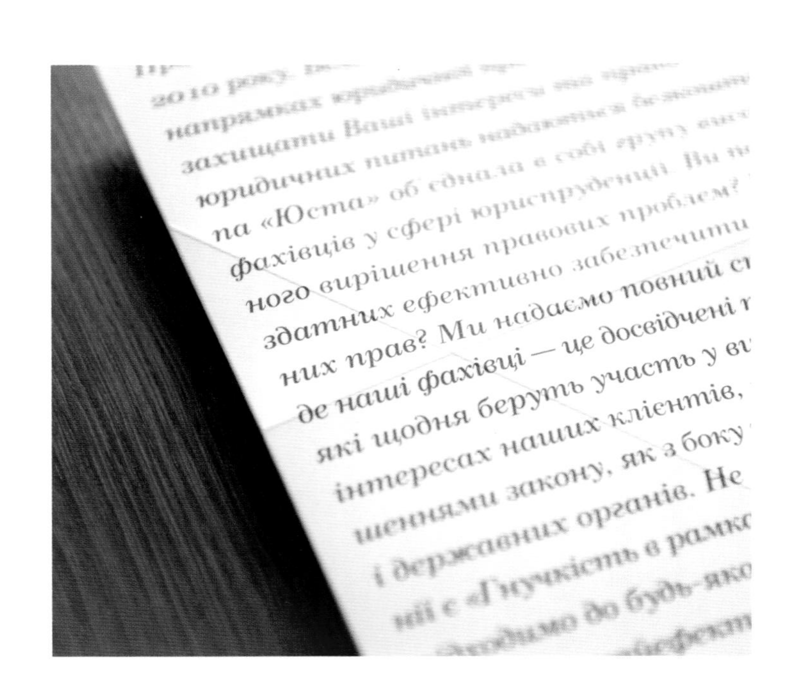

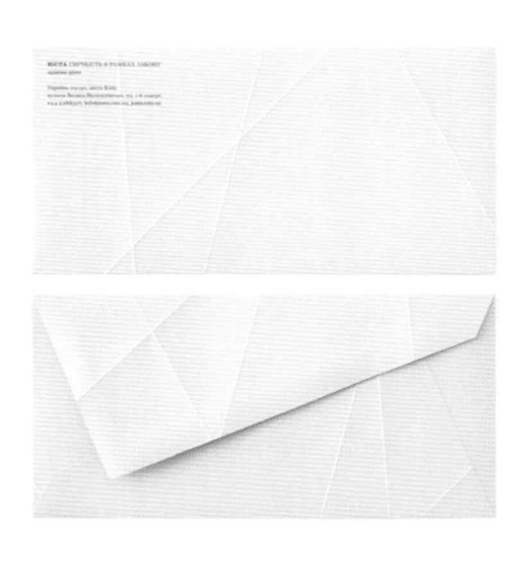

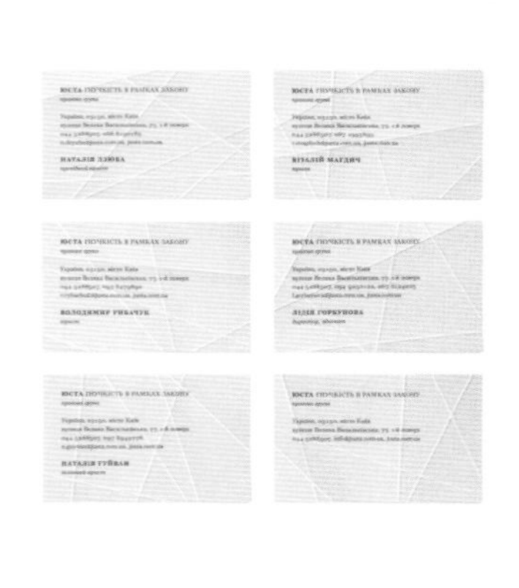

ЮСТА ГНУЧКІСТЬ В РАМКАХ ЗАКОНУ
правова група

Україна, 03150, місто Київ
вулиця Велика Васильківська, 77, 1-й поверх
044 5288507, 097 8979776
n.guyvan@justa.com.ua, justa.com.ua

НАТАЛІЯ ГУЙВАН
головний юрист

55 x 87mm
Sirio Color Sabbia 290gsm
Spot colour
Embossing, screenprinting

Maria Freydina

Coming with a birch plywood card holder, these veneer-based business cards is part of Russian art director Maria Freydina's self-promotional kit. In two colourways, the cards feature a custom angular logotype derived from a grid that bears resemblance to traditional Russian patterns and Union Jack. Visual elements were laser etched to the cards, each comes in three tiers for extra sturdiness and durability.

DE Maria Freydina

50 x 90mm
Mahogany & Birch Wood Veneer 3mm
Laser cutting

Steve Li

A brand identity entirely composed of apertures may seem natural for practised acupuncturists like Steve Li. Tailored for a business that is predominantly driven by word of mouth, Li's card design strengthens and takes this personal recommendation process to its best advantage by punching Li's details onto his happy clients' business cards. The combination equals a real endorsement and a physical proof of visit as they are passed on to new potential clients in need.

DE RE **CL** Steve Li

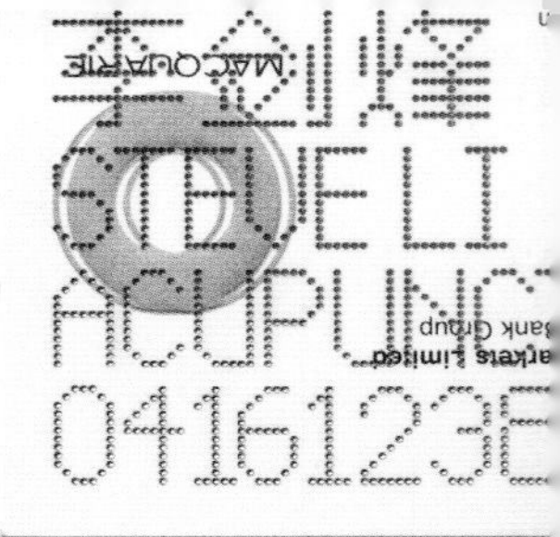

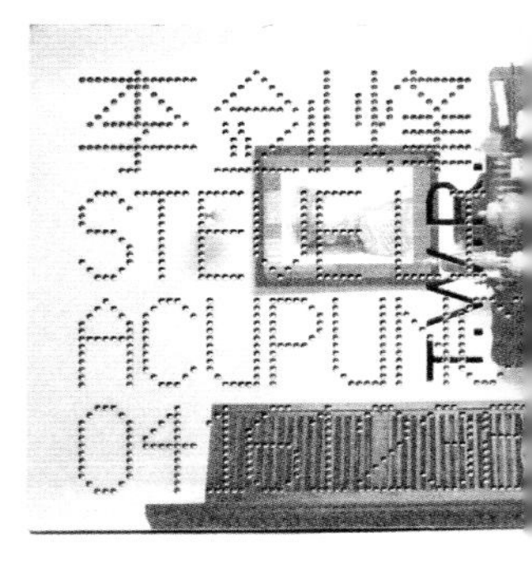

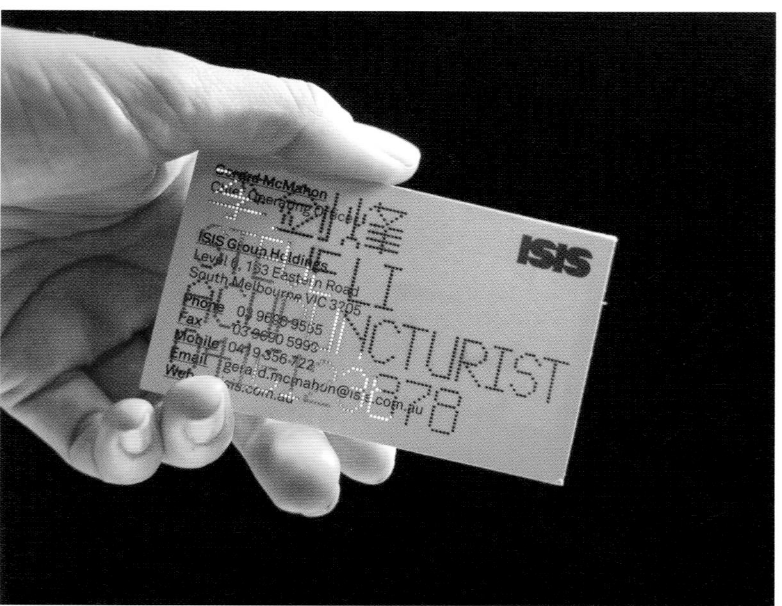

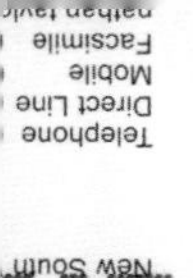
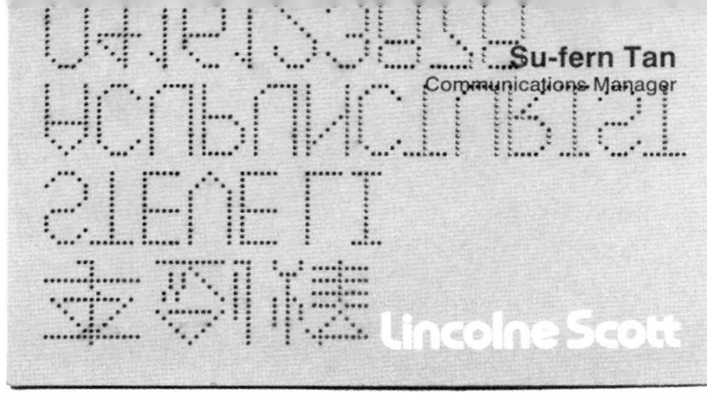

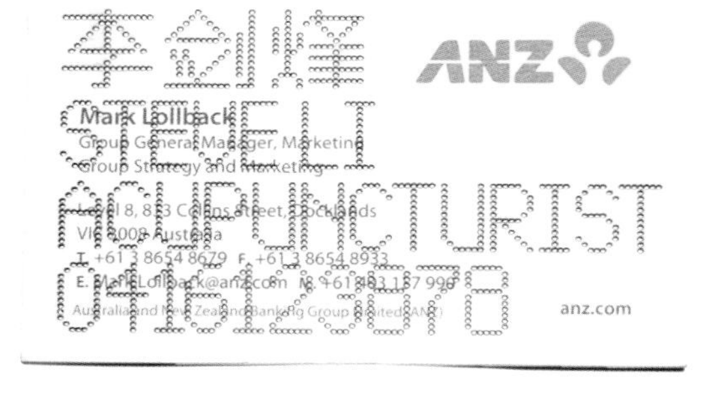

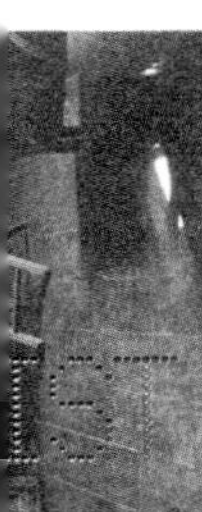

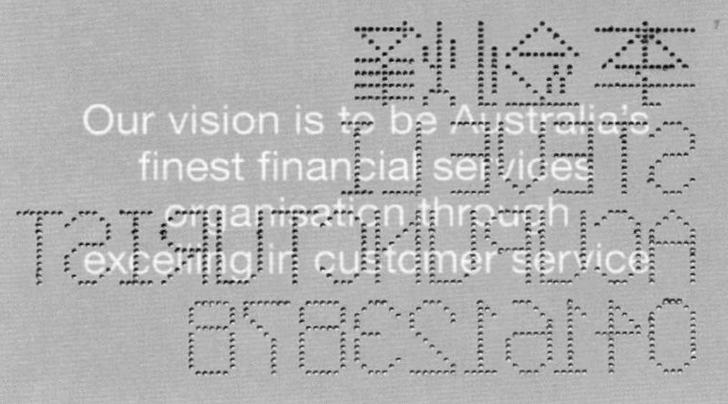

Various

Various

Laser cutting, perforation

CUB animation studio

Sprinkles of colours, baby-blue and orange and chubby stencil logotype deliver the dynamism in Hungarian animation studio, CUB. Colours exchange on the two founders' business card, effortlessly creating two distinctive yet coherent designs that speak as one. As for their company website, a gif-version of the three-letter logo, hand-rendered using the same stencil and different pens and paints, interprets CUB's specialty and energy in the most evident way.

DE Agnes Herr & Nóra Demeczky **CL** CUB animation studio

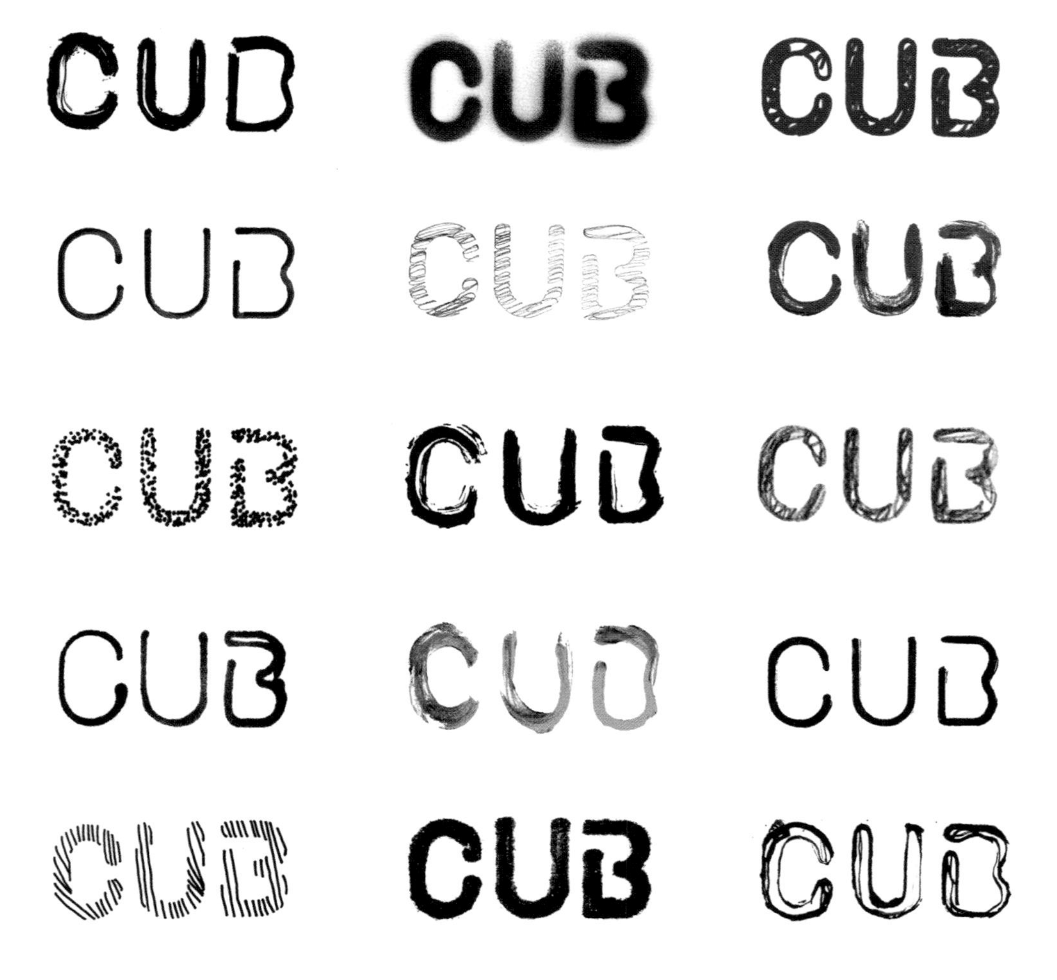

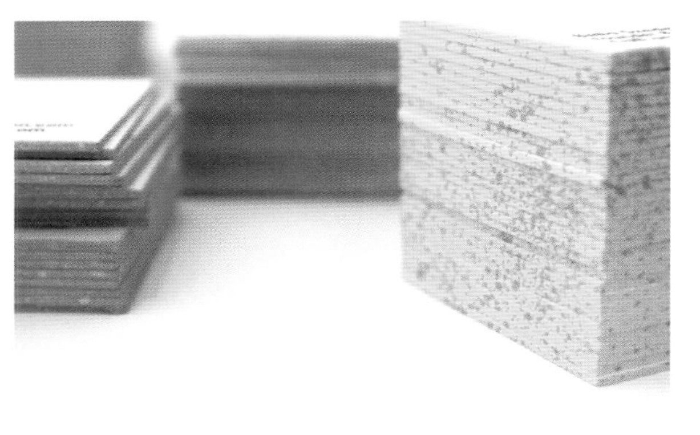

50 x 90mm
Museum Paperboard Extra White 400gsm
Spot colour
Edge dipping, screenprinting

Cocoon Labo inc.

Cocoon Labo Inc.'s identity is a graphic interpretation of the brand's commitment and the influences their work could possibly bring. Where a bright sky blue connotes Cocoon's environmental focus on communication, white takes to represent the word "cocoon" in a literal sense. A geometric uppercase logotype projects a strong sense of conviction in the brand's daily communications, and repeats to create a ripple effect on the envelopes' back.

DE Motoi Shito **CL** Cocoon Labo inc.

55 x 91mm

Araveal Snow White 200gsm

Spot colour

Edge dipping, embossing.

3Five Media

Aspiring to expand their core operations around film and TV post-production to include photography and corporate infomercials, 3Five Media has asked for a minimalistic and scalable logo that will fit all medias. Victor Malin's solution is a mathematically calculated, stamp-like emblem where the name "3Five" is distilled into a numeral compound. Simple structure and bold strokes enhance the logo's legibility whether it's applied singly as favicon or as 3Five's primary logo with the name by its side.

DE Victor Malin **CL** Dries Smulders (3Five Media)

50 x 90mm

Colorplan Ebony Black 700gsm

Debossing, hot stamping

Amperian

Amperian's brand identity is as equally sweet as the dessert bars the Singaporean specialist arranges for new couples. In accord with the meaning of wedding that celebrates love matches, 150 pastel combinations were rendered to set off the bold, classy Amperian face and establish Amperian as the ideal contender for different personalities. The design was coupled by MOO's Quadplex technology to boost a sense of individuality for each of service provider's business cards.

DE BÜRO UFHO **CL** Amperian

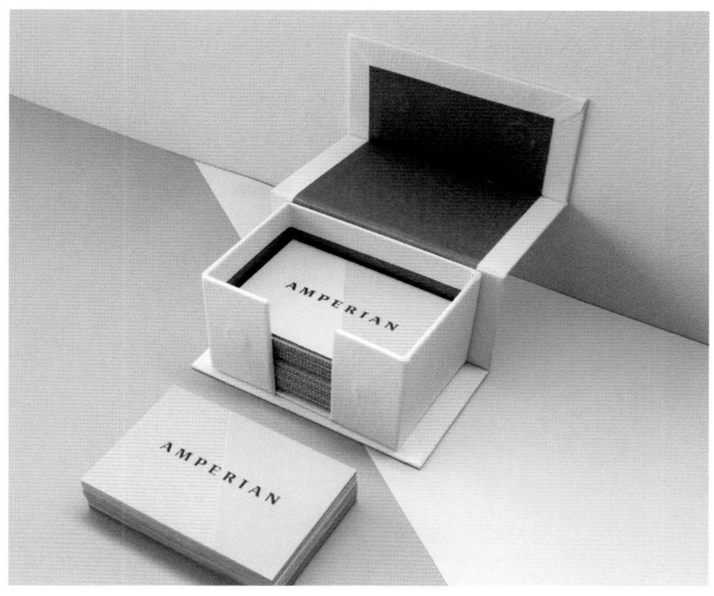

55 x 84mm

Quadplexed Mohawk Superfine Paper 600gsm

CMYK

Media Tube

Media Tube is a Shanghai-based gallery dedicated to exhibiting and presenting contemporary media artists within a progressive curatorial framework. Movements, abstract conceptions and the evolving forms of media art are encapsulated in colour patches inspired by the unique art of broadcast and frequency bands. A custom typeface incorporating visual disturbance was also designed for the gallery's publication containing art news and reviews.

DE not available design **CL** Media Tube

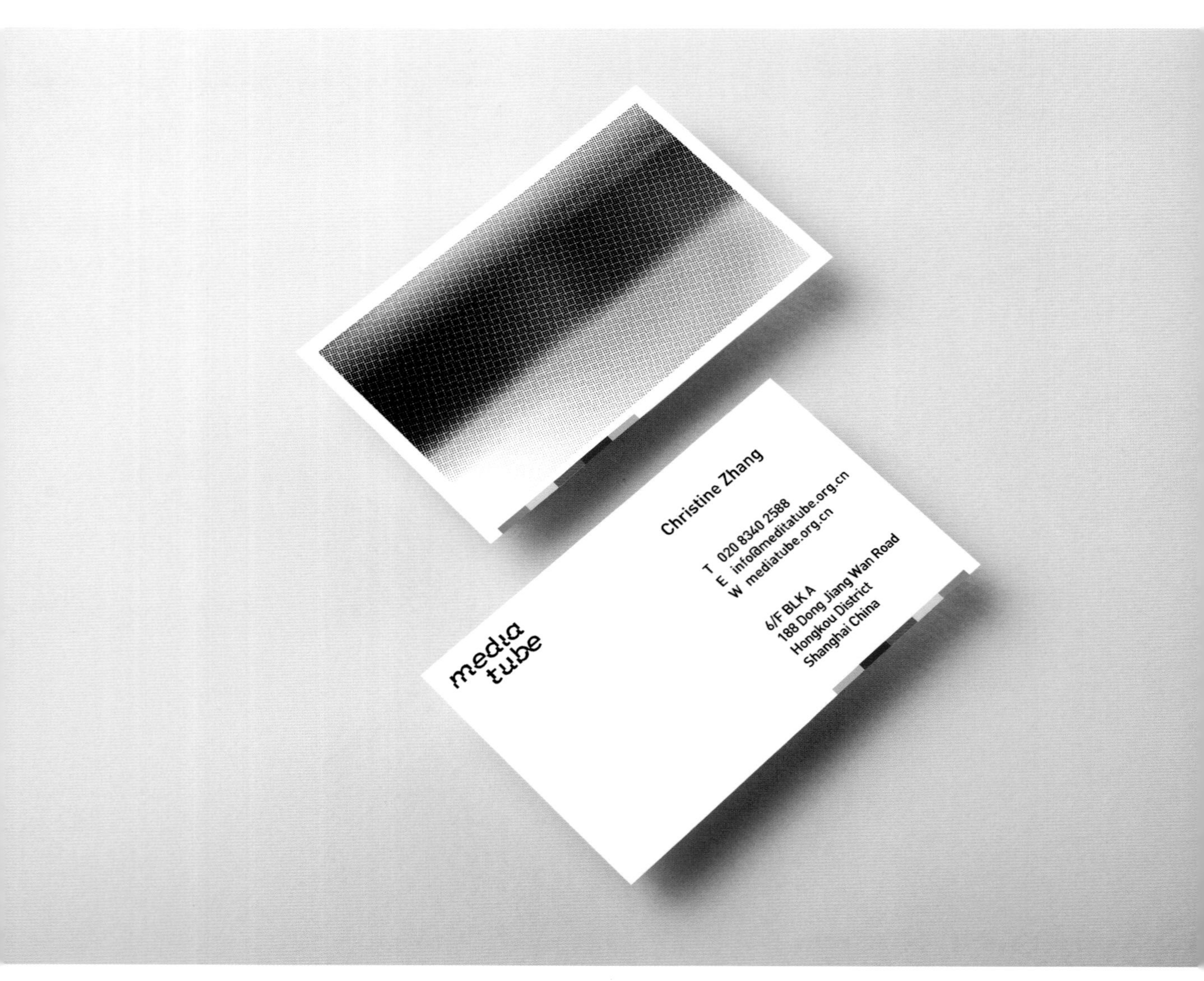

54 x 90mm

Antalis Matter Goya White 380gsm

CMYK

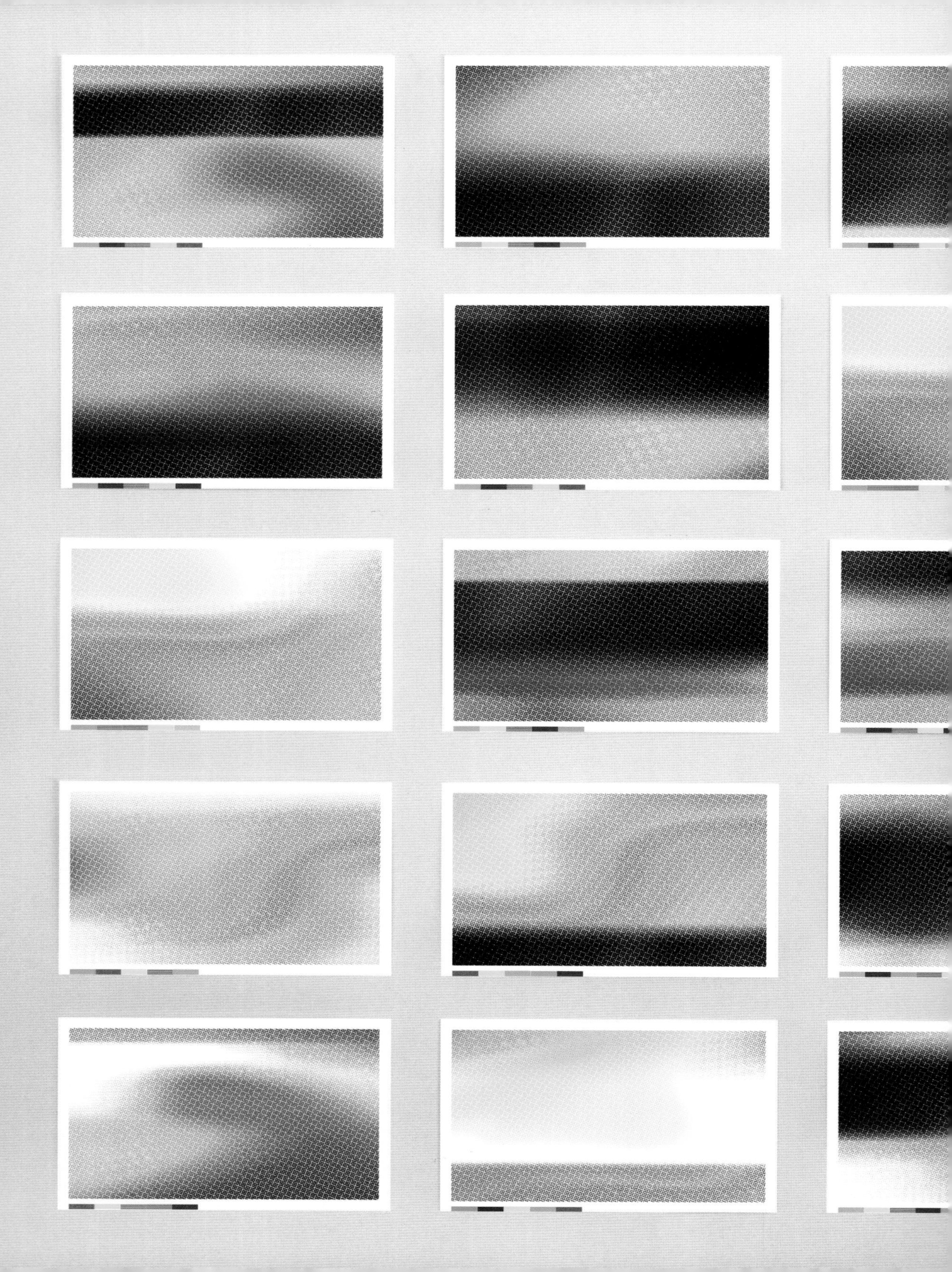

Art Business Card

Art Business Card is a collection of blank cards with face templates that target stylists, makeup artists and hairdressers — creatives who are constantly in need of handy tools to pencil down their ideas and designs for clients or their own reference. Provided with a face over a blank surface, creative individuals are free to improvise these ladies' looks with varying face shapes using colours, markers or cosmetics.

DE Lesha Limonov

90 x 50mm PRISMA Flux Soft White 270gsm CMYK Duplex, screenprinting

#ArtBusinessCard
art
business
card
with love ...
ArtBusinessCard

Ryan Romanes

A year after going freelance full-time, graphic designer and art director Ryan Romanes has decided to make his occupation official and produce his own business cards. With both his first and last name starting with a "R", Romanes adopted the uppercase letter as his mark. A stencil letterform, Dala Floda by Commercial Type, enables the die cut mark to stand prominently with pride on his single-sided card, over contact details foil stamped with white ink.

DE Ryan Romanes **CR** Stitch Press (PD)

84 x 55mm

Stitch Press Black Card 450gsm

Die cutting, hot stamping

Fibra

Fibra is a Peru-based multimedia agency aspiring to make brand vision tangible and breath life into every brand they touch. One way to manifest this promise and creative capacity is through their business cards that come with a lavish touch offered by a heavy debossing applied to both sides of bulky cardboard. A bright coral colour accents Fibra's name on the card as well as its edges painted by hand.

DE Fibra **CR** Quimera digital, Daniel Bengoa Photography

55 x 90mm

Smurfit Kappa Compact Recycled Paper 2mm

Spot colour

Duplex, edge dipping, letterpress printing, screenprinting

Alexander Palkin

A human resource management specialist and leadership trainer by profession, Alexander Palkin leads three types of training programmes with an objective to enhance individual client's leadership skills, career and productivity. Three geometric ripples convey Palkin's diverse orientations and the course of progression with a blue rhombus offering a clear, focused goal that both Palkin and his clients move towards.

AD & DE Vladimir Shlygin
CR Nick Tokarev (PH)

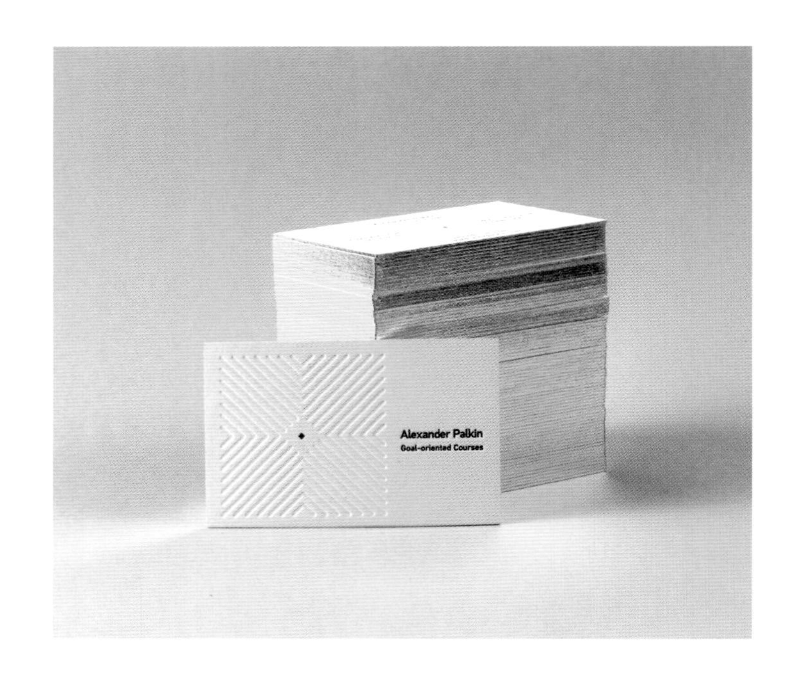

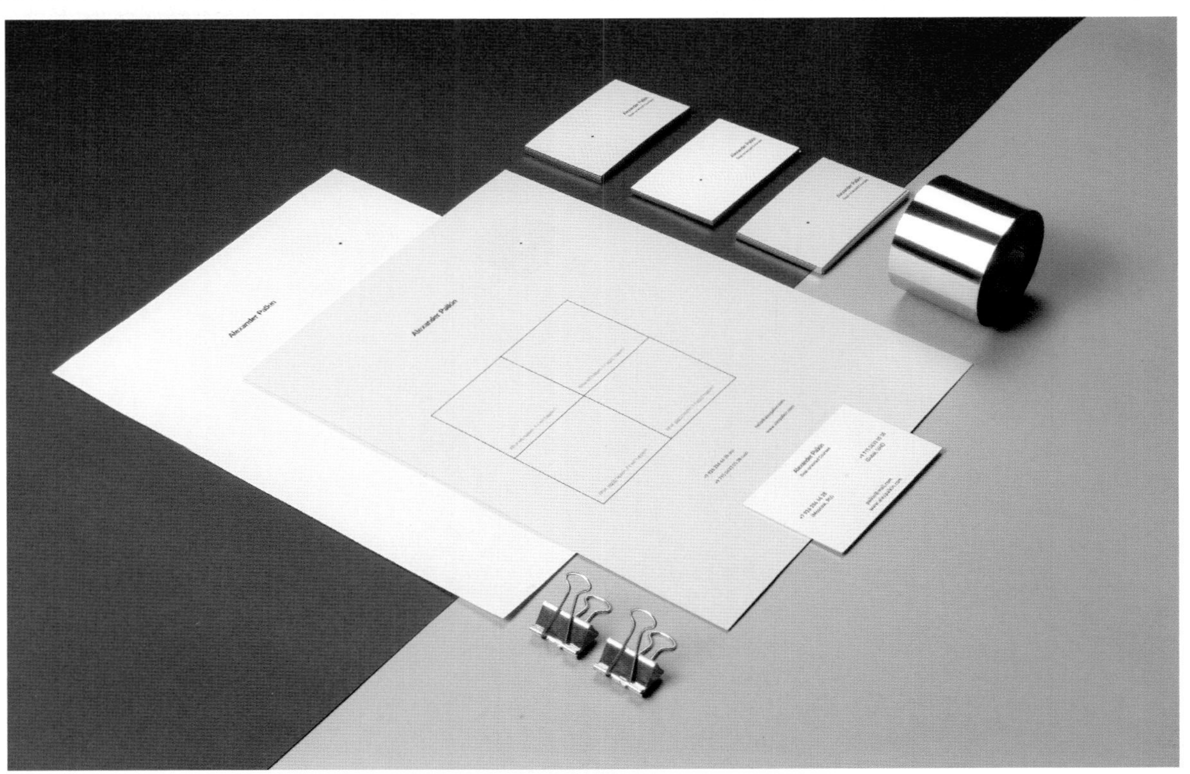

55 x 85mm

Gmund Gentlemen Blue, New Gray, Linen Cream 320gsm

CMYK

Edge dipping, hot stamping, letterpress printing

TU DESIGN OFFICE

The single Chinese character "TU" represents designer Tu Min-shiang and his namesake design office. Pairing a bulky stock with simple visual elements and a reduced palette, Tu's visions are condensed into a double-sided business card with a custom logomark hinting at the designer's cultural root, respectful attitude as a service provider, and prudent approach to design. Tu's business card has a metallic version bronzed with gold ink.

DE TU DESIGN OFFICE

90 x 55mm
Gray Cardboard 650gsm
Spot colour
Hot stamping

Business Cards

Confetti

Confetti's letterpressed business cards with gold foiling and a perky red is a material extension of the design studio's website design and result of meticulous manual colour matching. It has taken three hits of custom to achieve the current colour that is visually comparable to the RGB red initially optimised for computer display. The cards are produced at an old family-run letterpress business based in Melbourne.

DE Confetti Studio

55 x 90mm Stephen Chilled White 330gsm Hot stamping, letterpress printing

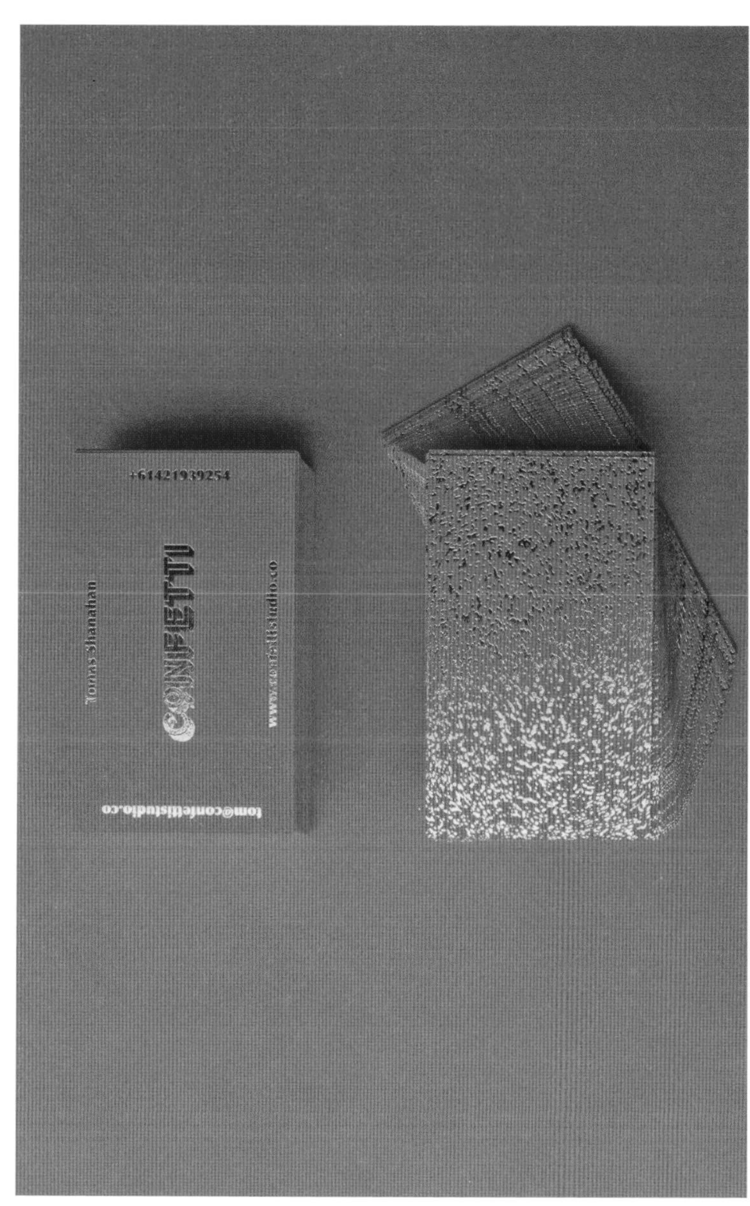

Brigitte La

Fresh design graduate Brigitte La's business cards were produced at the cusp of completing her studies and venturing out into the business world. Eschewing the consideration of strategic branding from a designer's perspective, the young professional decided to have fun with the task and delivered her passion for life in an array of delicious motifs and funky designs. Inside the frames made of colourful patterns find Brigitte La's address that leads to Brigitte La's online portfolio.

DE Brigitte La **CR** MOO Inc. (PT)

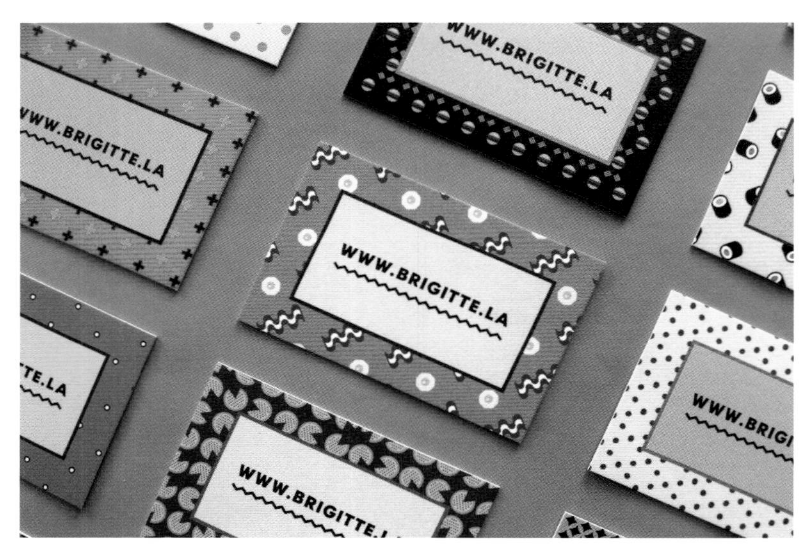

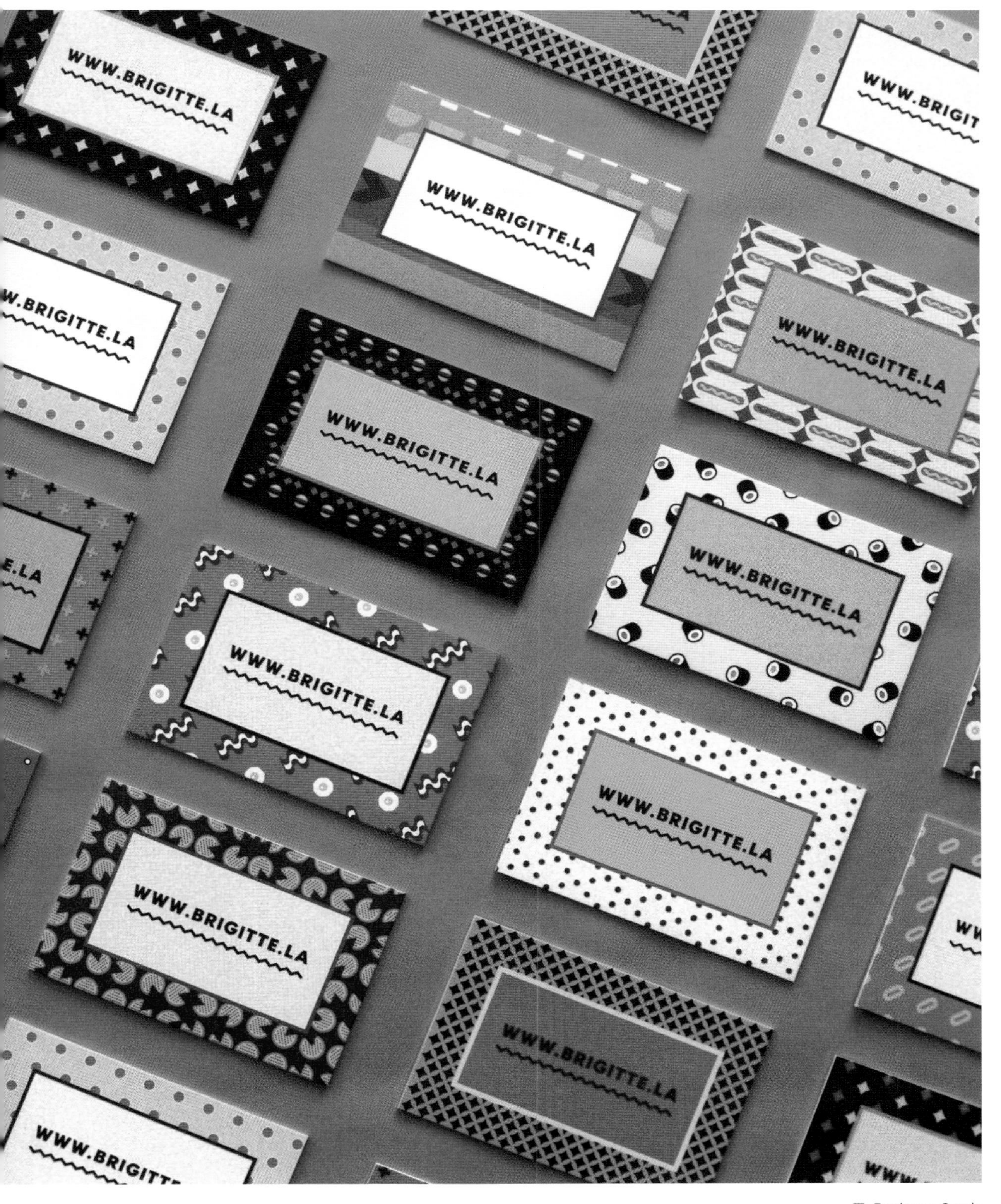

54.86 x 83.82mm Quadplexed Mohawk Superfine Paper 600gsm CMYK

Aleatoria

Aleatoria is a Madrid-based architecture firm that seeks to provide wide range of architectural and interior design services to fit client's' different needs. Drawing inspiration from optical art and the firm's enthusiasm for constructing, el estudio™ created a deck of cards with a beautifully patterned back that are strong enough for construction games. Aleatoria's logos coheres with this construction theme with a structural appeal.

DE el estudio™
CL Pablo García de Madariaga
CR María Laura Benavente (PH)

arquitectura & interiorismo

ALE
ATO
RIA

MADRID

—

arquitectura & interiorismo

A

ALEATORIA
MADRID

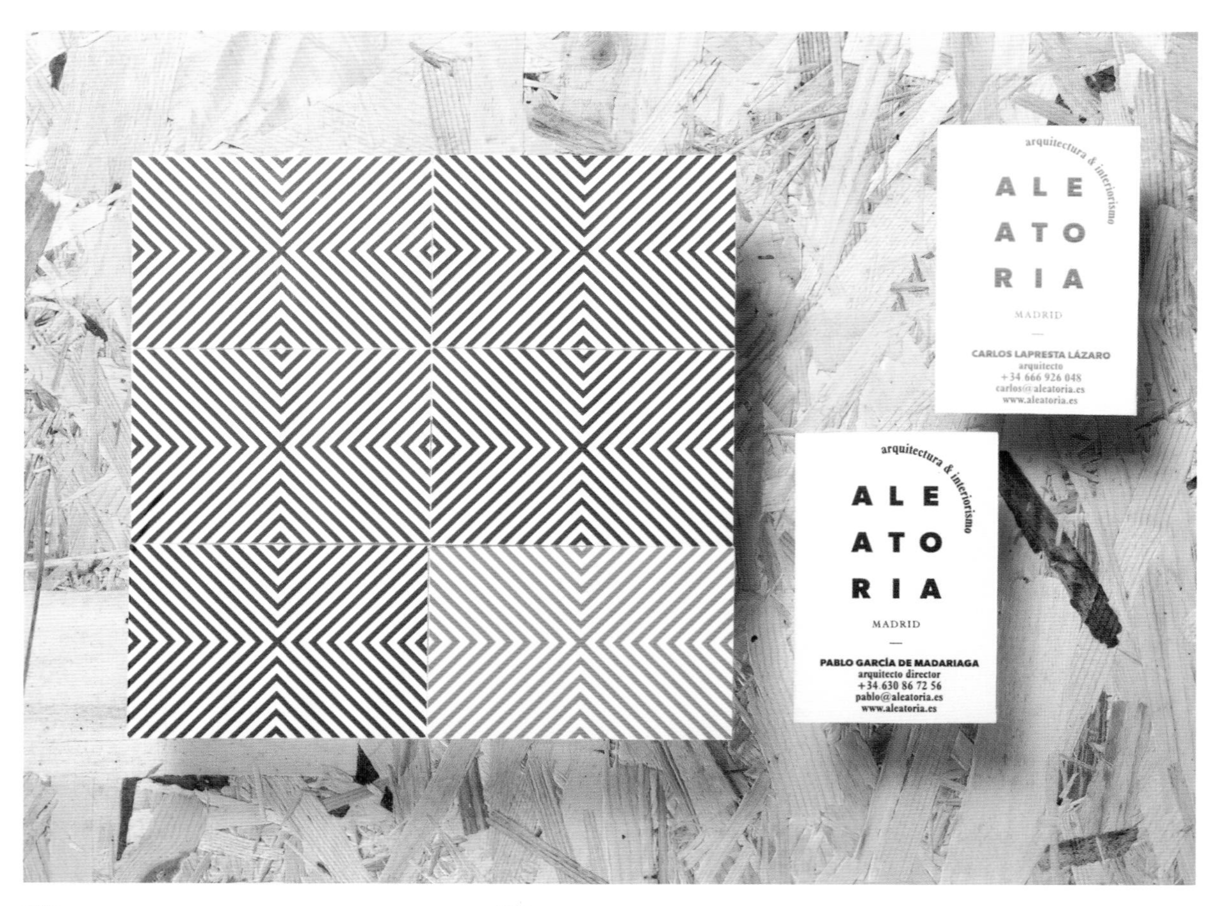

90 x 60mm
100% Cotton White Paper 600gsm
CMYK

How to Use a Business Card

Marco Oggian's business cards are but a simple piece of paper stationery. Bearing certainly no practical information that guarantees further association with this designer after the first encounter, the card is still fully functional as icebreaker as Oggian starts to introduce its alternative functions at current times. Chances are the unorthodox approach makes for a good risk and brings in friends and clients that share the same way of thinking.

DE Marco Oggian

55 x 85mm SBS Matte Black & White Cardboard 450gsm UV ink

Fonda Mexican

Primarily inspired by the Mexican tradition of people gathering at a local house for a mother's cooking, Fonda is a Melbourne based restaurant that offers authentic and healthy Mexican food. A Fonda, which refers to a local house with an open kitchen in Mexican culture, is warm, familiar and relaxed. The idea founded the bases of an overarching brand and print collateral, where a symbolic colour scheme is visible across formalised corporate stationery and interior space.

DE Wildhen Design **CL** Fonda Mexican

55 x 85mm Colorplan Ebony 350gsm CMYK, spot colour

Andia Angelidou

Just as significant as Paper is in the world of graphic arts, paper plays a leading role in designer Andia Angelidou's business card design. With one side displaying Angelidou's mark and contact details, the reverse is a vivid colour card with a corresponding die-cut symbol that emotionally matches the stock's colour. The die-cut hole reveals the monogram underneath, appearing as a mirrored design of the logo on the front.

DE Andia Angelidou **CR** Georgios Soumelidis (PH)

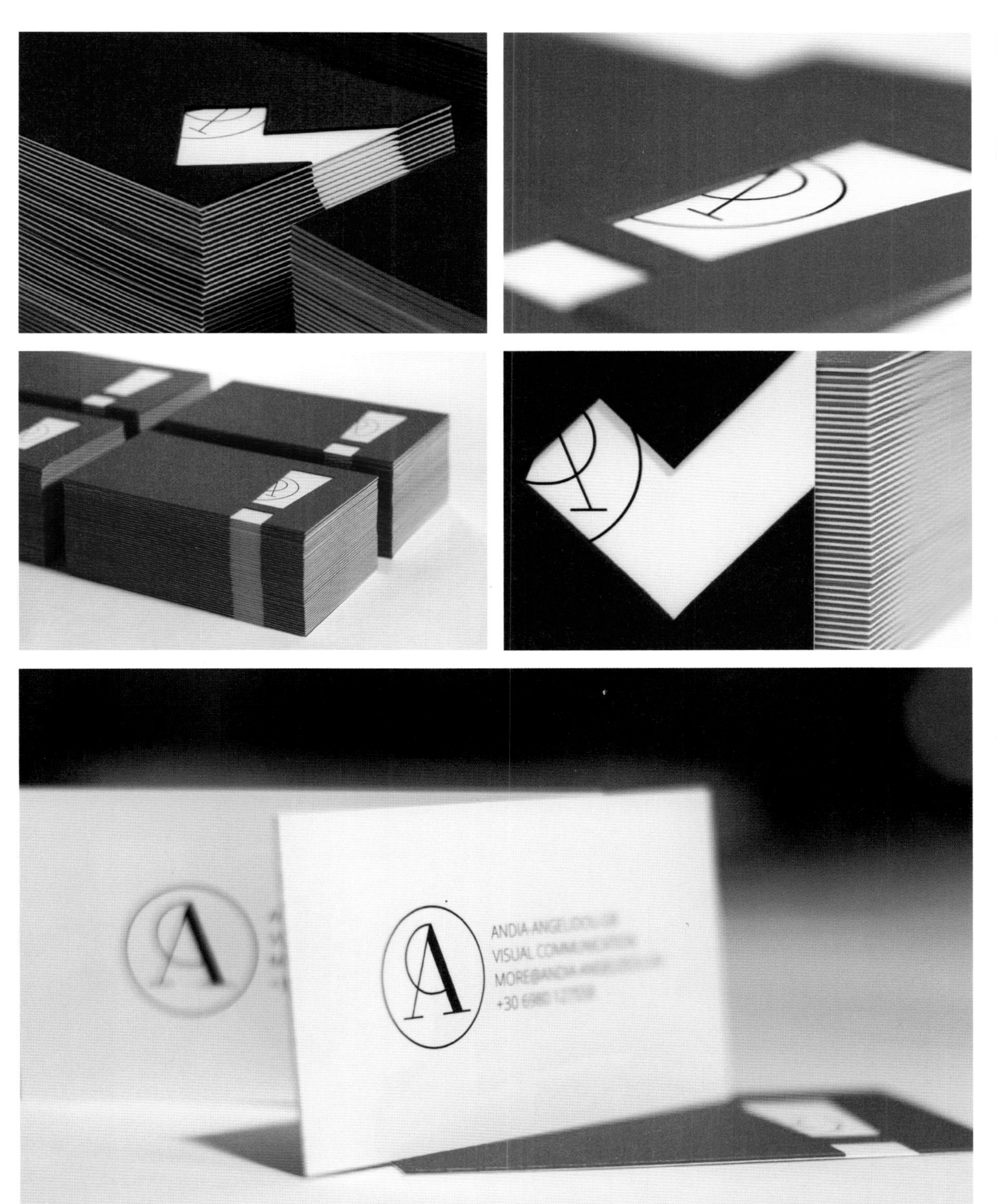

50 x 90mm
Curious Matter Désirée Red 380gsm, Adiron Blue 380gsm, Goya 270gsm
Spot colour
Die cutting, duplex

GRAF

GRAF is short for "Get Rich And Famous", which perfectly describes the purpose of this one-man music management army. With just the right amount of self-irony, WAAITT™ created a gold foiled design that reflects the lifestyle of the rich and famous.
The primary logo is a coat of arms consisting of music notes, a gold LP and an anvil, with a simplified version for the letterhead.

DE WAAITT™ **CL** GRAF

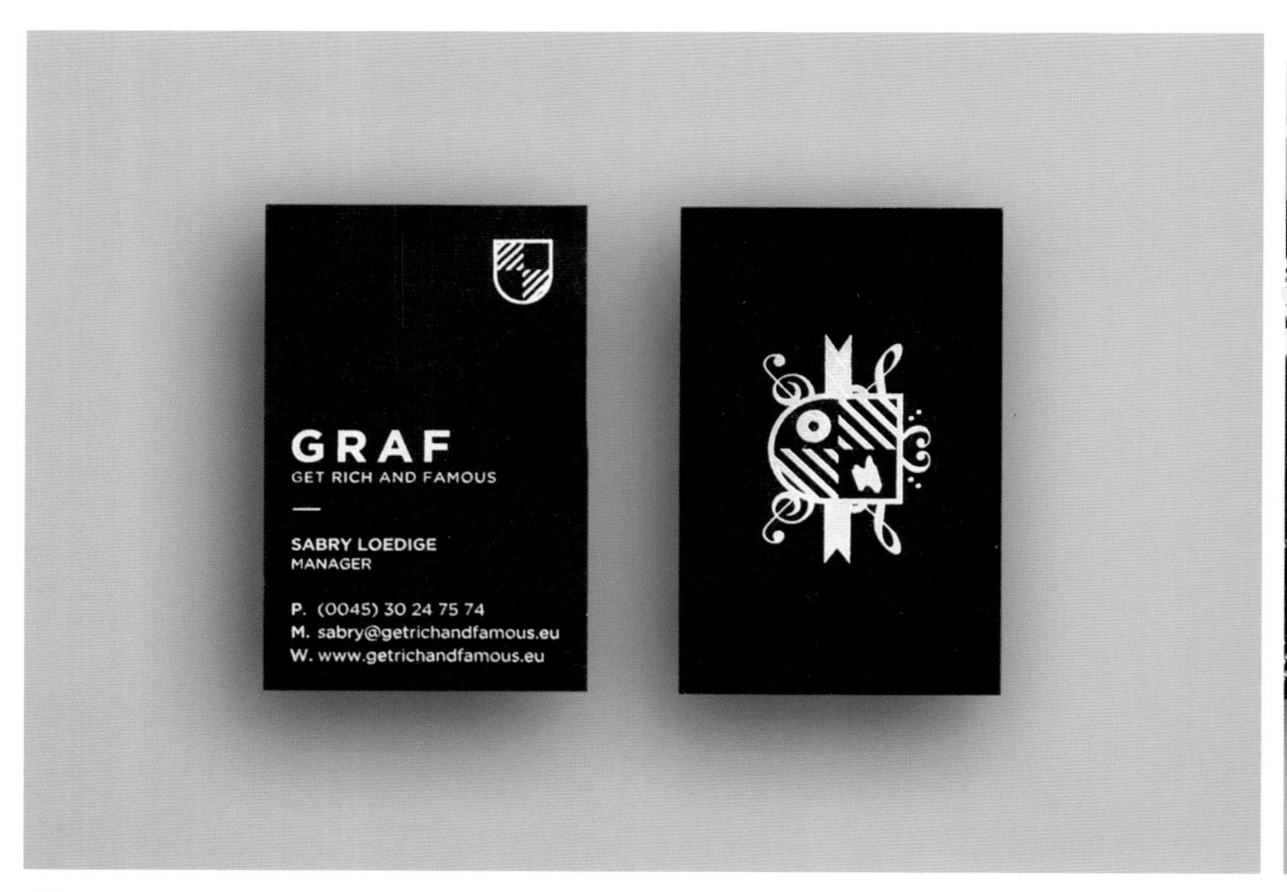

85 x 55mm

Black Uncoated 300gsm

Hot stamping

+ wolframgrafik

Athens-based visual artist and graphic designer Paschalis Zervas, aka + wolframgrafik's, business cards are a stack of print art, all made based on a single portrait of the late German conceptual artist, Joseph Beuys, taken before the 1944 plane crash, debatably a turning point for Beuys. Produced using random colours for each print, no two of Zervas' cards are the same. On the reverse side, contact details of the designer stand out in a prominent tangerine.

DE & PH + wolframgrafik
CR tind, Chrysanthos Angelakis (PT)

53 x 85mm Munken Pure Rough, Polar Rough, Lynx Rough 300gsm, etc. Screenprinting

Michael Barley

Photographer Michael Barley's business cards are meant to bring maximum impact as a promotional item when it's handed out to Houston agencies and design firms. Presented as a mailer, holding a couple of Barley's work inside in a windowed sleeve sealed with a tab sticker, these cards serve as Barley's miniature portfolio as well as a note announcing his relocation from New Mexico. A mail stamp containing the photographer's address completes the message.

DE 3 Advertising **CR** Michael Barley (PH), Studio on Fire (PT)

57.15 x 92.075mm
French Speckletone Natural 80C
CMYK, spot colour
Die cutting, letterpress printing, rubber stamping

CROP Salon

CROP's visual identity is unmistakably rooted in the confident, cutting edge and robust. Featuring a laser-etched logo where hairline decorative strokes meet a distinctively bold lettering, the letterpress business cards reference the salon's refurbished walnut interior, as well as their services that promise to deliver an innovative and harmonious experience. A light grey label helps to personalise each card with contact details of individual crew members and the salon.

CD & DE Device Creative Collaborative
CL Crop Salon
CR Public Letterpress (PD & PT)

88.9 x 50.8mm

Walnut wood, French Paper Pop-Tone Sno Cone 140# Cover

Spot colour

Laser etching, letterpress printing

Les Sales Gosses

French for "The nasty kids", Les Sales Gosses is a restaurant in Quebec that serves a menu influenced by both French and Italian cuisines. Asked for a visual identity that projects a rebellious and elegant image at the same time, Figure created a total package united by a black and white tone, from stencil logotypes to posters and the restaurant's interior — enriched by unique finishes and a breakage theme. Each business card's bottom was manually ripped to reinforce the impact.

DE Figure **CL** Les Sales Gosses

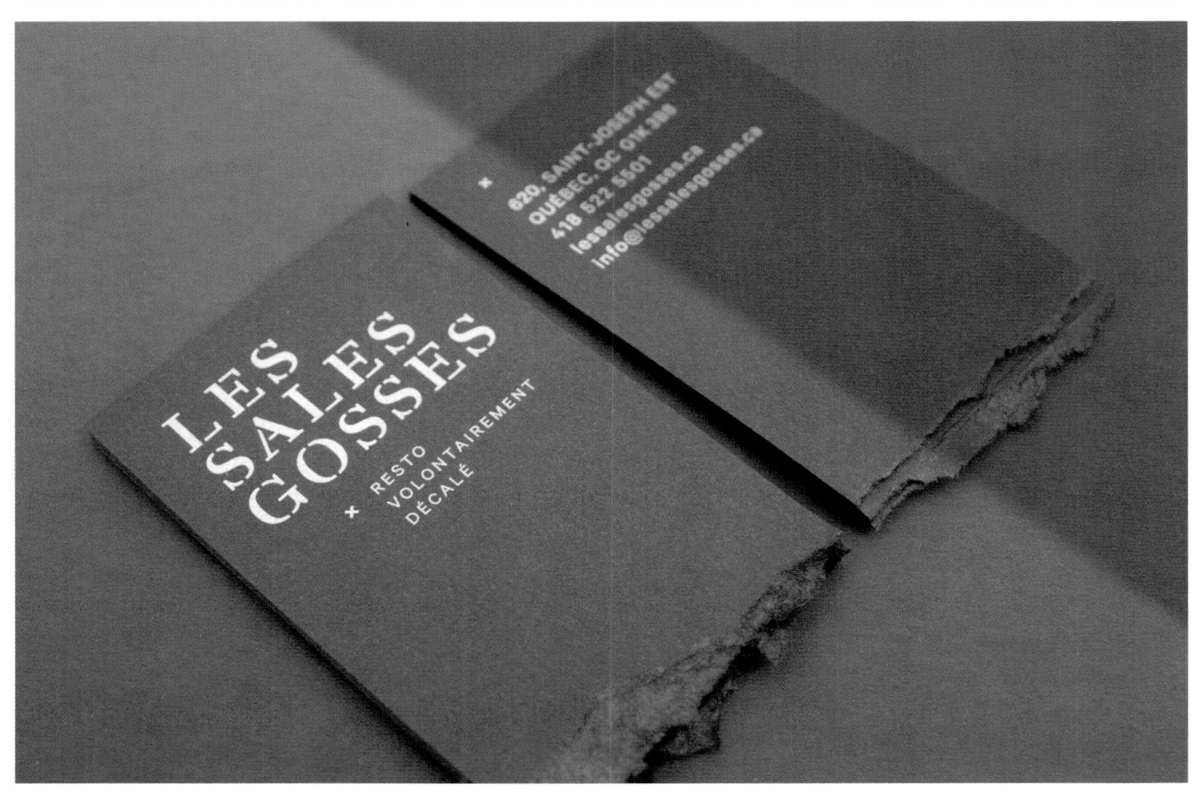

89 x 51mm
Neenah Classic Crest Epic Black 260gsm
Screenprinting

archimesh

archimesh is a Japanese manufacturer of decorative metal mesh for interior and architectural use. With two netted patterns foil-stamped to the card's brim, their business cards recreate the intricate touch and sheen of the meshes' fabrics in textured print. At the bottom of the card stands a logo 'M' with intersecting strokes, another detail to emulate the beauty of fine weaves.

DE Kamimura Typografie Gestaltung
CL Taiyo Wire Cloth Co., Ltd.
CR NSSG Inc. (AD & AG), OVERKAST(PD), Cosmotech Inc. (PT)

91 x 55mm GOJO Paper Kohaku Rough Dream 360.5gsm Hot stamping

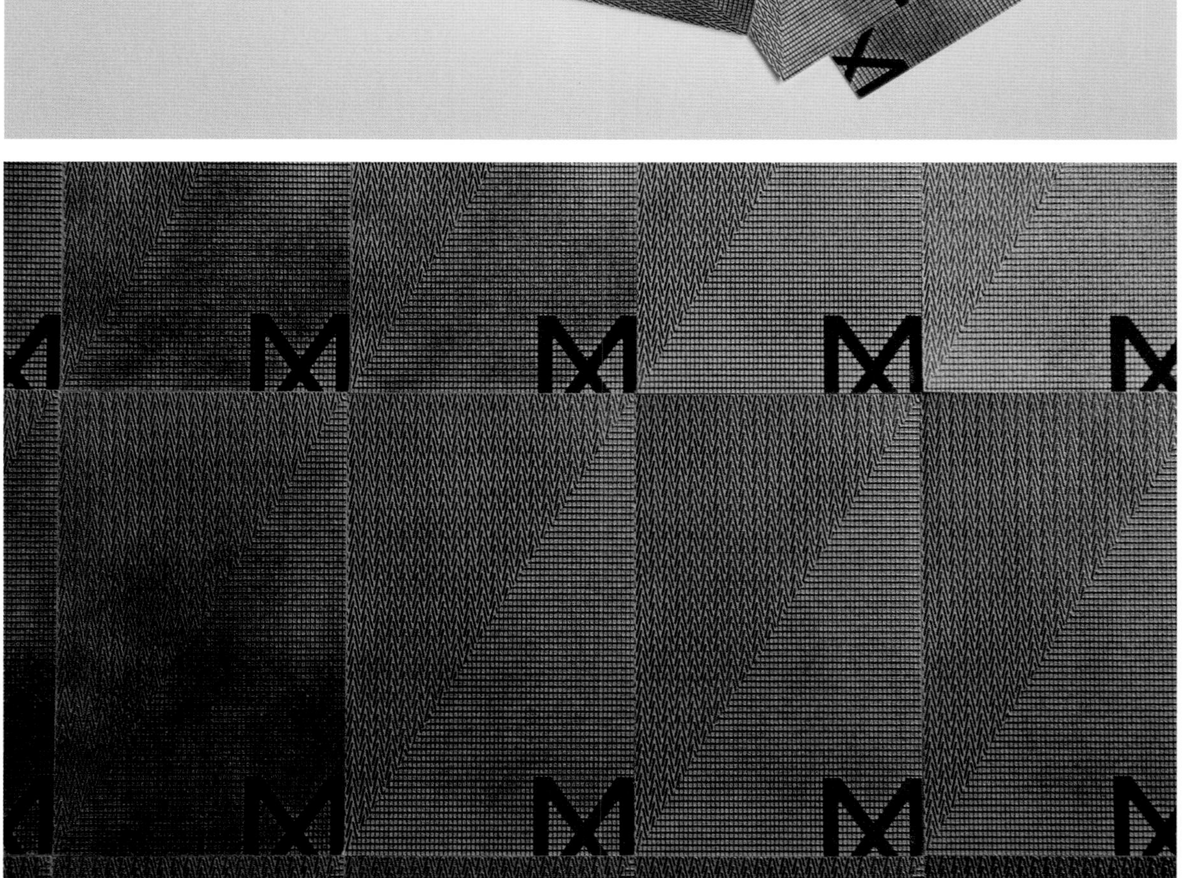

Dynora

Dynora develops smart software for daring applications. In the spirit of Dynora's technical field and area of expertise, this card captures the interest of the recipient with its subtle engineering and interaction. The thermal ink responds to anything that generates warmth: A kiss, a hard day of programming, or simply a firm handshake.

DE Taken By Storm **CL** Dynora **CR** Booxs.nl (PT)

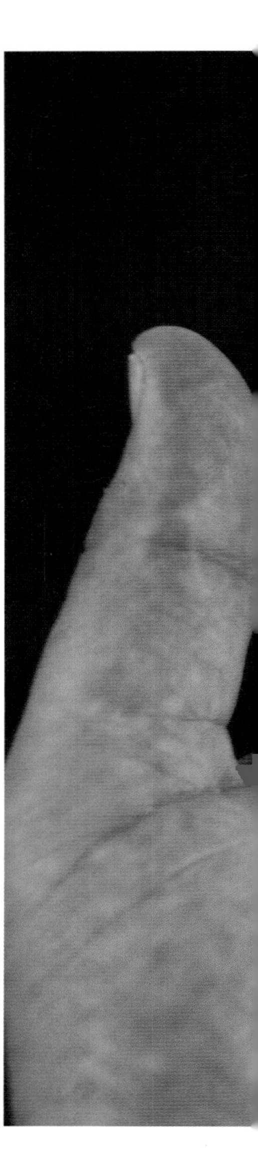

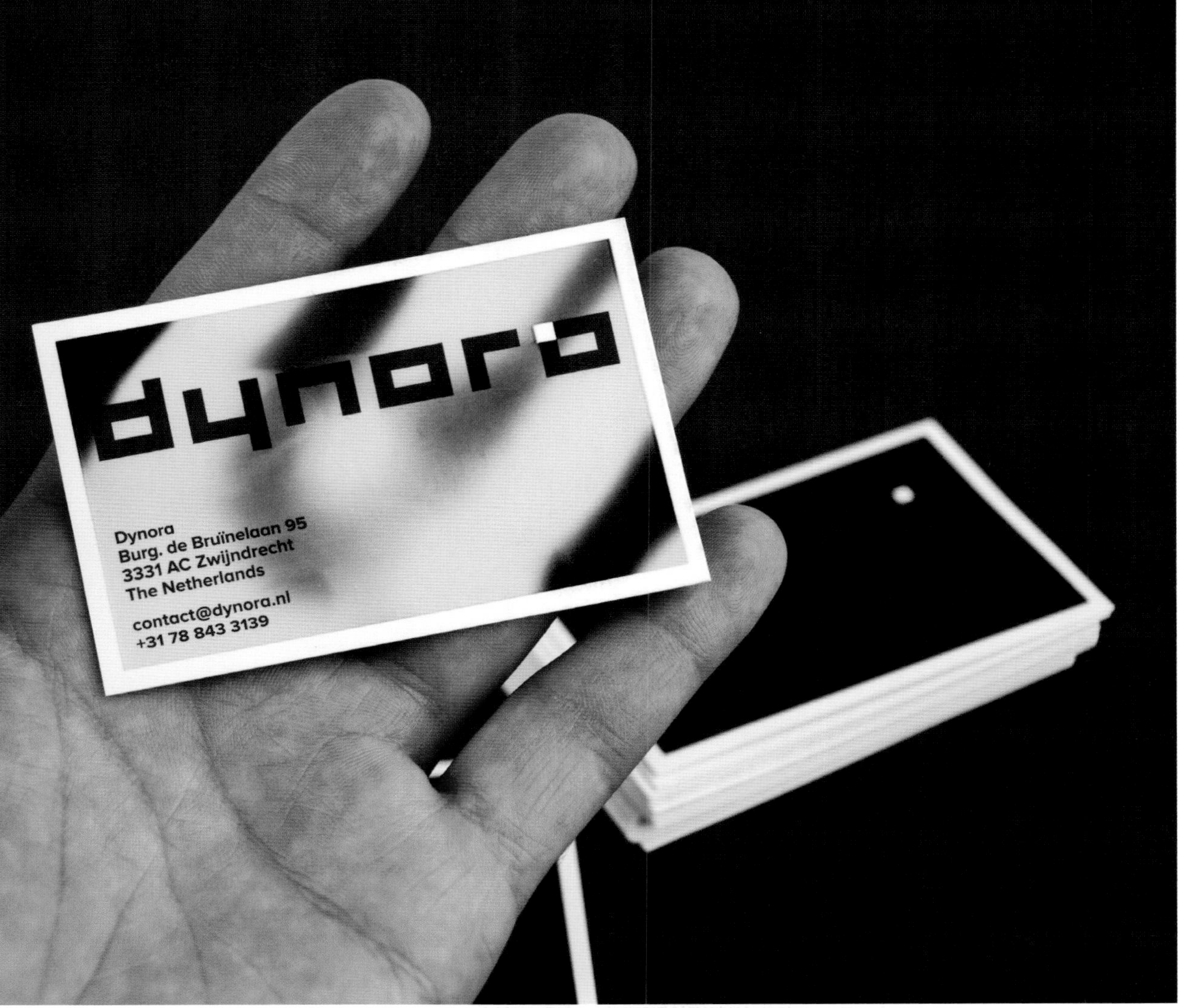

55 x 85mm

300gsm

Black

Heat sensitive ink

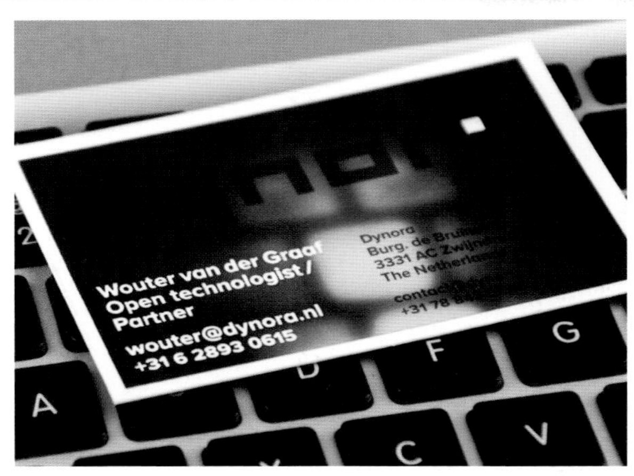

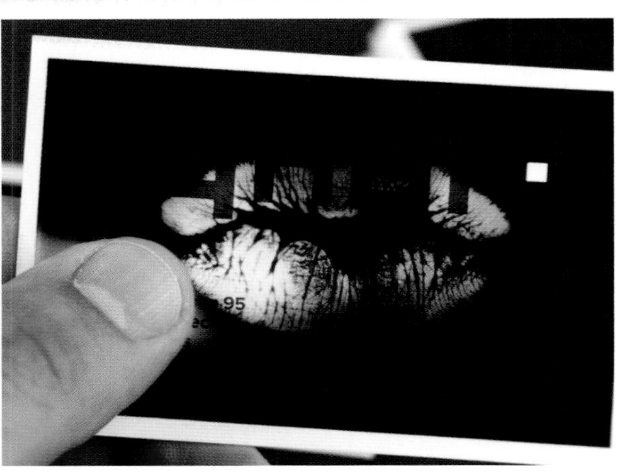

Background Bars

Background Bars is a London-based creative agency specialising in bar design and management as well as event production. Playing around the literal interpretation of Background Bars, Campbell Hay developed a set of tactile bar patterns as the backdrop of the agency's visual identity. Blind deboss adds a subtle layer to the monotone business cards and sets off the vibrant parties and colourful drinks they created.

DE Campbell Hay

50 x 90mm
GF Smith Colorplan Ebony 270gsm
Spot colour
Debossing, duplex

Tourean

Tourean is a British multinational brand design and venture capital company with lifestyle subsidiaries across the fields of music, social media, beverages and fashion. The compound word made of "taurean" and "tour" rounds up the brand's fortitude, courage and integrity, well matched by a solemn blue, cream paper and gold foil. A hybrid Gotham roman-like serifs derived from Gotham Black and Copperlate Gothic merges modernity with the more earnest business side of Tourean.

DE Anagrama **CL** Tourean **CR** Caroga (PH)

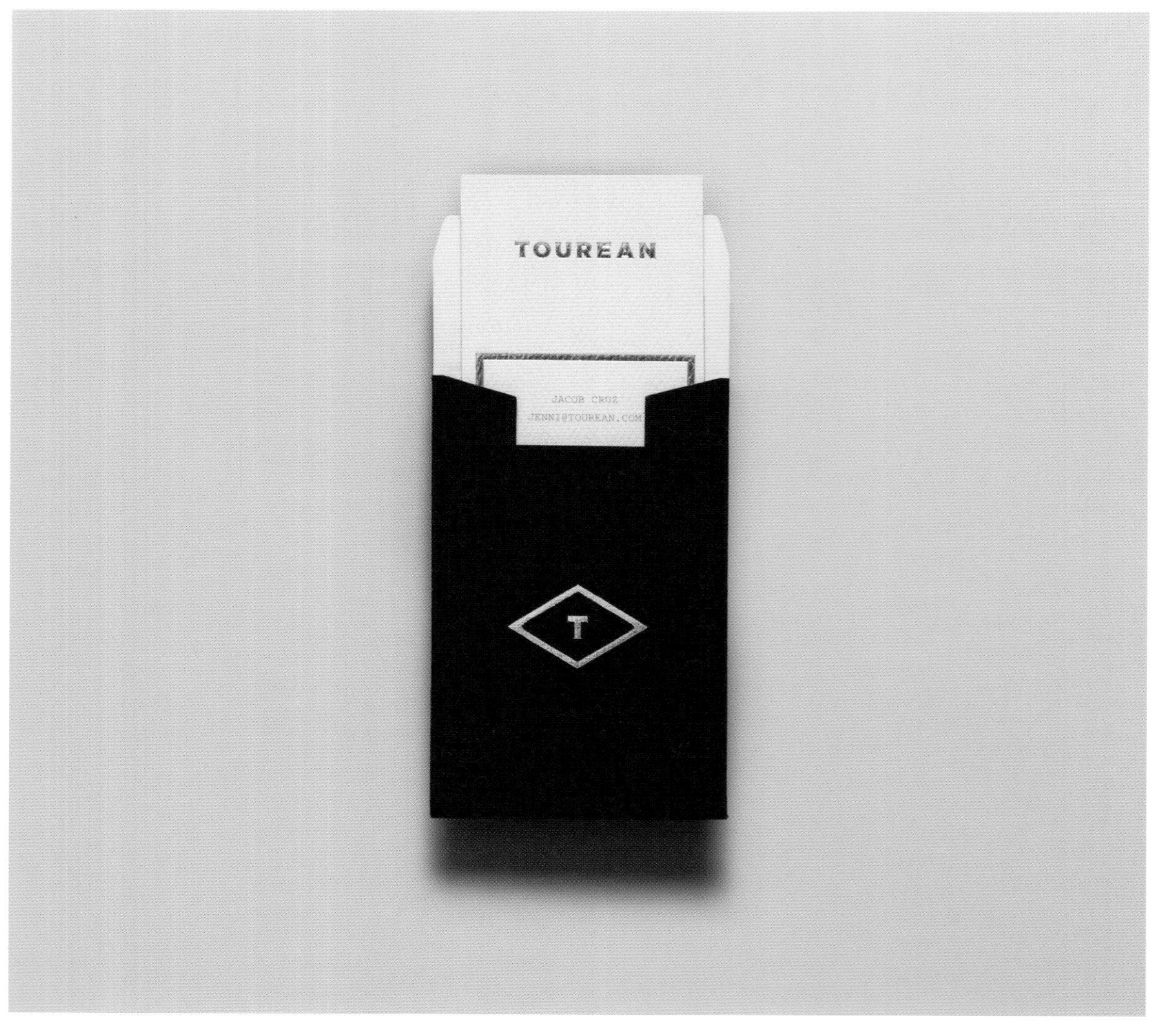

90 x 50mm ROYAL SUNDANCE® Sundance Felt Natural White 216gsm, CLASSIC® Linen Papers Patriot Blue 216gsm Spot colour Duplex, embossing, hot stamping

Business Cards

BOGL

BOGL is a Copenhagen based landscape architecture practice that work to find their way into the unique quality, poetry and unfulfilled potential of environments. The studio's dedication epitomised by four viridescent patterns, an integrated representation of landscapes, maps and textures that the team deals with everyday. The rebranding project also produced three logotypes, with a custom ampersand resembles an "o" on top of a "g", which forms the danish word "and".

DE WAAITT™ **CL** BOGL (Bang og Linnet)

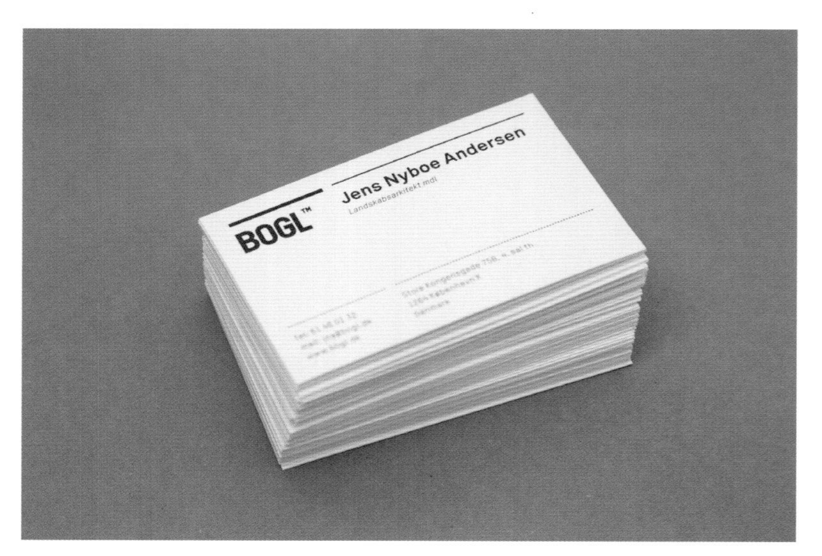

55 x 85mm Munken Pure 400gsm CMYK, spot colour

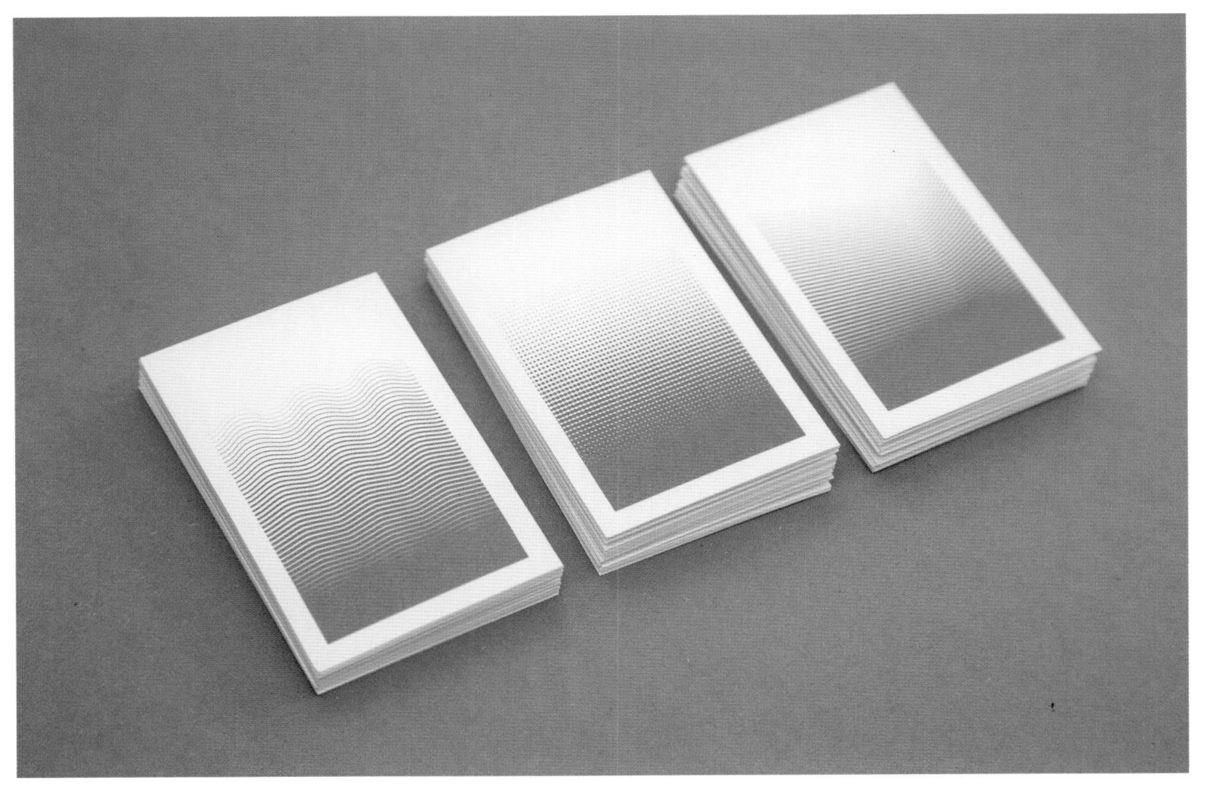

Ben Chen Photography

Being Ben Chen's pure photography territory, Mount Tate in Japan becomes a key visual in Chen's business cards. The need to rotate view to peruse all written details illustrates Chen's dynamic viewpoints taken into his art. Details were also added to stress precision. The two holes on the backside, commonly visible in negatives, are hot stamped with black on the top to visually strengthen Chen's identity on the card.

DE sionhsu **PH & CL** Ben Chen

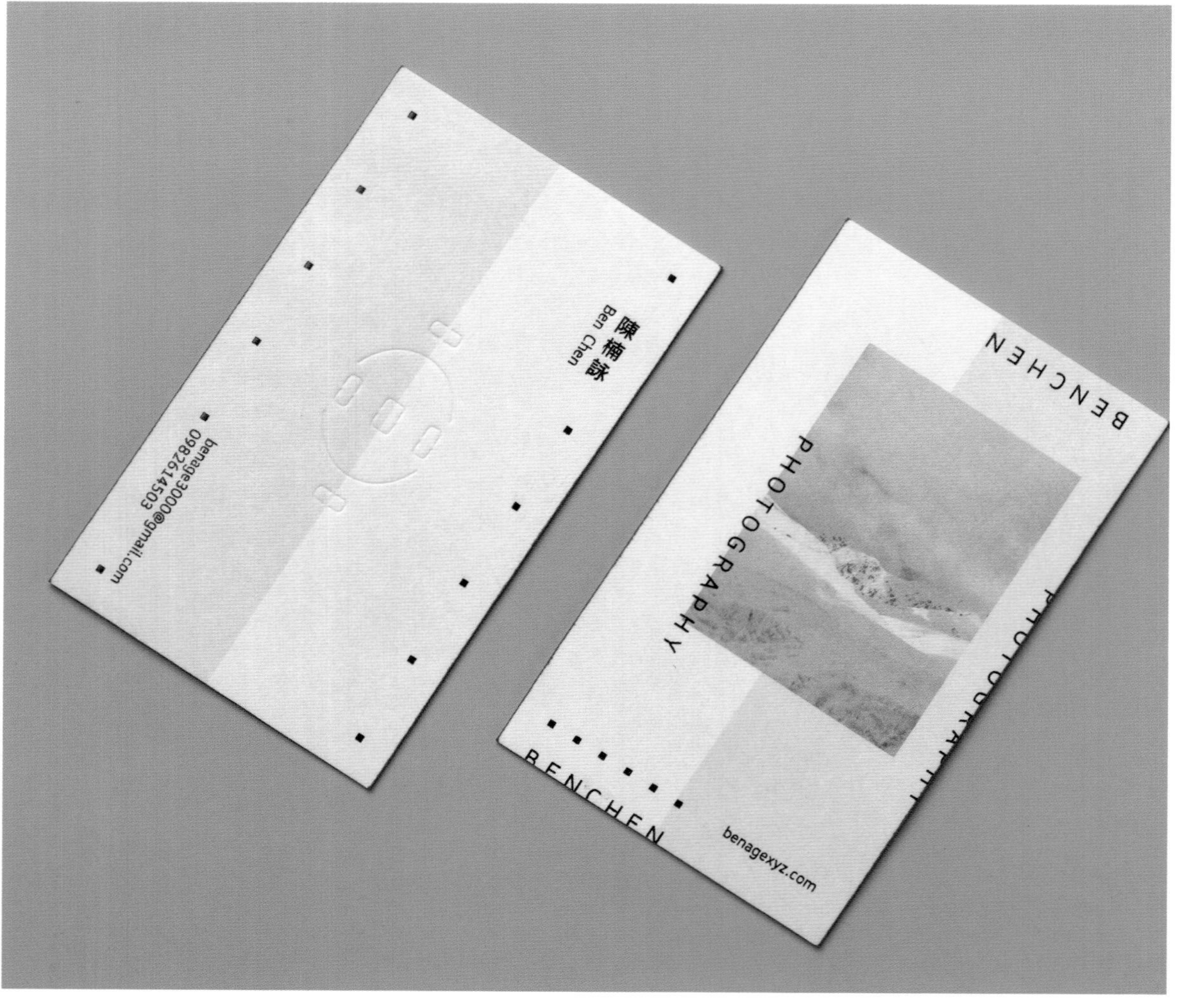

90 x 54mm

Ivory card 720gsm

CMYK

Debossing, duplex, edge dipping, hot stamping

Condé Nast College of Fashion & Design

The renowned publisher Condé Nast was planning to take the bold step from publishing to education by opening a college of fashion and design. In response, Together Design created a timeless brand that honours the group's glamour and history. A selection of archived fashion images were matched with a greyish tone and modern types in varying weights and style. The visual identity was implemented throughout the college and across everything from the school's signage to ad campaigns.

DE Together Design **CL** Condé Nast

55 x 85mm · Munken Polar 300gsm · CMYK, spot colour · Duplex, edge dipping

Willoughby Architecture

Willoughby Architecture works across bespoke residential, small to medium sized commercial buildings and everything in between. The brand identity was developed through the exploration of the architect's observational eye, looking into brilliant architectural elements through a specialist frame. Monochrome images reinforced the practice's grounding on the business cards, in the juxtaposition of low-fi and hi-tech building methods.

DE Grosz Co.Lab **CL** Willoughby Architecture

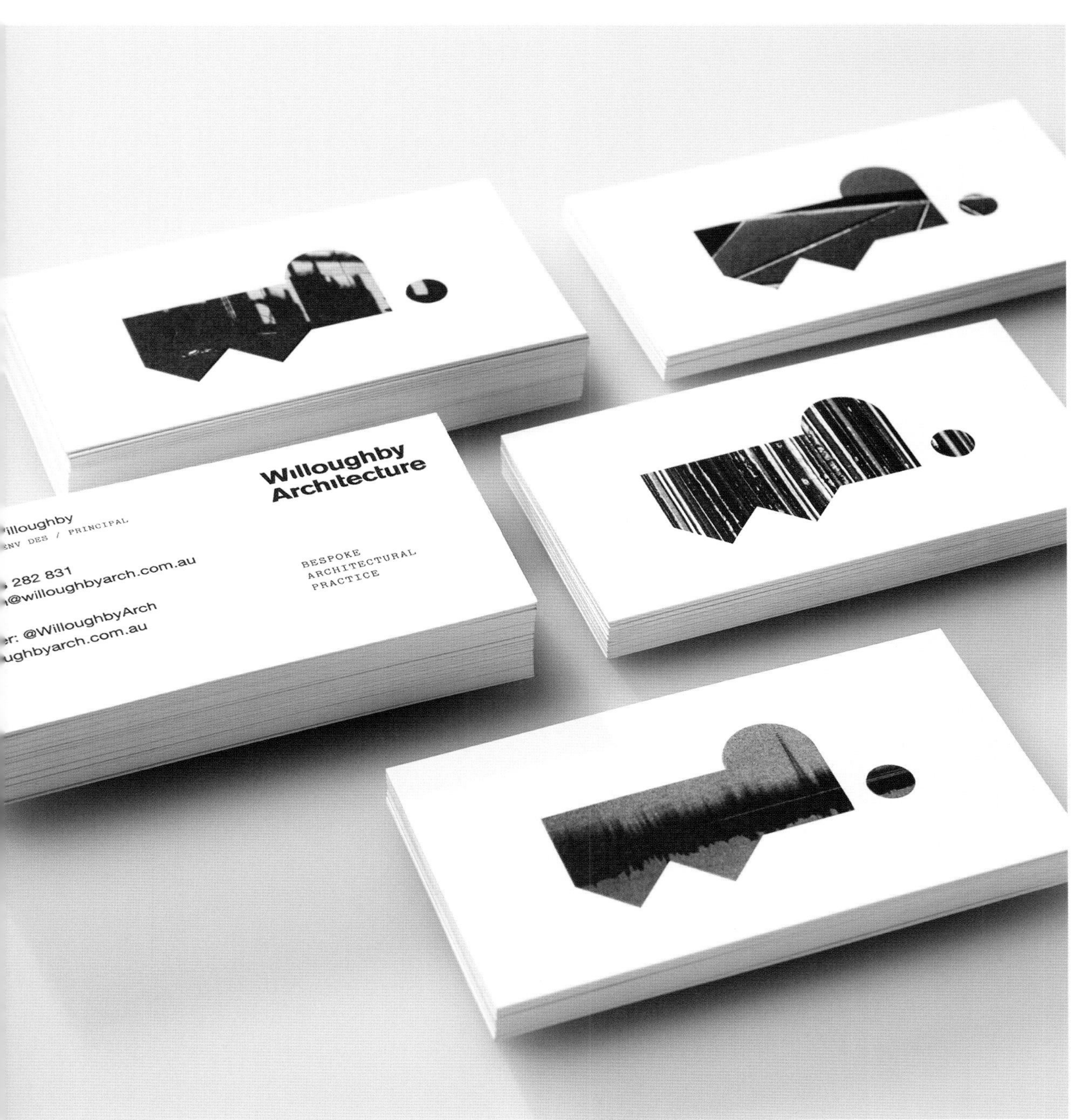

50 x 90mm
K.W Doggett Strathmore Premium Wove Ultimate White 352gsm
CMYK
Hot stamping

Dots and Lines

Text editor and proofreader Monika Buraczyńska works under the alias Dots and Lines. Eschewing a single logo design, STUDIO 2x2 developed a visual identity with a strong and unified character literally based on dots and stripes derived from the editor's professional name. Punctuated by required information, the bands and spots formed a symbolic text column neatly edited by Buraczyńska. The design was implemented across her corporate stationery, invoice template and website.

DE STUDIO 2x2
CL Monika Buraczyńska (Dots and Lines)

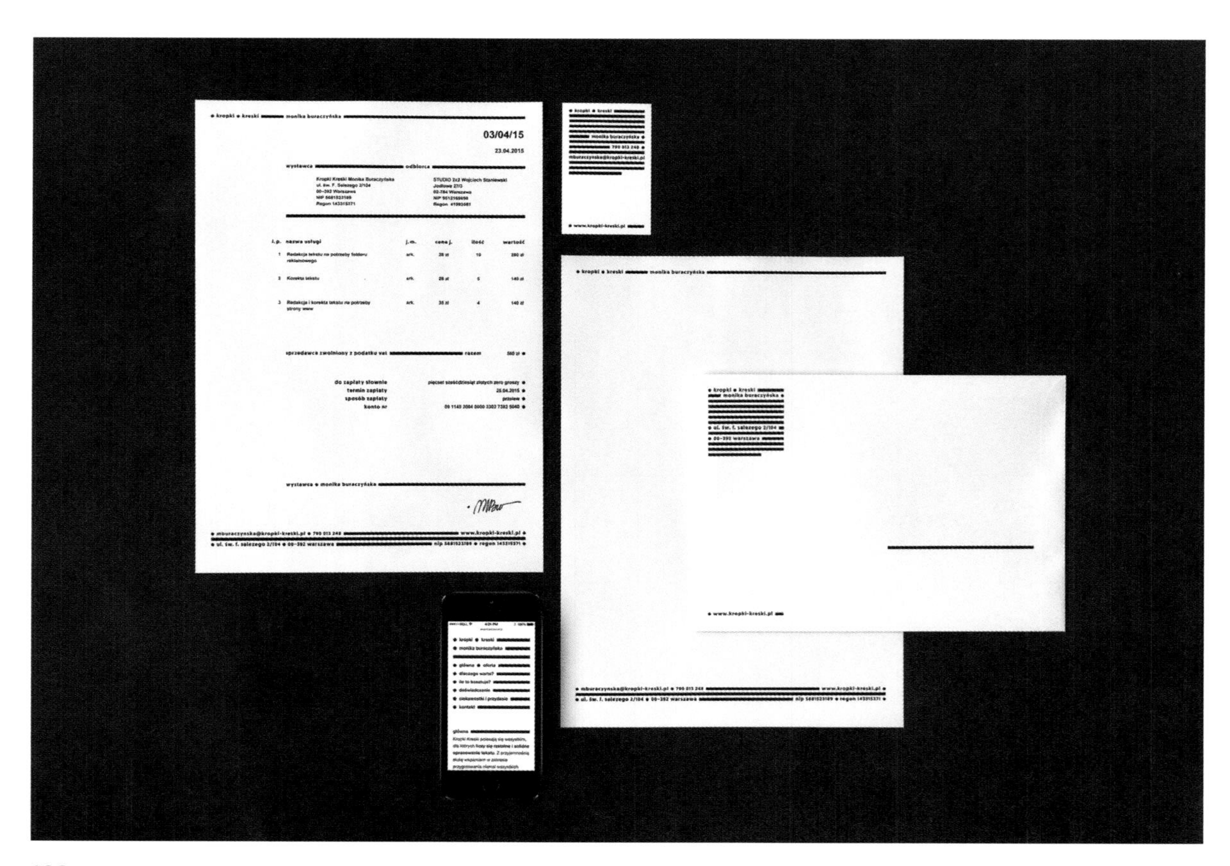

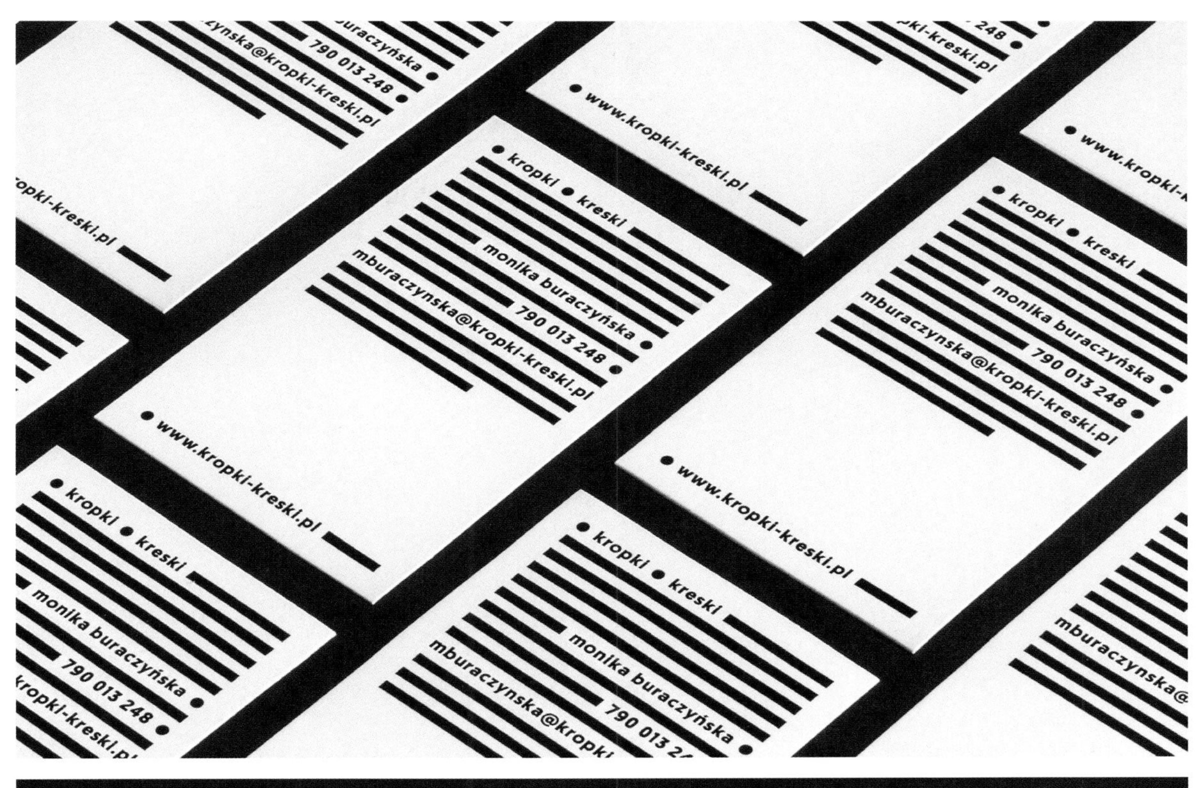

85 x 55mm
Munken Polar 400gsm
CMYK

Redscout

As the confidential advisory behind game changing innovations for top global brands, Redscout was ready to step into the light with theirs own public image. Inspired by their diverse team of loyal strategists and designers, Franklyn created a new identity system highlighting the diverse backgrounds and interests of these Scouts. Stylised illustrations of each employee were decorated with iconographic tattoos representing the who, what and where of these talented individuals.

DE Franklyn **CL** Redscout **CR** Simone Noronha (IL)

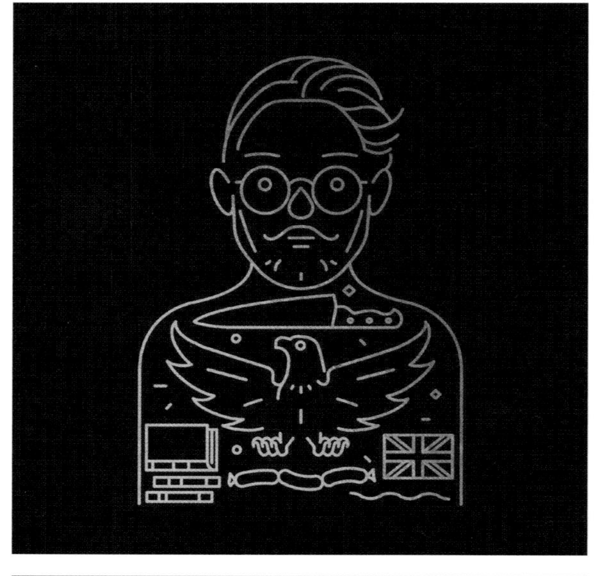

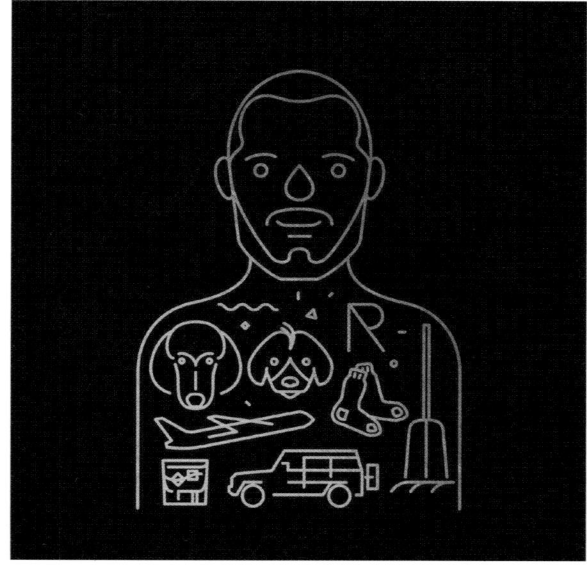

88.9 x 50.8mm
Colorplan Bitter Chocolate 270gsm, Neenah Classic Crest Smooth Solar White 216gsm
CMYK
Debossing, duplex, letterpress printing, screenprinting

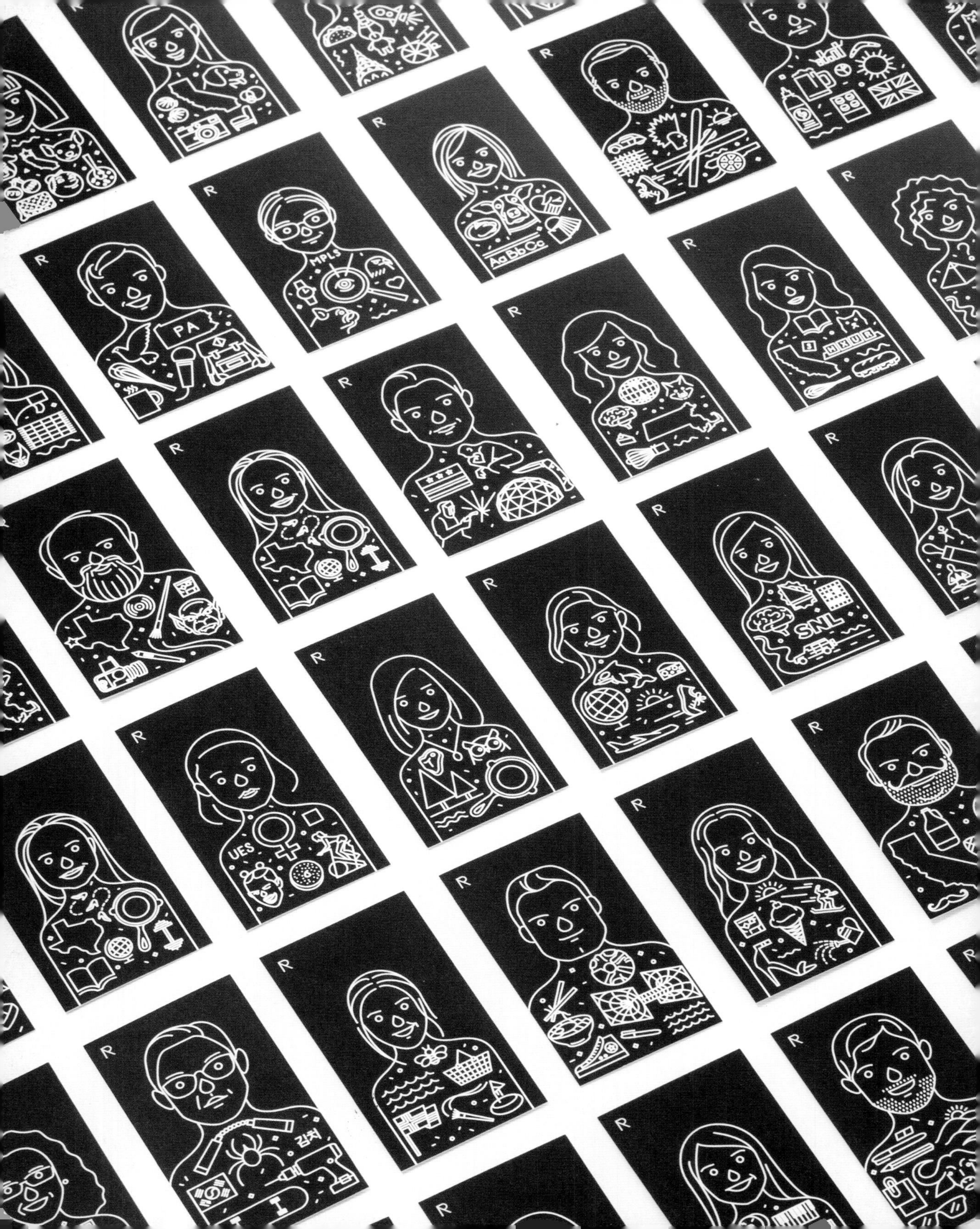
PA
MPLS
AaBbCc
SNL
UES
김치

R
NJ
MPLS
IN
PA
MI
Aa Bb Cc

Maggy Villarroel

Based upon a sans serif with some geometric touches in its structures, graphic designer Maggy Villarroel's visual identity gives prominence to the materials and details of her business cards. Three neutral colour paper were used to set off bold black types, emphasising Villarroel's name, occupation and contact methods. A clean blind embossed mark containing the designer's initial in a circle adds a dynamic contrast to the stock and the types.

DE Maggy Villarroel

55 x 85mm
Fedrigoni Woodstock Giallo, Noce, Camoscio 285gsm.
CMYK
Embossing

Good Design

Set in an extra bold, black lowercase sans serif on an ebony black or natural card, Murmure's maxim "Good Design — is for good clients" immediately catches the holders' eyes at first glance. Produced as the French agency's new business cards, the art directors assume their graphic in strategic ways. Flecks of gold oil around MURMUR's logo echos the gold full stop in the punchline, conveying values the agency created for their good clients.

DE Murmure **CR** Julien Alirol, Paul Ressencourt (AD)

55 x 85mm · Colorplan Ebony Black, Natural 540gsm · Debossing, hot stamping, letterpress printing

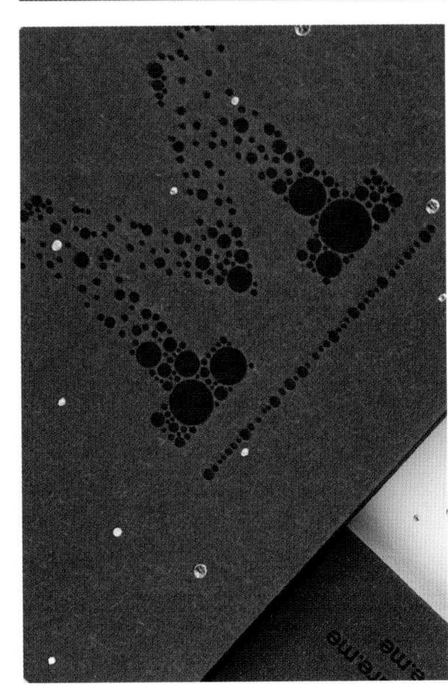

Finta Dorottya

Lakosi Krisztián created a clean and minimal identity for young restorer Finta Dorottya, who could easily remake and customise herself. The simple design comprises a stamp design and a gold stroke, which are interchangeable to create varied compositions on any little white cards or wrappers. The stamp marks and gold paint are taken to reflects the the visuals with which she works.

DE Lakosi Krisztián **CL** Finta Dorottya

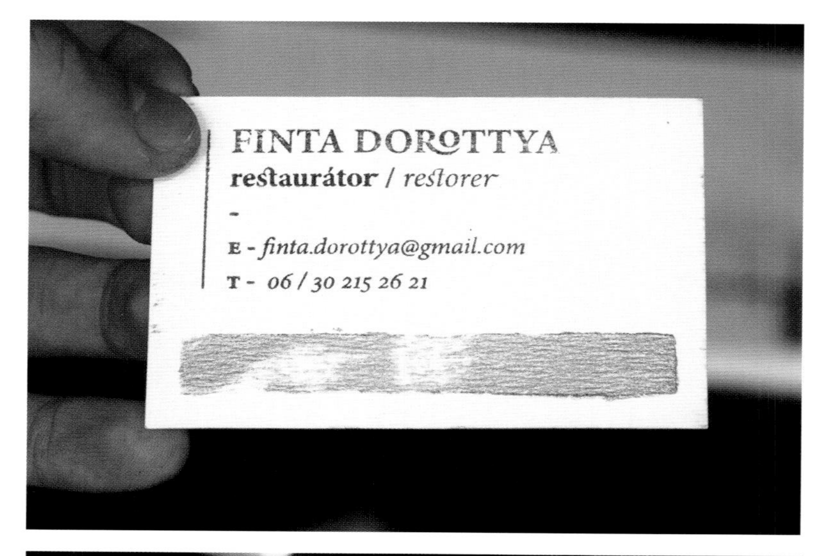

55 x 85mm
Acquarello Bianco 300gsm
Rubber stamping

Cradle to Cradle

Studio Mosgroen is a specialist infographic design house with a yen for sustainable designs. With an objective to minimise his footprint, the studio took on a cradle-to-cradle approach — using dried autumn leaves from the Platanus and blind embossing — to produce their business cards. Produced entirely free of ink and added materials, these cards presumably would cost zero damage to the environment even if they are discarded in the park after use.

DE Studio Mosgroen

55 x 85mm
Dried Platanus Leaf
Die cutting, embossing

Birdcage Films

Birdcage Films is a production house incepted by film producer Rachel Higgins. Making reference to thaumatrope, one of the first "motion" graphic illusions, Studio Worldwide brought about a typographic version of the Victorian optic game. Split in half, the name "BIRDCAGE" appears on either side of the card attached with two pieces of string. Once twirled quickly, the card creates the shortest film possible ever using only two frames.

DE Studio Worldwide **CL** Rachel Higgins

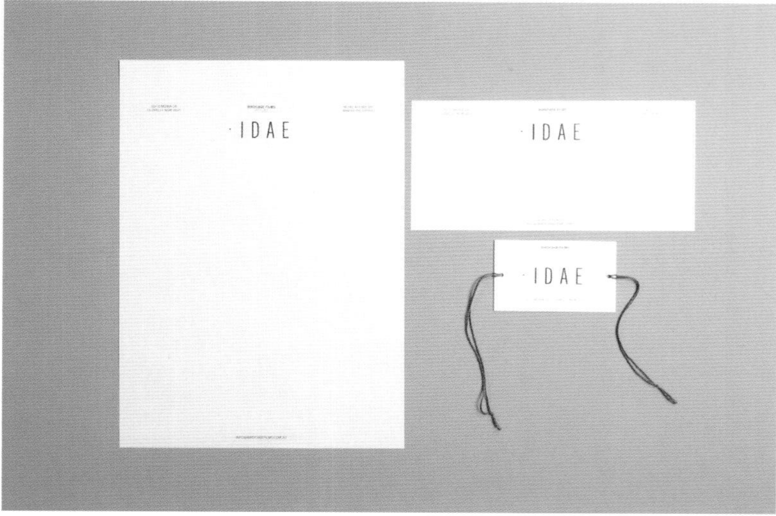

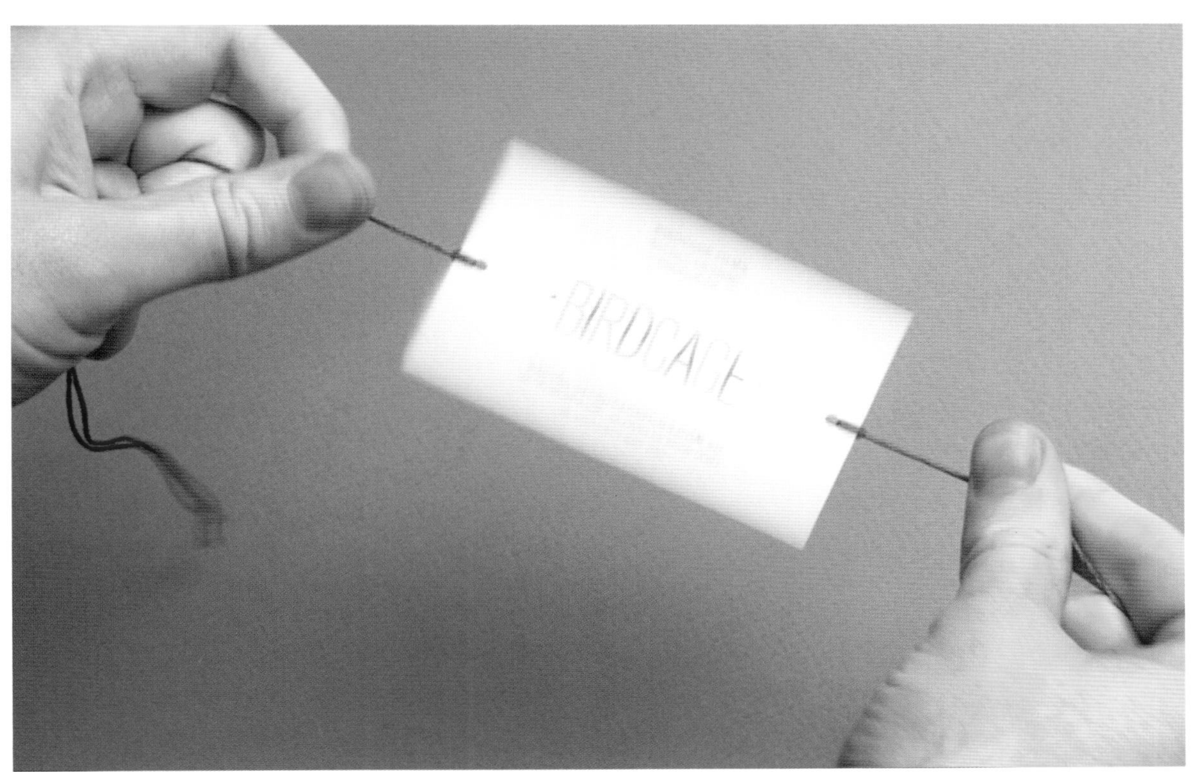

55 x 85mm 12-Matter Papers N/E-Old Offset Uncoated 300gsm CMYK Die cutting

Studio Fiz

Studio Fiz is a young interior design studio committed to exploring possibilities in architecture, interiors and events. The studio's brand identity, which includes a logotype, business cards, custom corporate communications and website, delivers a spirited yet professional resolution of architectural cues. Debossed structural forms and simple white lines engendered new dimensionality on flat surfaces in navy blue and white.

DE Studio 10 **CL** Studio Fiz

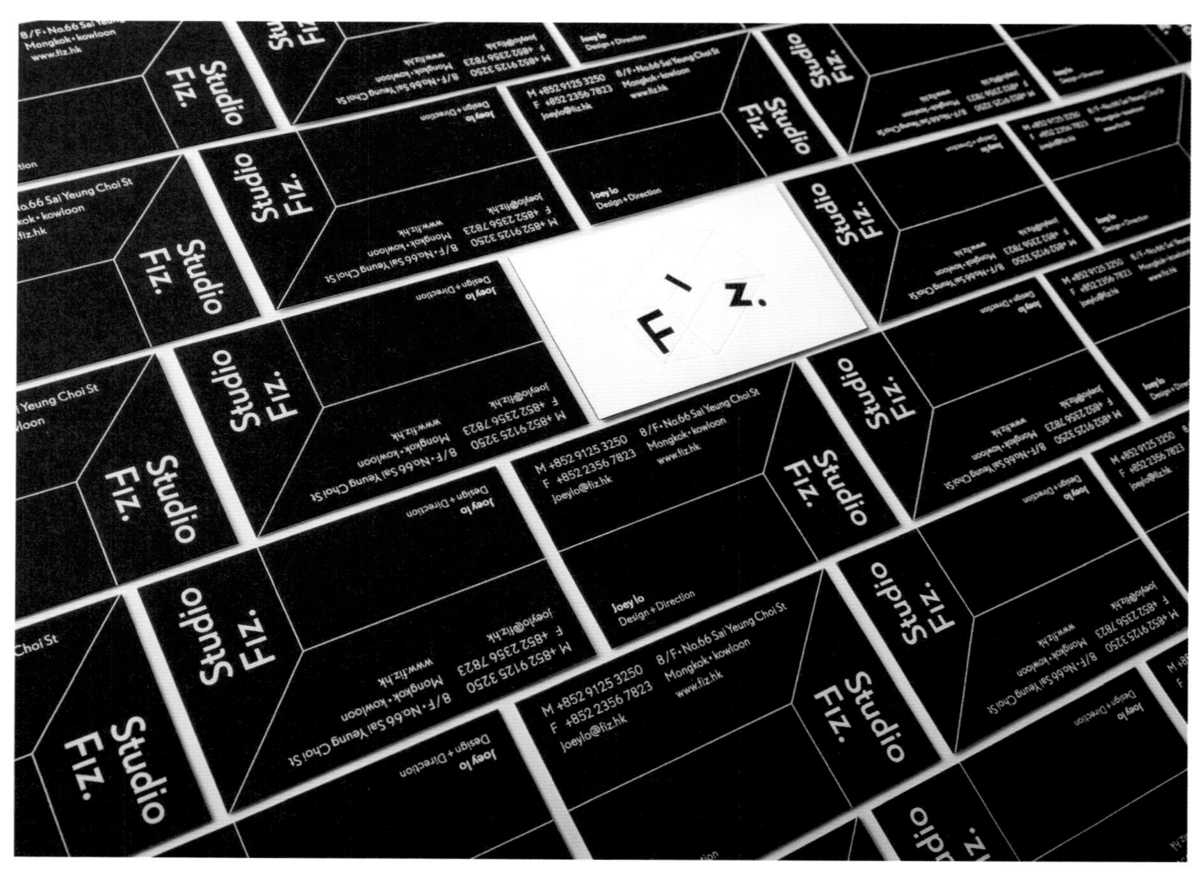

54 x 87mm Mohawk Loop Antique Vellum Iris 298gsm, Mohawk Options Vellum True White 270gsm Debossing, die cutting, duplex, hot stamping

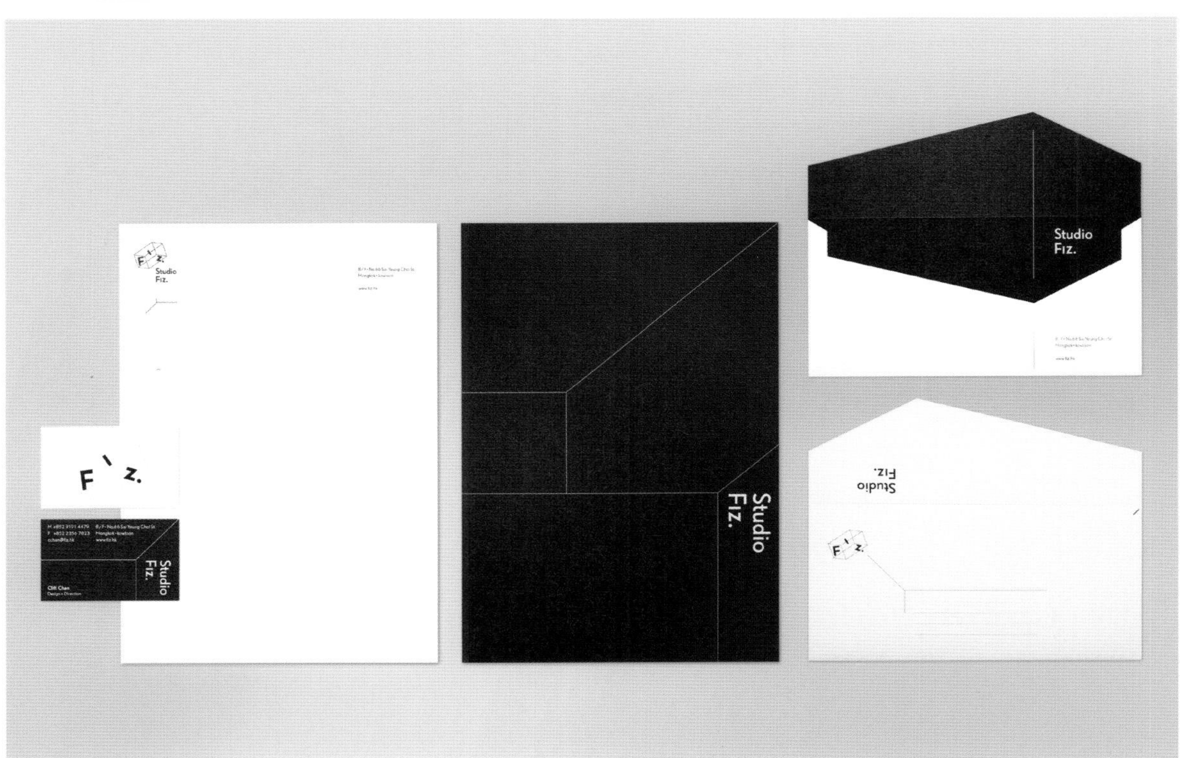

HOUTH

Taiwan based creative studio HOUTH takes inspirations from real life experience. Finding beauty in simplicity and purity, the creative duo infused such quality into their own corporate identity, with a blind embossed logo, decorative line patterns and contact details modestly mix a true attitude. Three colour stock ascents the pared-down design in the slightest sense.

DE HOUTH

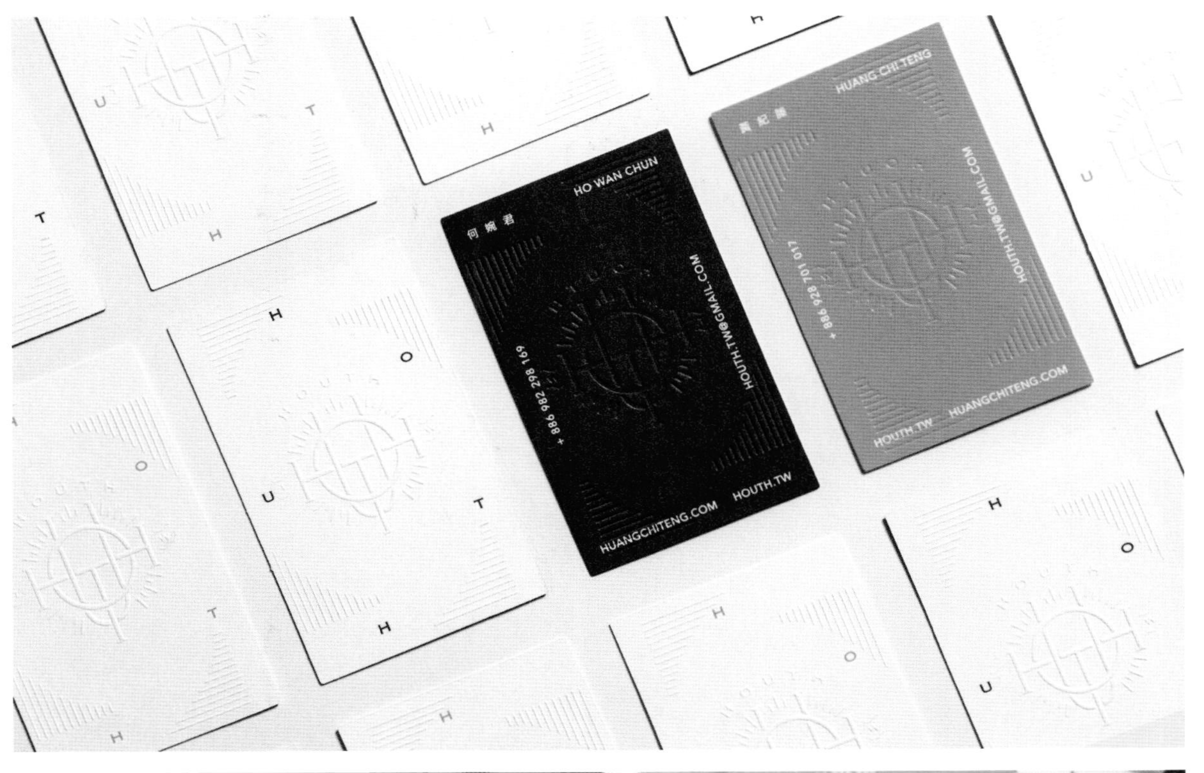

90 x 55mm
Neenah Solar White System Classic Crest 446gsm
Spot colour
Embossing

7Cycle

7Cycle is an indoor cycling studio with charismatic instructors, curated music and a rave-like atmosphere. A holistic identity, which includes towel labels and corporate stationery, was devised to project healthiness, fun and a sense of community onto 7Cycle. A pastel-like gradient palette is used against a contrasting neon orange alongside an animated logo, with seven spinning strokes suggestive of "group cycle" that the studio runs. Under ultraviolet light, the neon glows, illustrating 7Cycle's intensity and dynamism.

DE ACRE **CL** 7Cycle

85 x 65mm
Maple Stucco 320gsm
CMYK, spot colour
Edge dipping

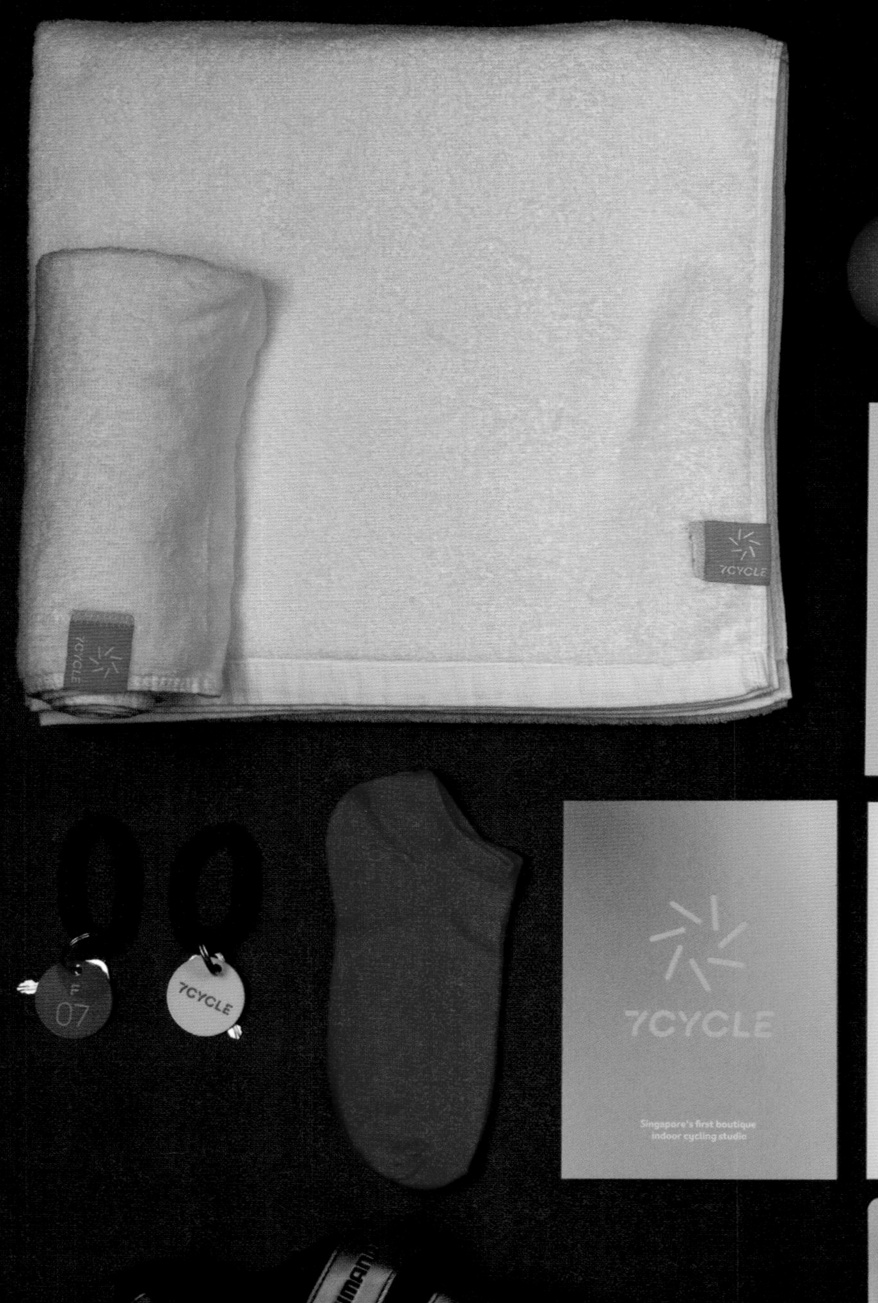
7CYCLE
F
07
7CYCLE
7CYCLE
Singapore's first boutique
indoor cycling studio
SHIMANO

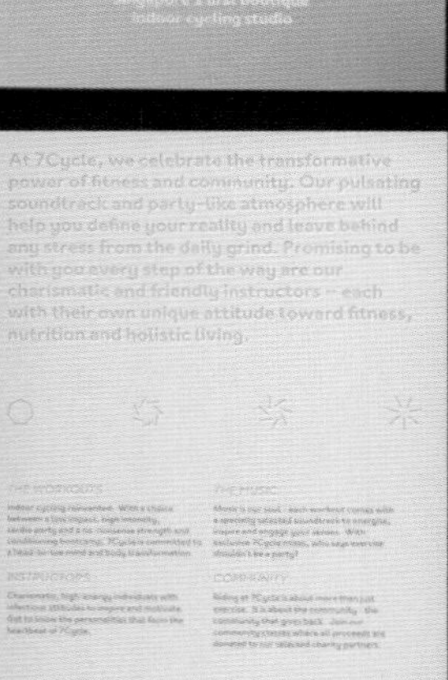
At 7Cycle, we celebrate the transformative power of fitness and community. Our pulsating soundtrack and party-like atmosphere will help you define your reality and leave behind any stress from the daily grind. Promising to be with you every step of the way are our charismatic and friendly instructors — each with their own unique attitude toward fitness, nutrition and holistic living.

Single Class
Card

7CYCLE

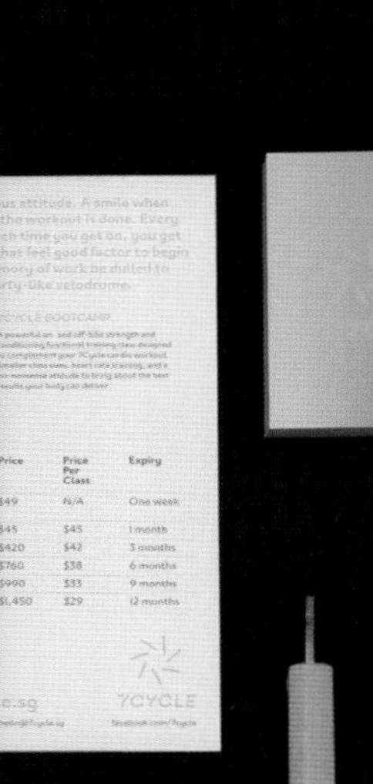

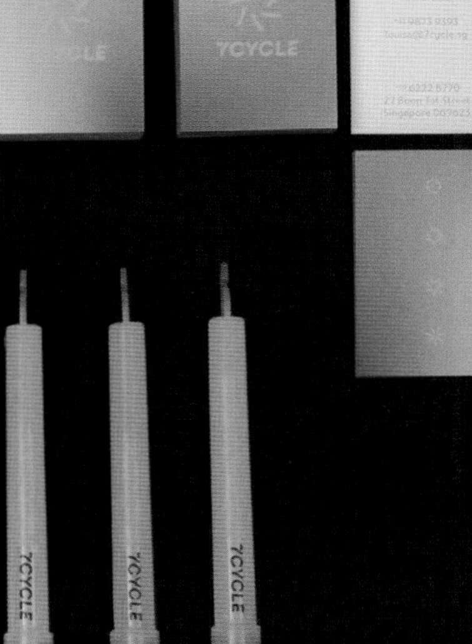

EMBARK.

Minority Women in Fashion

Minority Women in Fashion is a non-profit organisation that supports creative, remarkable women of all origins in fashion scenes. Julia Kostreva created a compelling black on black business card with a custom logo comprising the group's abbreviation in a serif typeface with distinctive strokes. The compelling black emanates strength, vulnerability, elegance and depth at once as an authentic portrait of the women MWIF represent.

DE Julia Kostreva Studio **CL** Minority Women in Fashion
CR Madelene Farin (PH), RockDesign (PT)

88.9 x 50.8mm

Black uncoated paper 280gsm

Duplex, hot stamping

The Counter Press

The Counter Press is a contemporary letterpress studio working with traditional hand set wood and metal type. Capitalised as a perfect stage to show off their craft and a mini type specimen for a wood letter font range held by the press, their business cards demonstrated the press' old-meets-new aesthetic with 8pt Monotype Plantin contact details on the fronts and loud greetings on the backs. Fluorescent orange edge painting finishes the cards off with a vivid flash of colour.

DE The Counter Press

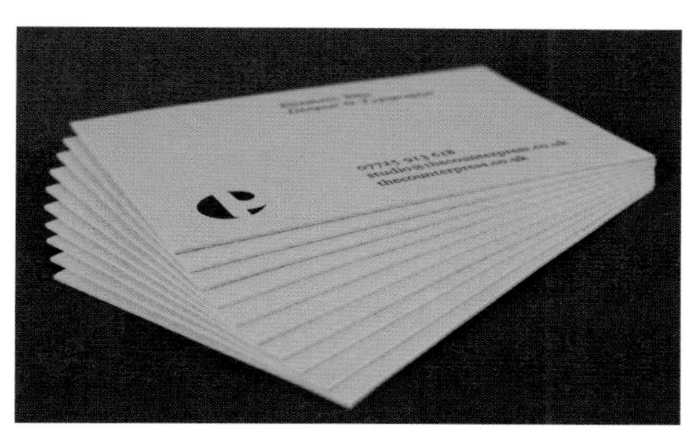

55 x 85mm

Fedrigoni Materica Clay 360gsm

Edge dipping, letterpress printing

KK Kwong

KK Kwong is a fashion stylist and makeup artist who offers tailored image styling to her clients. Studio Much created two sets of business cards for her consultancy KK Concept to reflect her two fields of work. Individually numbered and bound with a fabric wrapped spine, the business card book comes in handy without a card holder and offers Kwong a register for recording cards handed out. The fresh green lines and details accentuated the artist's identity against grey and white.

DE Studio Much **CL** KK Concept

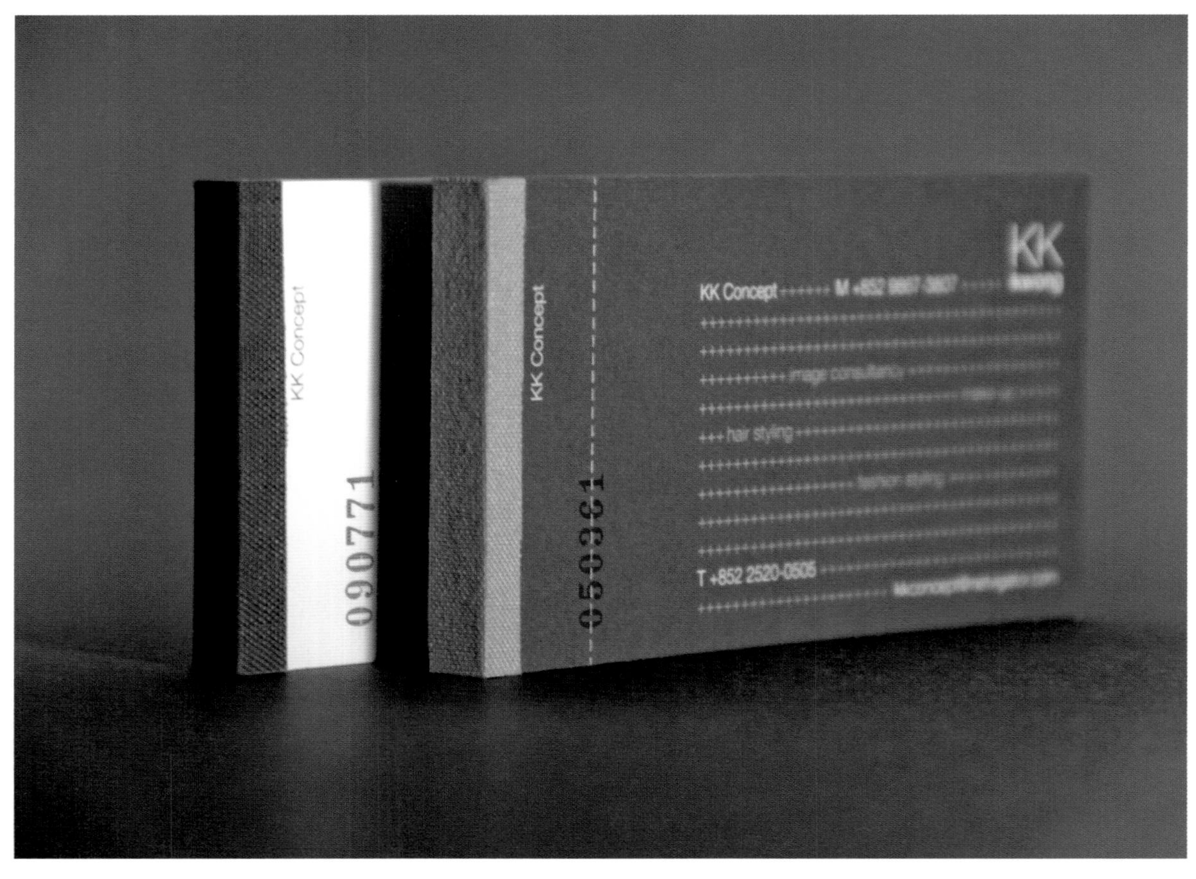

55 x 85mm | Curious Touch Soft 300gsm | Spot colour | Fabric wrapped spine, perforation, technical binding

White Monkey

Saint Petersburg-based White Monkey is a wood workroom that produces handmade jewellery and accessories. Believing 'a white cat is best seen in a dark room', F61 Work Room created two business card designs that adheres to the saying. Its new identity is a simple but bold combination of a monoline weight logotype, strikingly applied to a jet black card or veneer. Both stained black ash and maple veneer were used in the final design.

DE F61 Work Room **CL** Anna Kerbo

55 x 85mm

Stained black ash & maple veneer 1mm, Keaykolour Original Pure White, Jet Black 250gsm

Debossing, duplex, hot stamping, laser cutting, triplex

B.O.I.D. Journal

B.O.I.D. is an online journal where the best branding projects in the industry are carefully collected like genuine treasures. The journal's own brand story was told with references to the legends of the dragon who guards his jewels in a dark cave, with a logo rendered based on traditional European heraldic dragon images and triplex design to imply hidden gold guarded between two black layers. Each new journal project corresponds to a golden coin in the dragon's treasury.

DE Eskimo design studio **CL** B.O.I.D. journal **CR** Anatoly Vasiliev (PH)

85 x 55mm

Arjowiggins Curious Touch Texture Black 250gsm, Favini Majestic Gold Shine 290gsm

Hot stamping, triplex

Sanrun Mining Co.

Sanrun is a mining company recognised for excavating, processing and distribution of manganese in Chongqing, China. Representing Sanrun's main areas of activity, contour lines in the shapes of opencast mines were designed as the main visual on the white identity. Both the distinctive forms and the business cards' edges were tinted in the same holographic colours to resemble manganese alloy, manifesting mining as a highly developed industry in modern terms.

DE Necon **CL** Sanrun Mining Co.
CR Kolor24, Pakato (PT)

54.5 x 89.5mm
Olin Regular Absolute White 250gsm, cardboard 1mm
Spot colour
Edge dipping, screenprinting, triplex

Exclusive Bike Services

The brand identity for Eric, who provides exclusive bike repair service and maintenance in Singapore, is set in black and gold. Familiar features like fingerprints, grease and bolts that define a mechanic's everyday work background Eric's greetings and contact details with a remarkable feel. Taken as Eric's initial, 'E' in the logo also stands for his assurance of being exclusive, excellent and efficient.

DE Kong Studio **CL** Exclusive Bike Services

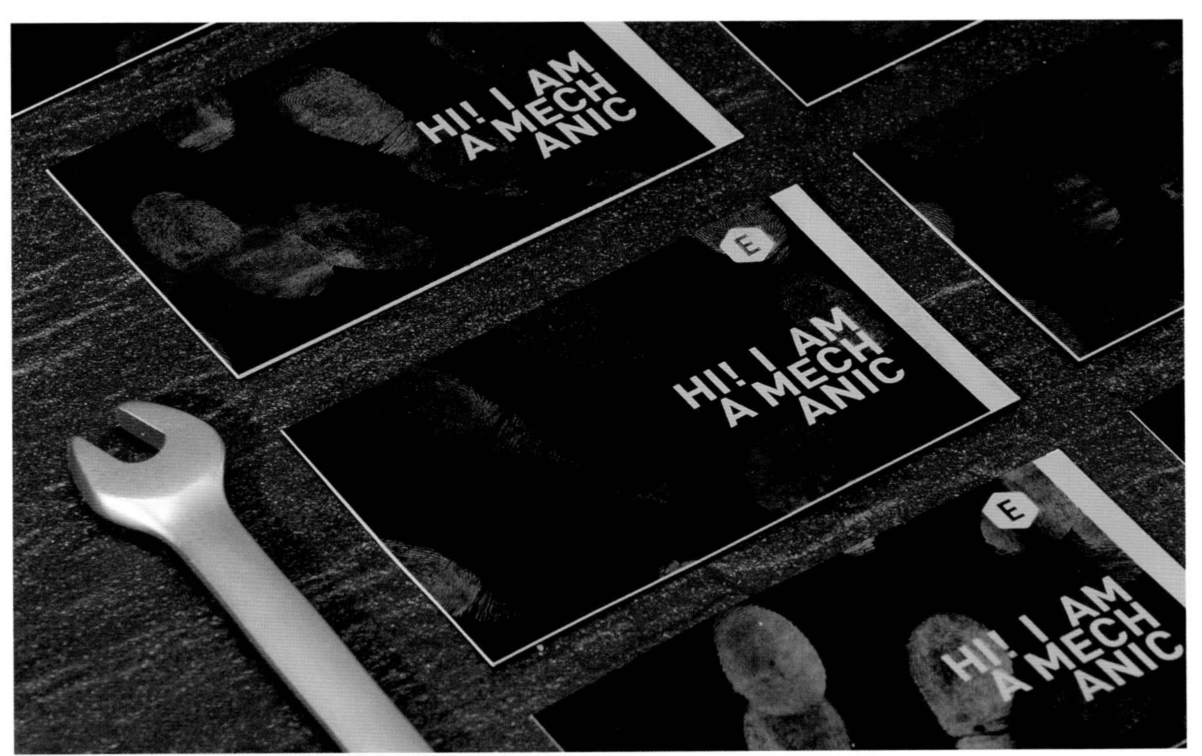

55 x 90mm Strike Bronze 300gsm CMYK

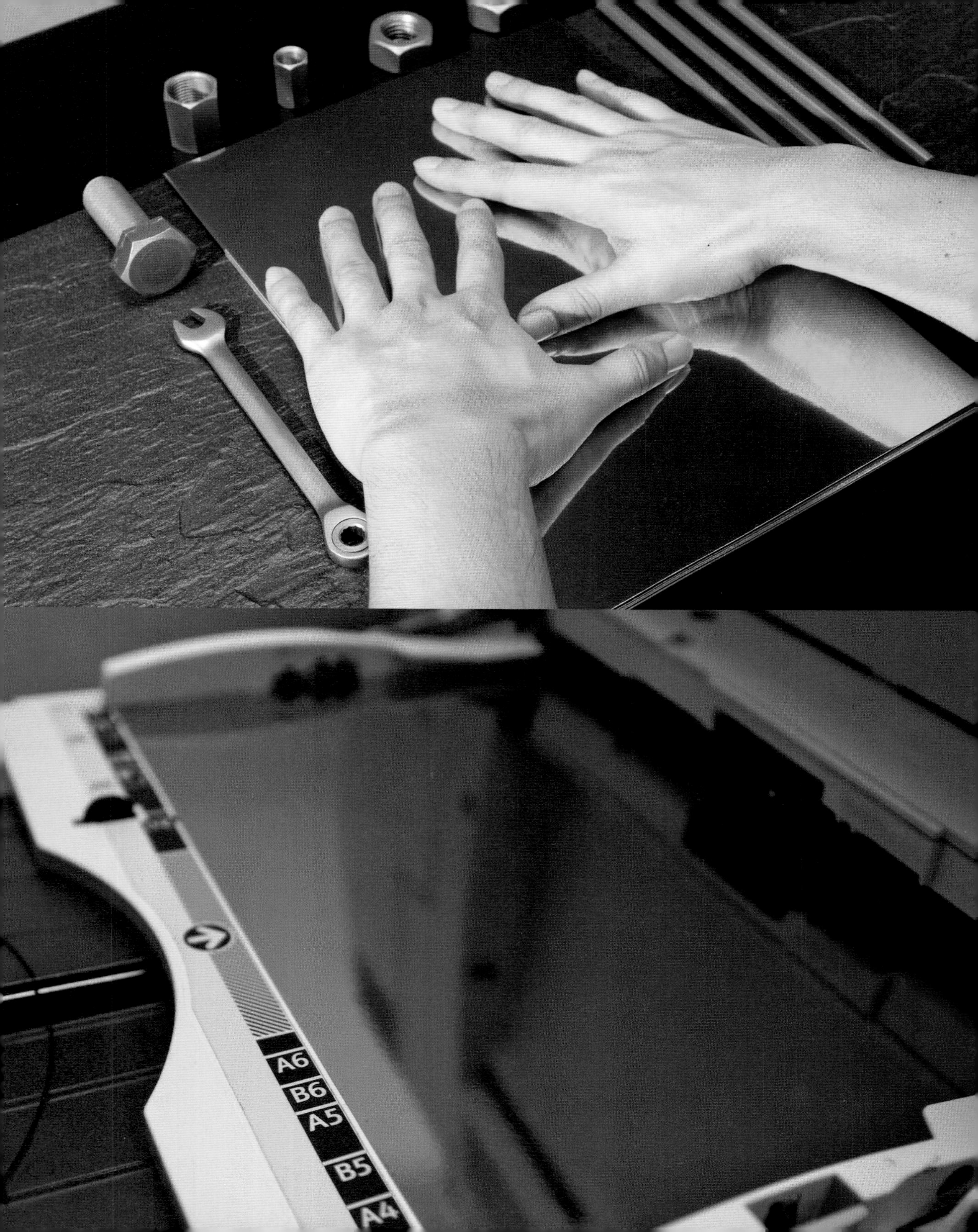
A6
B6
A5
B5
A4

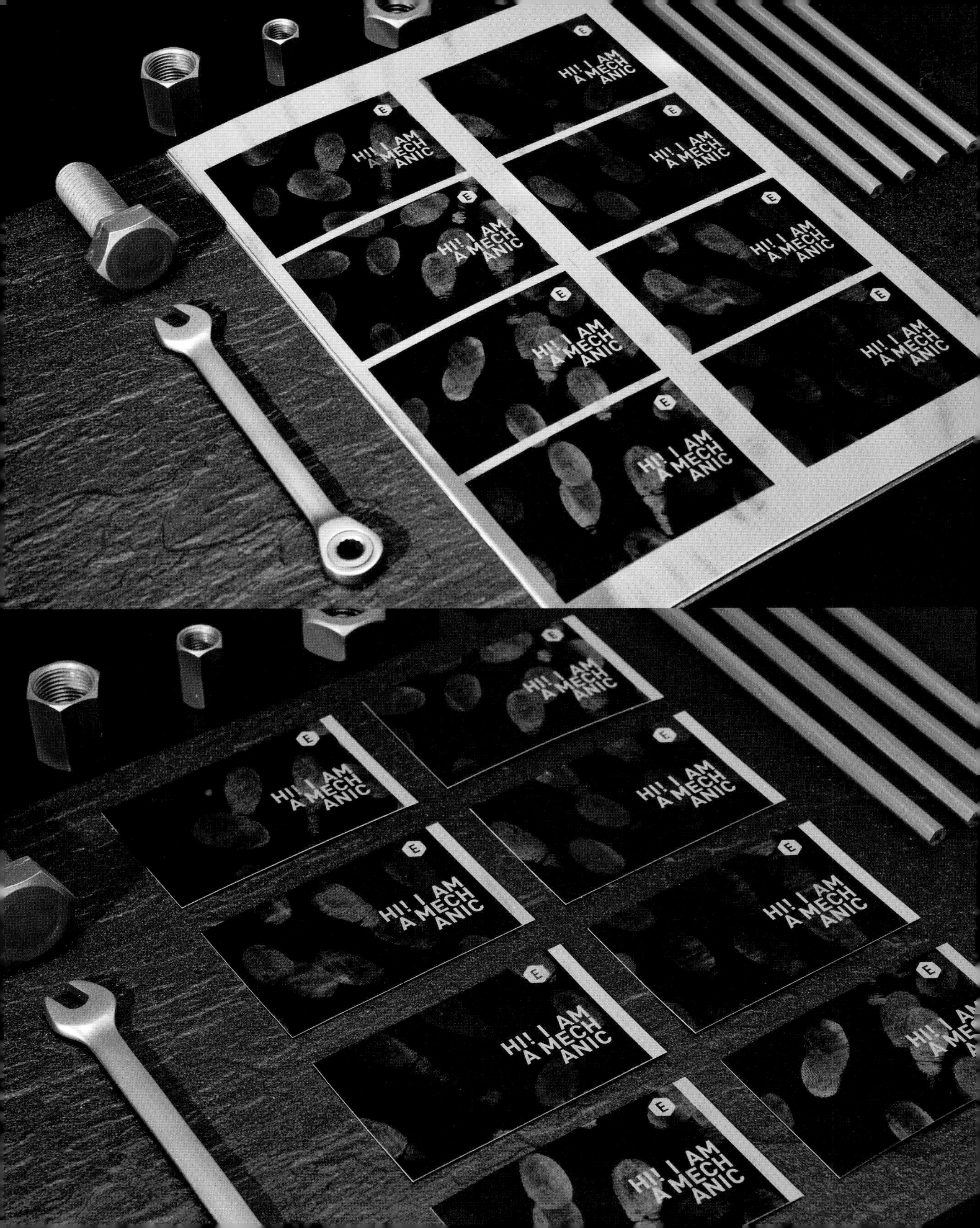
E
HI! I AM
A MECH
ANIC

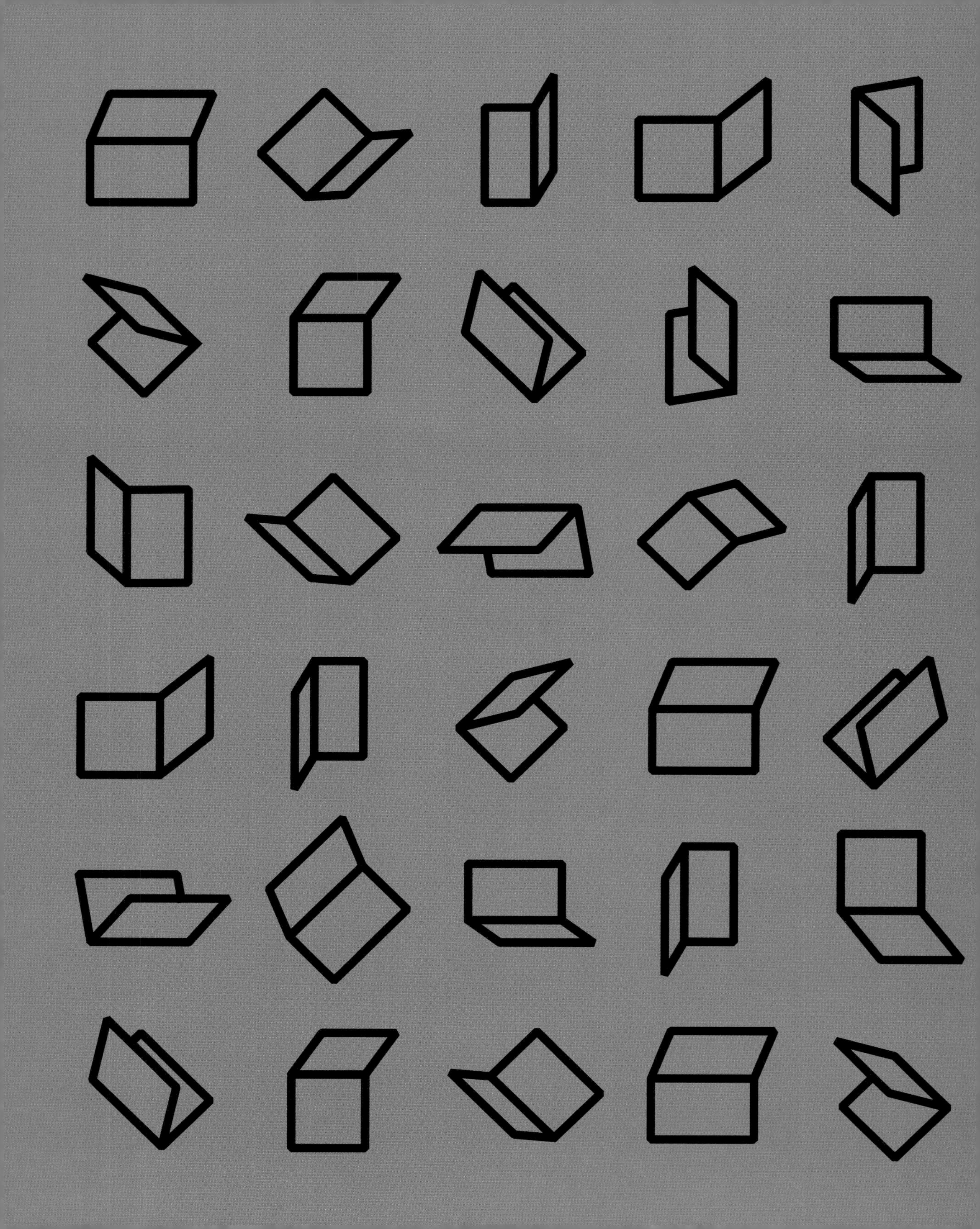

Invitations and greeting cards

Invitations and greeting cards need to grab target recipients' attention straight away. Taking advantage of their unrestricted format and size, designers spice them up with interactive elements and sculptural builds. Whether they are cast into origami high heels, paper marionette or standard printed form, the end products never fail to surprise recipients with mesmerising graphics.

Forest Christmas Mailer

Creative studio Tofu believes Christmas should be magical, and Christmas would not be special without the glitter and sparkle of a Christmas tree. Yet the Singaporean studio understood that few could afford the time and space for a life size one, which led them to create and mail out not just a single tree, but a snow-capped forest to each of their loved ones and clients. The exquisite slipcase was marked by a north star and encased with a miniature landscape decked in gold foil for the sparkle.

DE Tofu

80 x 170 x 25mm
Antalis Conqueror Bamboo 250gsm
CMYK, spot colour
Die cutting, hot stamping

Chisako Imagaki Greeting Card

Japanese designer Chisako Imagaki opted for the beauty of tradition paper craft when she created the greeting card for 2013 New Year. The card contained abstract motifs of the year's zodiac, snake as well as the blessings of camellia flowers. These graphic elements were created by kami-zogan, a time-honoured Japanese decorative technique of placing different coloured paper into delicate carved motifs.

DE Chisako Imagaki **CR** To-hoku Paper Industry Co.,Ltd. (PD), Takeo Co.,Ltd. (PP)

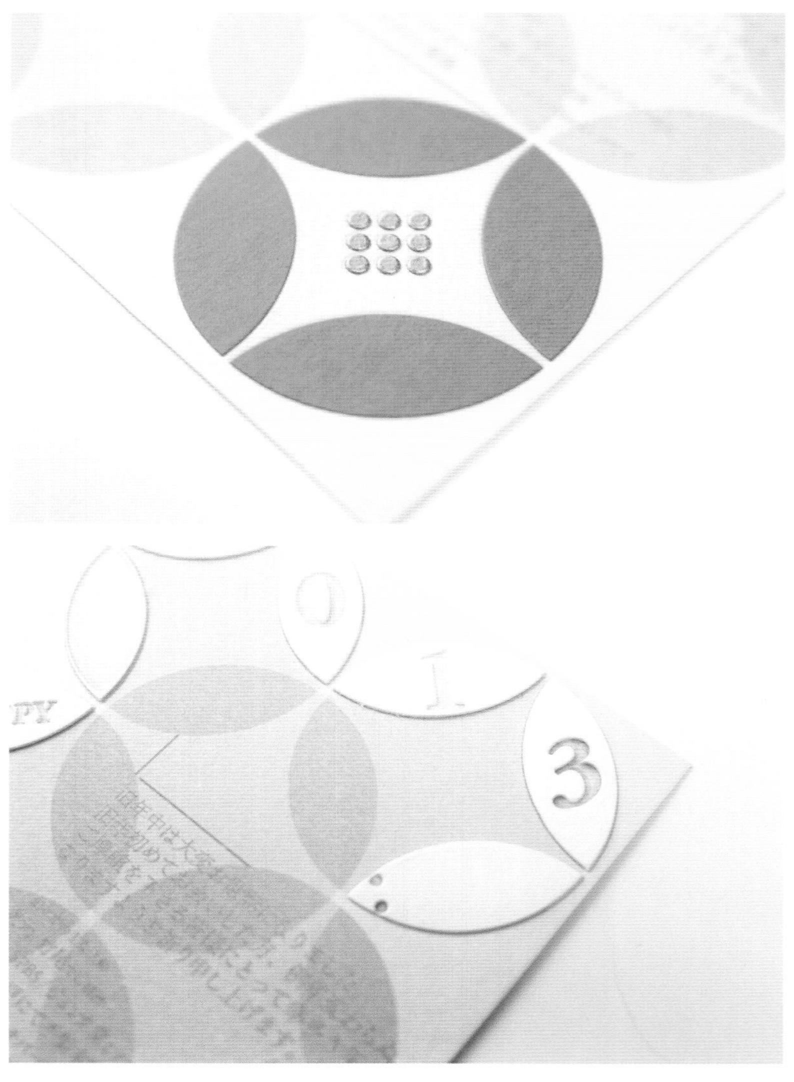

146 x 100mm Biotope GA-FS Cotton White S/G 244gsm, Pachica 233gsm, Youhishi Beni 110kg, Hi-pika E2F Gold 95kg CMYK Hot stamping

Your Christmas to Make Mailer

Christmas is a wonderful season of gifting, but sometimes we can't help getting what we get. Recreating the moment one getting a fuddy-duddy Reindeer knitted sweater from their aunt, creative studio Tofu came up with a 'scarf card' for their friends and clients in 2013 Christmas. The tongue-in-cheek paper craft contained a guide that taught the recipient to pop the intricate knit stitch-imitating cut outs so they could at least choose a more favourable pattern.

DE Tofu

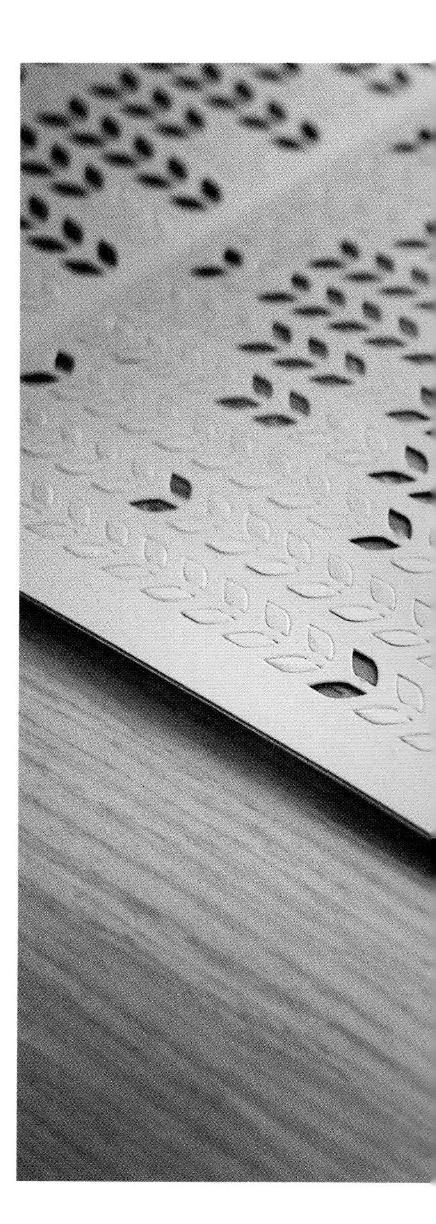

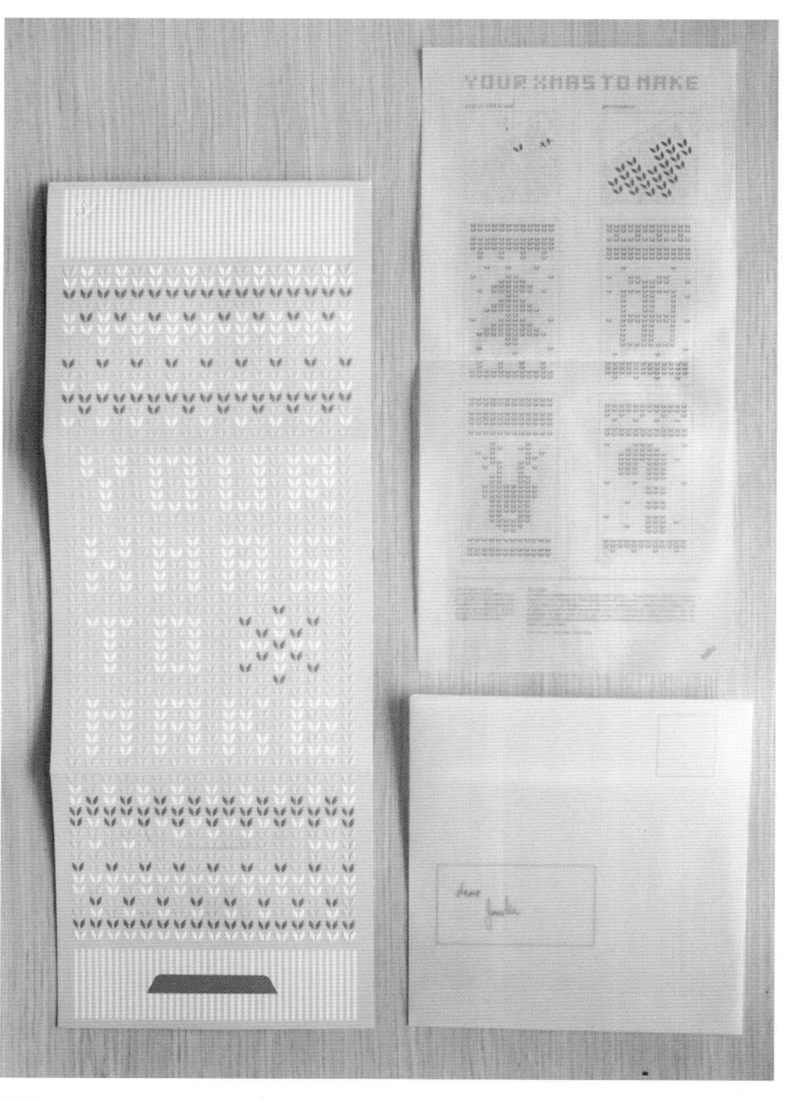

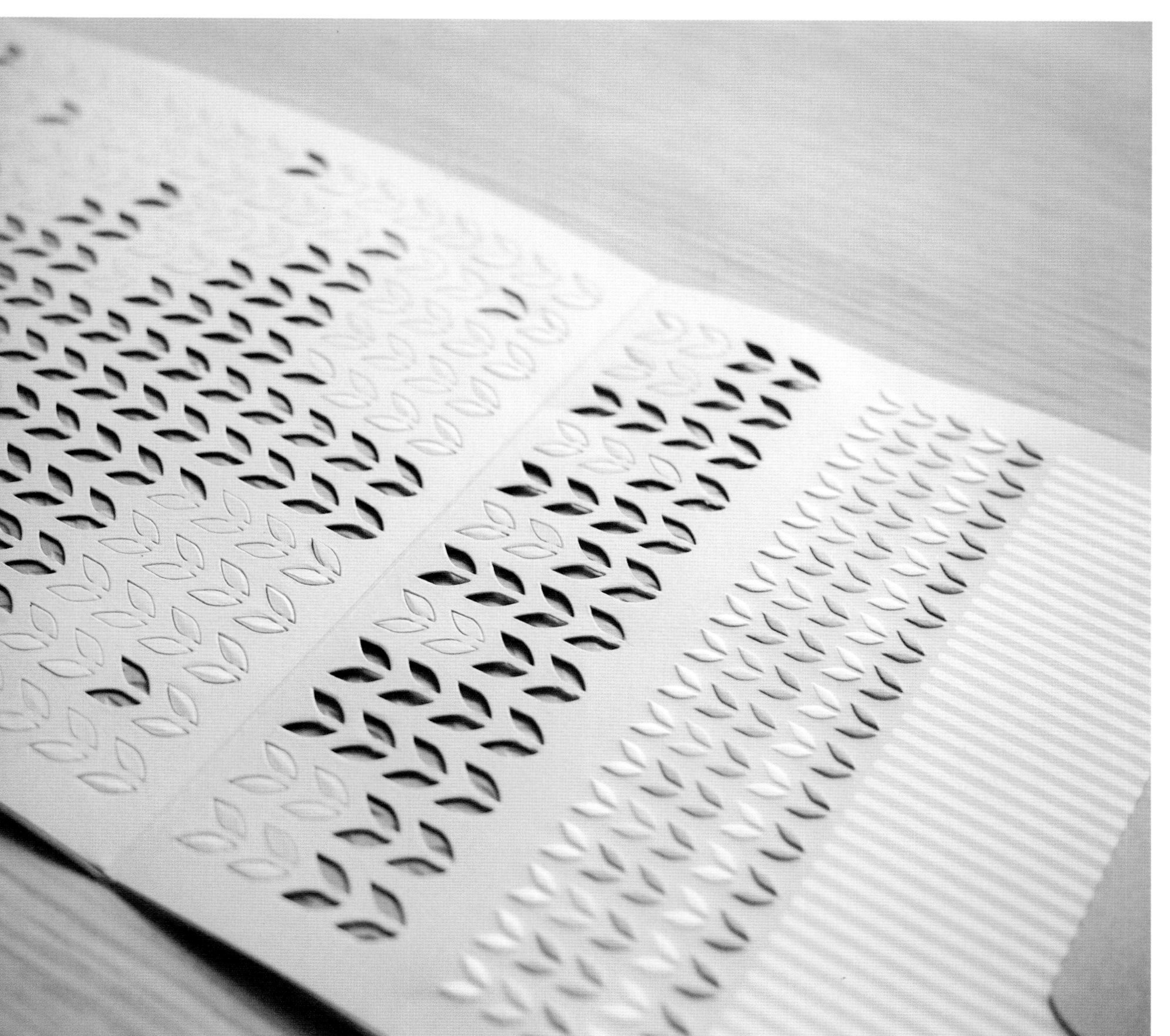

180 x 170mm
Conqueror Iridescent Sillica Blue 160gsm
Spot colour
Debossing, die cutting, embossing

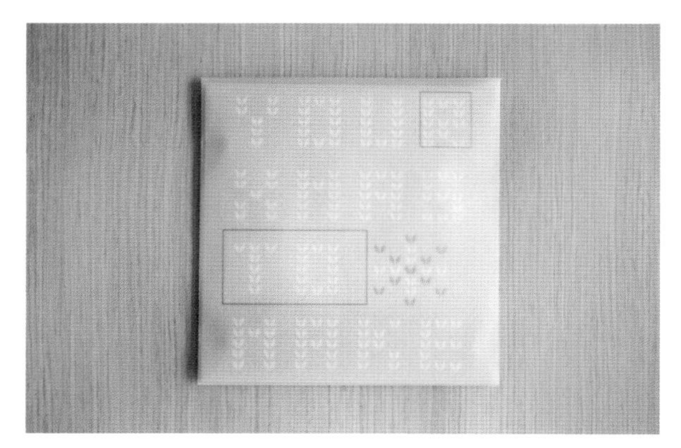

TAKEO Greeting Card

Characterised by fine embroidery, TAKEO's 2014 greeting cards also served as an announcement for the renewal of their NT RASHA paper stock. Embodying a warm, wool-like texture, the vibrant cards were embroidered with Japanese style patterns in Christmas colours, combining into a unique mail item for overseas suppliers that displayed the quality of one of the Japanese paper trading company's signature collection.

DE cosmos **CL** TAKEO
CR Katsuhiro Kagota, BIHAKU WATANABE (PT), Daichi Okabe, GRACE-EMB (PT)

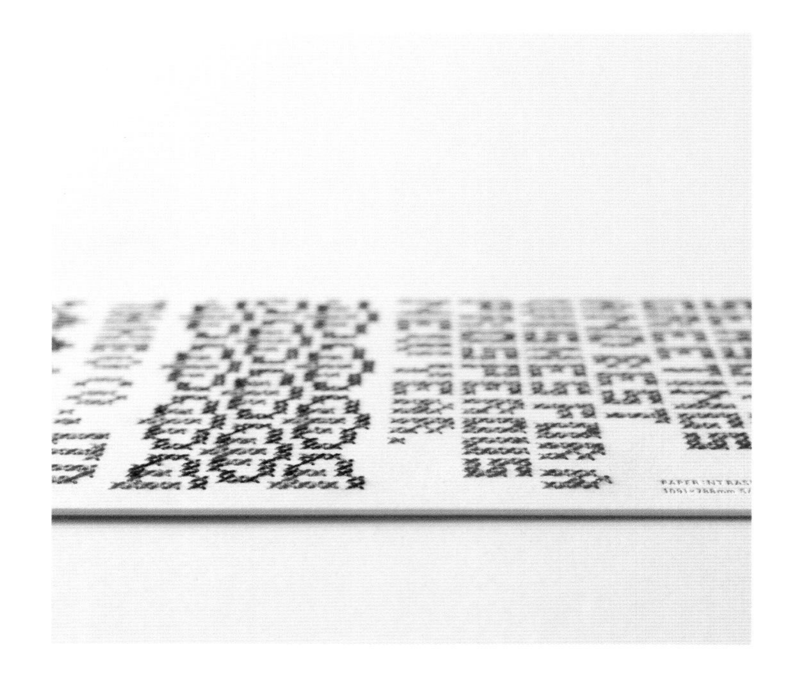

210 x 95mm

TAKEO NT RASHA Koiaka, Green, Dark Blue, Muku, Shikkoku 244gsm

Embroidering, hot stamping

Mistle-Tofu Christmas Mailer

As the first Christmas promotional mailer of creative studio Tofu, the Mistle-Tofu was inspired by festive mistletoe decorations. Came in a laser cut plywood board, recipients were able to have fun putting together a wooden mistletoe crafted to set hearts aflutter and spread Kiss'mas cheer.

DE Tofu

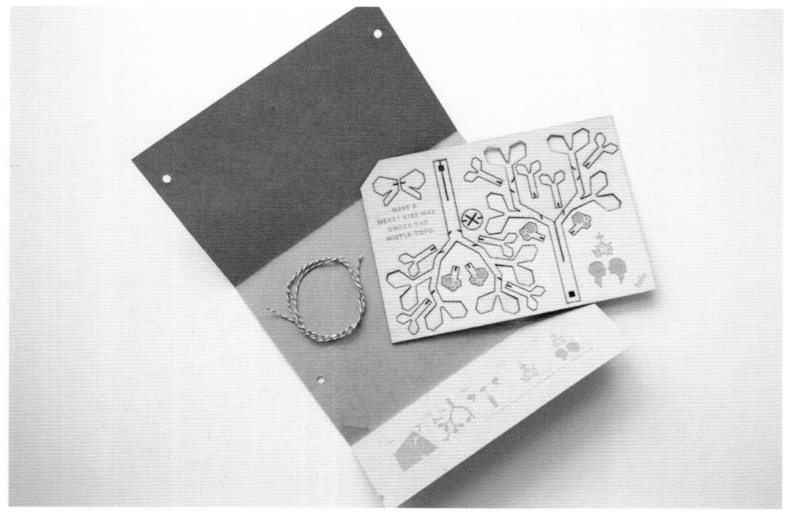

158 x 220mm
Plywood
Laser cutting

HAVE A
MERRY KISS'MAS
UNDER THE
MISTLE-TOFU
tofu

tofu

M & Y Wedding Invitation

Creative studio Tofu designed an interesting wedding identity for a nature-loving couple. Celebrating their marriage in a simple yet romantic layout, the set of collateral included a pop-up invitation featuring the silhouette of the couple's favourite moment, a programme booklet that spins out to form a fan and a crossword puzzle at the back of a menu. They were designed to keep guests entertained and let them leave the wedding knowing the couple a little more.

DE Tofu **CL** Mark & Yilin

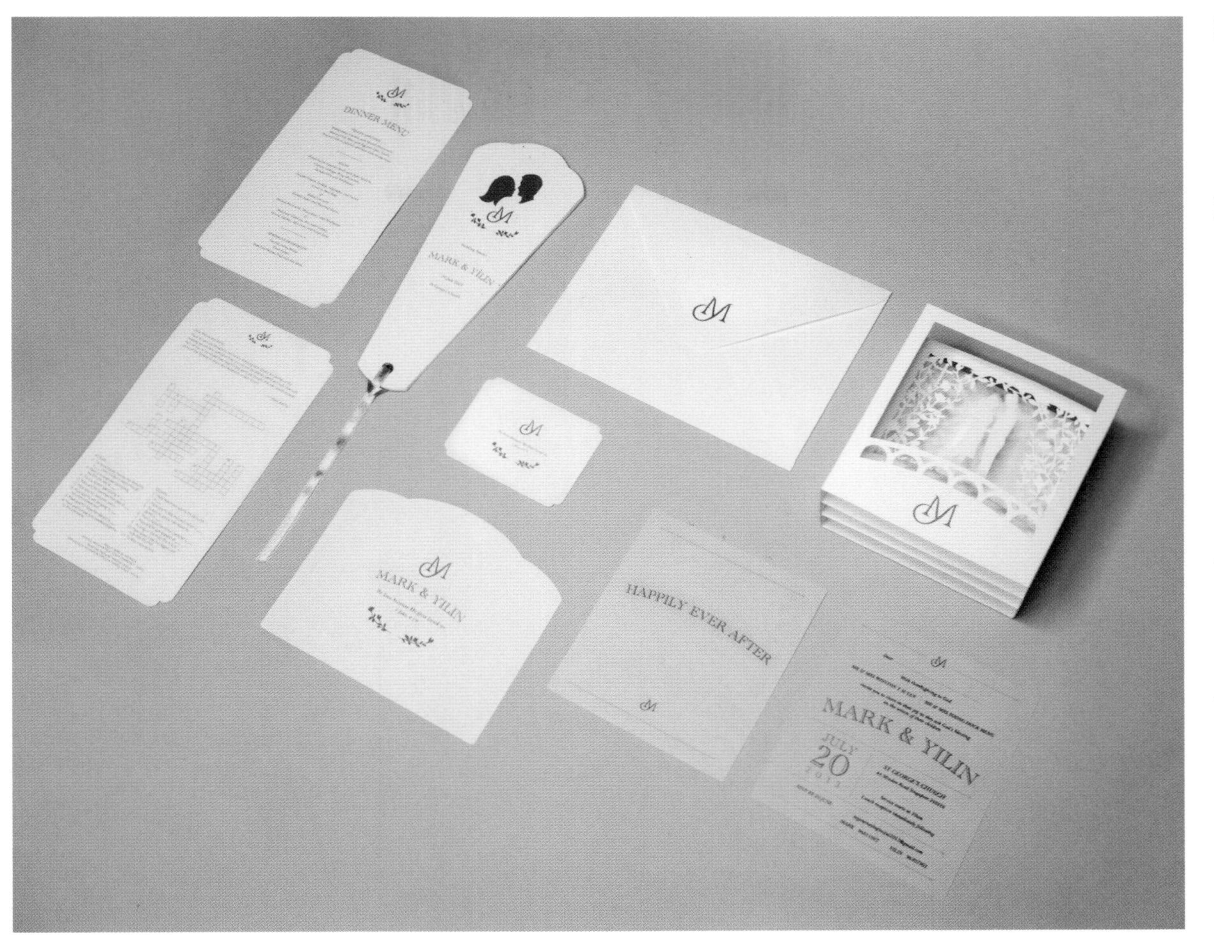

140 x 126 x 64 mm
Naturalis Smooth Absolute White 250gsm
Spot colour
Die cutting, hot stamping

Deer Card

Deer Card is a Christmas card in the shape of a reindeer. With versions made of vegetable tanned leather and various kinds of metal sheets, the card came in as a flat pad inside the envelope and with a simple step of fastening the belt lock became a small sculpture that stands on its own. The Deer Card not only epitomised tactility of printed cards, but also fulfilled the role of a delightful Christmas decoration.

DE PLEASANT by Hank and Maxwell Design Studio

130 x 145mm (card) 13.8 x 15.8mm (deer) Contact HB 250gsm (card) Cow leather, mental pad (deer) CMYK, spot colour Die cutting, hot stamping

National Historical Centres Day Brochure

Held in the city of Porto, National Historical Centres Day targeted both the senior and the younger public. In order to appeal to a diverse audience, visual identity for the event was set to address the dichotomy between the modern and the classic. Another Collective juxtaposed serif with non-serif as well as neutral colours with gold, which resonated well with the concept of the event.

DE Another Collective **CL** Porto City Hall

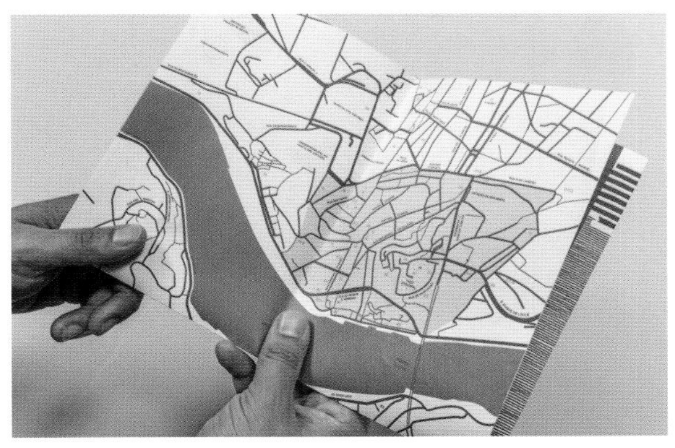

210 x 150mm Munken Pure 120gsm Spot colour

Little Prince Museum Identity

Inspired by the French classic "The Little Prince", Little Prince Museum resides in the Red Rock Desert, Nevada with a huge collections of prestigious Surrealist paintings by masters including Salvador Dali and Vladimir Kush. On the leaflets, monoline rectangles of different sizes frames the masterpieces, drawing a visual contrast against the centuries-old works. The Little Prince Museum is a school assignment composed by designer Leo Porto.

DE Leo Porto

88.9 x 50.8mm Pristine White 270gsm CMYK

Gianvito Rossi Origami Invitation

A limited edition of 100 miniature shoeboxes were sent out to the VIPs of luxury fashion store Harvey Nichols. As an invitation to meet up with Italian shoe designer Gianvito Rossi, the boxes contained origami paper in exquisite prints inspired by the legendary designer's latest collection. Following an enclosed instructional manual to turn them into heels, these loyal customers were able to have a sneak peek into the collection.

DE Fp7 Dxb **CL** Harvey Nichols Dubai

250 x 250mm
Plike Black 280gsm
Spot colour
Debossing, hot stamping

Process Exhibition Invitation

Chinese sculptural artist Mu Boyan held a solo exhibition titled "Process" in Beijing, 2013. The main visual of its event invitation breaks an entire course of action of Mu's iconic "naked fatty" into a sequence of movements. The theme of movement echoes the exhibition's theme of "process" and "the moments in between". The logotype in Chinese also falls apart and scatters on a line to represent the idea of continuity.

DE MANMANTEAM Design Office Inc. **CL** aye gallery

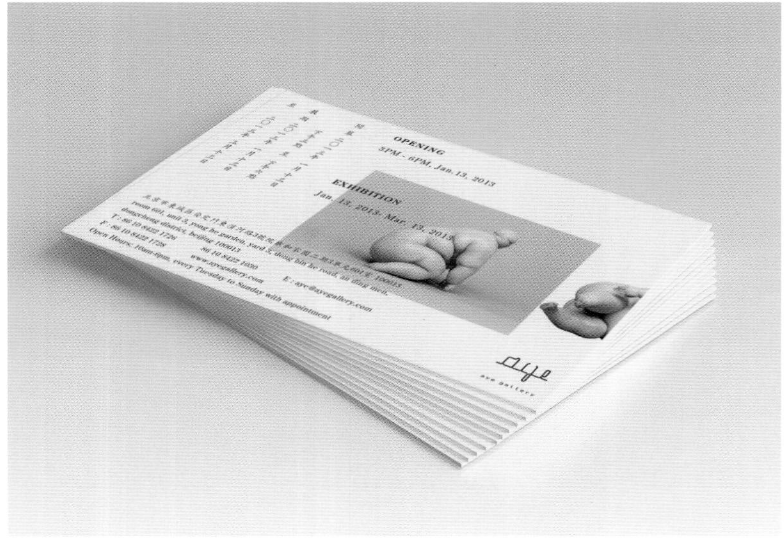

100 x 150mm
Conqueror Smooth Wove 300gsm
CMYK

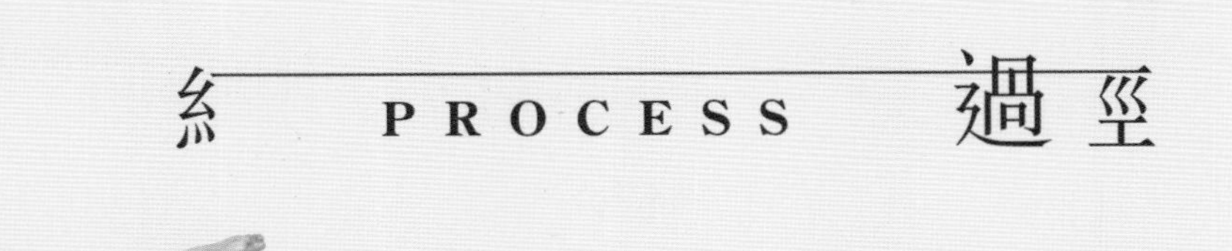

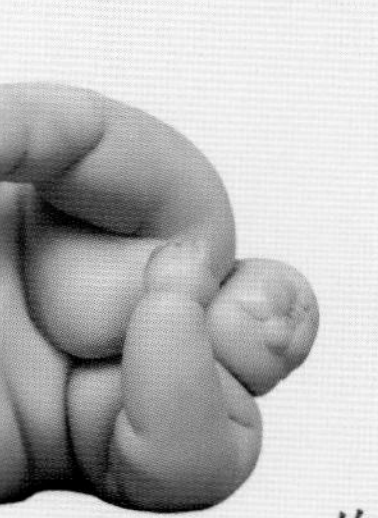

牟柏岩
二〇一二年
作品

Mu Boyan Works 2012

開幕 二〇一三年一月十三日
下午三點 至 下午六點
展期 二〇一三年一月十三日
至 二〇一三年三月十三日

OPENING

3PM - 6PM, Jan.13, 2013

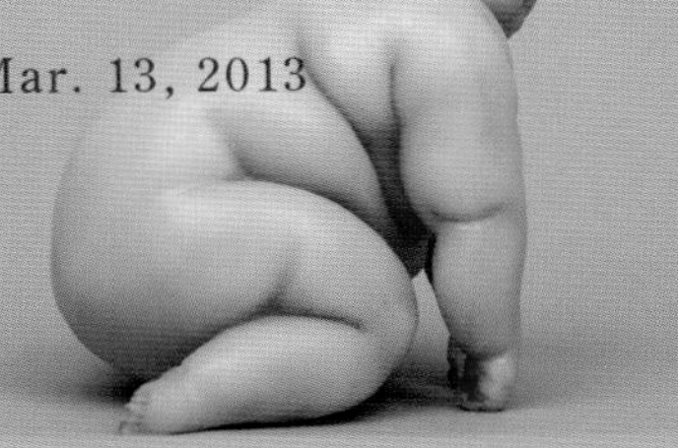

EXHIBITION

Jan. 13, 2013- Mar. 13, 2013

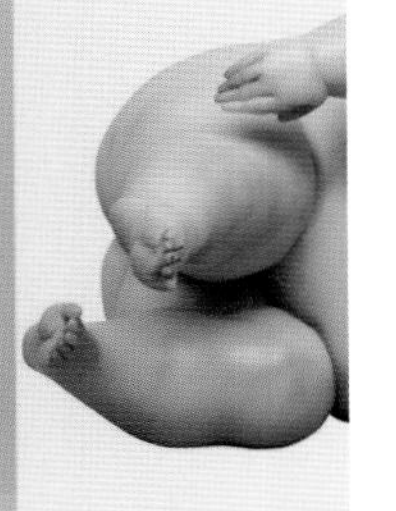

北京市東城區安定門東濱河路3號院雍和家園二期3單元601室 100013
room 601, unit 3, yong he garden, yard 3, dong bin he road, an ding men, dongcheng district, beijing 100013
T : 86 10 8422 1726 86 10 8422 1030 E : aye@ayegallery.com
F : 86 10 8422 1728 www.ayegallery.com
Open Hours: 10am-6pm, every Tuesday to Sunday with appointment

Awst & Walther Exhibition Invitation

Studio Hausherr was responsible for designing the invitation to the opening of artist duo Awst & Walther's "Ground to Sky" exhibition. Held at the PSM gallery in Berlin, the exhibition featured a surrealistic installation of a boxwood hedge afloat in the air. Similarly, the invitation also featured a suspending solid block at the centre of the front, revealing a small portion of the message. Event information can only be viewed when the block was scratched off.

DE Studio Hausherr

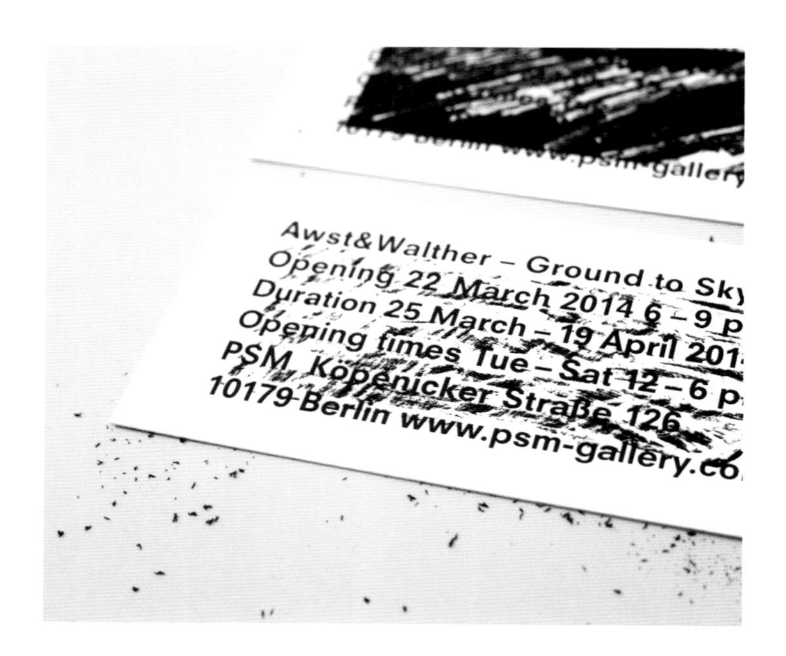

Awst&Walther – Ground to Sky
Opening 22 March 2014 6 – 9 pm
Duration 25 March – 19 April 2014
Opening times Tue – Sat 12 – 6 pm
PSM Köpenicker Straße 126
10179 Berlin www.psm-gallery.com

The Thief Opening Invitation

Located in Tjuvholmen, Oslo, The Thief is a Norwegian hotel and former 'home' to criminals and prostitutes back in the 1600s. Invitation card for the hotel's grand opening was designed as arrest sheets and identification papers to proclaim this notorious history. The heat sensitive ink on the envelope completes the design as every guests willingly leave their fingerprints on the invite.

DE Work in Progress

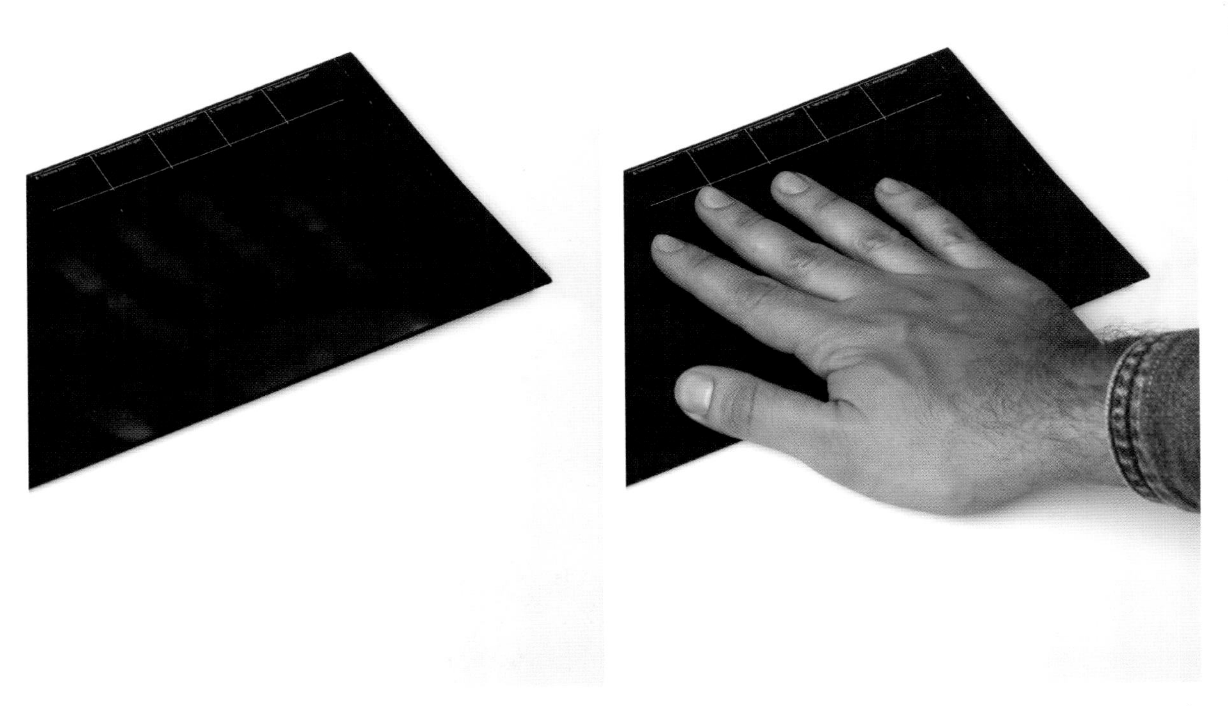

300 x 320mm Laminated MultiArt Silk 200gsm, MultiArt Gloss 260gsm Spot colour Embossing, heat sensitive ink, perforation

Christmas in July Invitation

Christmas in July is an event hosted by Spanish Cava label Freixenet. Set in a dark background, its invitation was brimming with gold foil spots that drew similarities between Cava bubbles and snowflakes in a dark winter night. The allusion graphically lowered the temperature for the mid-summer event. Use of gold foil on tactile paper stock also gave the invitation a lavish touch.

DE Them Design Ltd. **CL** Freixenet

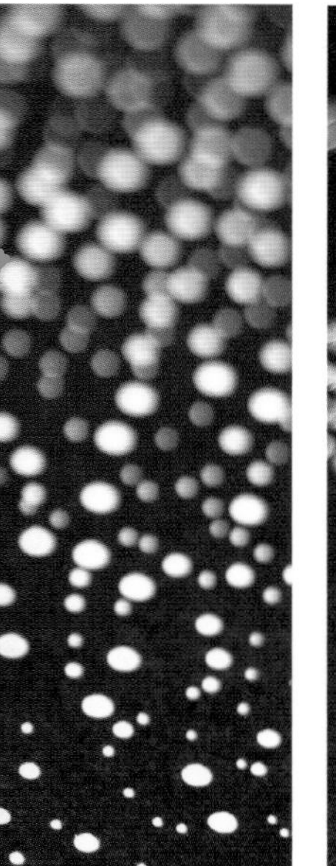

210 x 148mm

Colorplan Ebony 540gsm

Hot stamping

BASF Bespoke Invitation

This elegant invitation was for premium automotive partners of BASF Coatings. The invitations were exclusively handmade, with an edition of 60, intended for major clients from the automobile industries. Using a single palette to a showcase of the current colour collection, ONOGRIT played with laser-cut foil, adjusted and polished by hand. The envelope folding was inspired by traditional japanese folding techniques.

DE ONOGRIT **CL** BASF Coatings
CR 99Nos, Ruth Biniwersi (AD)

110 x 220mm

Gmund Colors Colour 38 300gsm

Hot stamping, laser cutting

tapas&co Identity

tapas&co's visual identity was created based a set of pictograms illustrating various tapas ingredients. Much like preparing the Spanish bites, each pictogram can be combined freely to innovate a vibrant dish or meanings. The pictograms can be used as independent graphic elements to identify with other entities, matched with custom colours to tell another colourful brand story.

DE Masha Portnova

50 x 90mm
Coated Paper 350gsm
CMYK

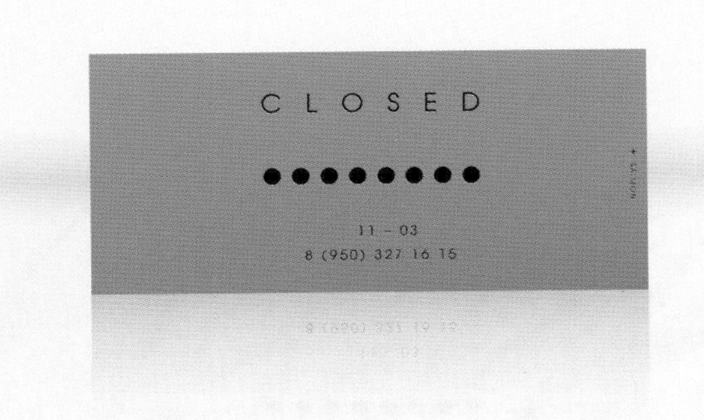

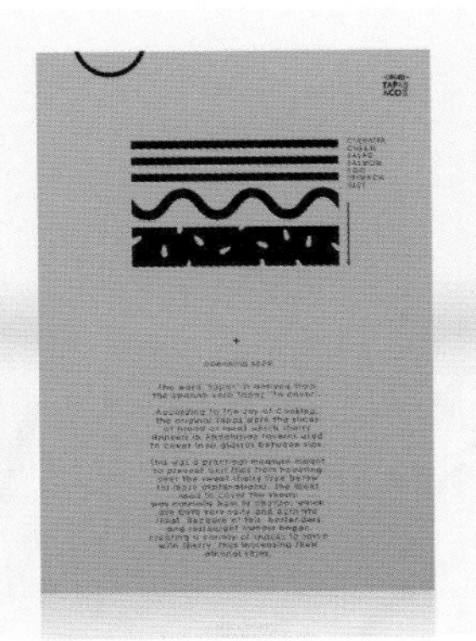

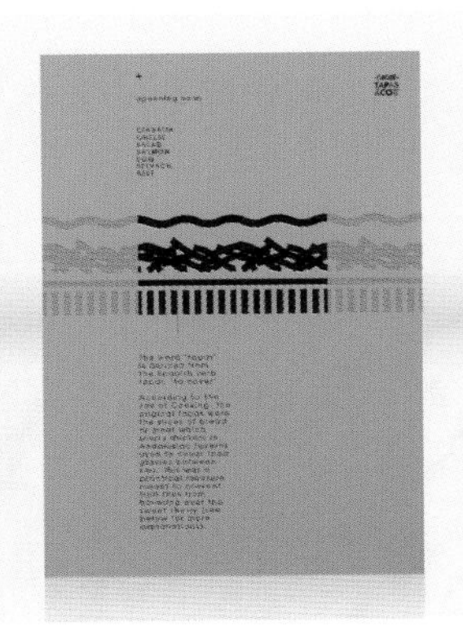

plat Greeting Package

To celebrate their opening, studio plat prepared a greeting package for their client and friends that consisted of a postcard, a matchbox and a coaster. These handy mediums were illustrated with the studio's interior, featuring four sets of posters and books, if you look close enough. The posters and books represented the four members of the studio. Knowing well local creatives' habit of enjoying coffee or beer at work, the coaster was made a useful reminder of the studio when they drink.

DE plat

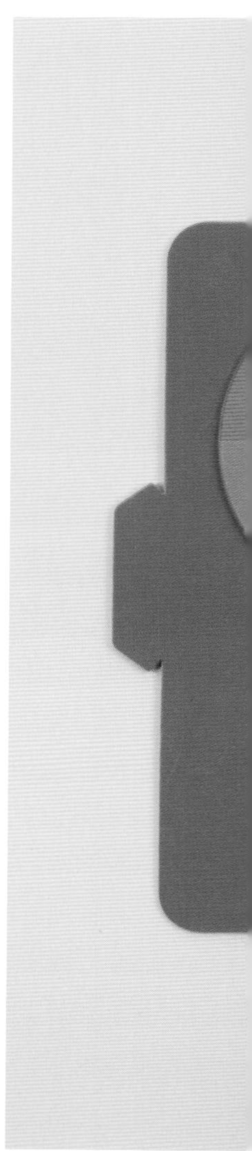

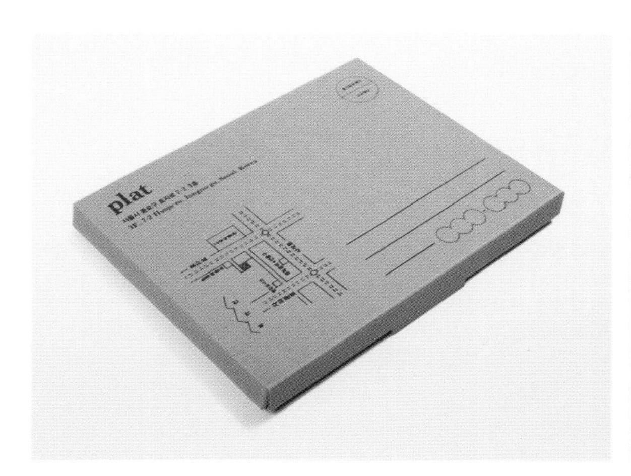

175 x 130mm Gentle Box 352gsm (postcard) CMYK

Invitations and greeting cards

Taidehalli Rebranding

Taidehalli, also known as Helsinki Kunsthalle, has rooted itself firmly in its 86-year history as one of the key spaces for exhibiting contemporary art in Finland. The distinctive facade of the respected institution guided the rebranding scheme and appears in the new logomark. To show the diverse and energetic personality of Taidehalli, a set of alternative logos were also designed to apply on different context and promotional materials.

DE Tsto **CL** Taidehalli / Kunsthalle Helsinki

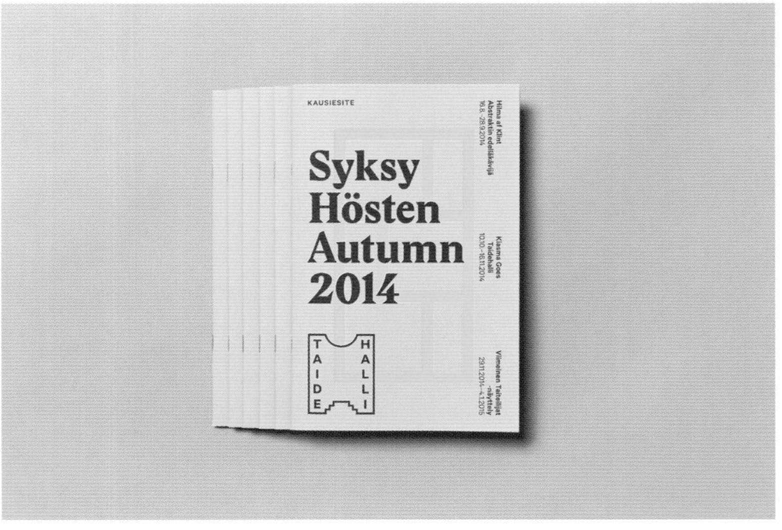

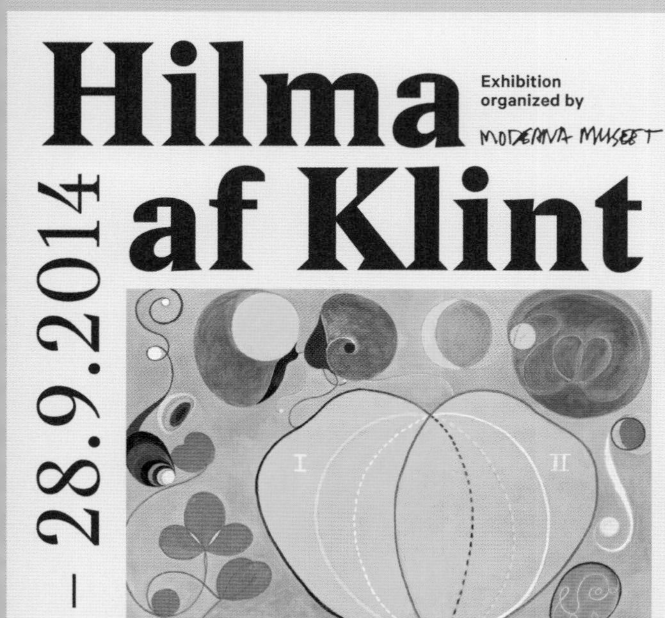

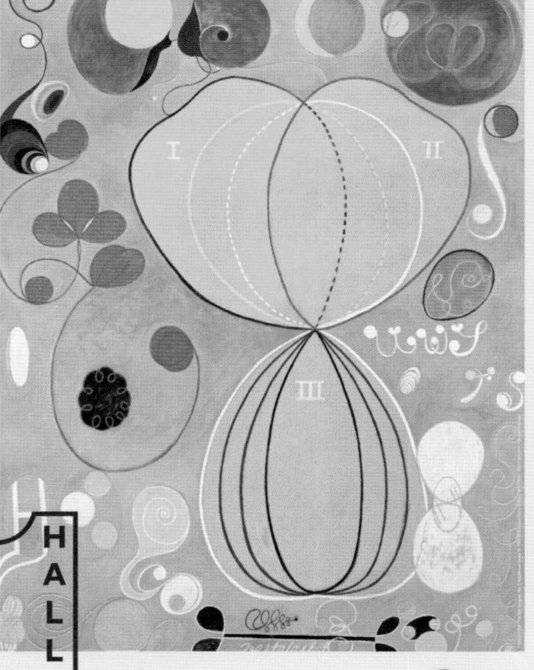

85 x 55mm
G.F. Smith Colorplan Plain Royal Blue 540gsm
CMYK
Screenprinting

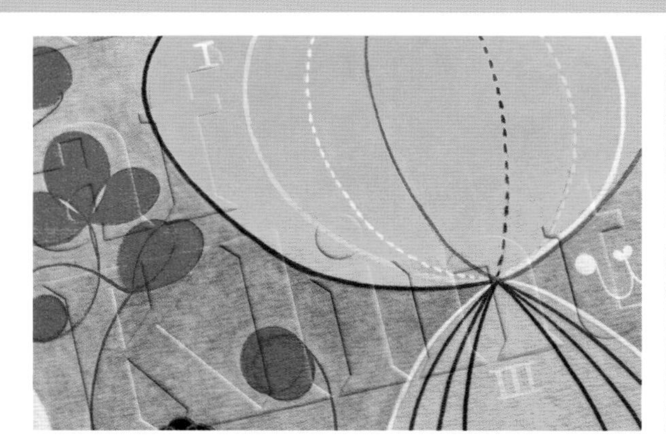

Stephanie Hundertmark Birthday Invitation

Studio Hausherr wittily made use of honeycomb paper party balls as the invitation to Stephanie Hundertmark's birthday party. Event information was hand stamped on both ends of the balls when pressed together, which can be turned instantly into a substantial decoration for the guests' home as well as the party venue.

DE Studio Hausherr

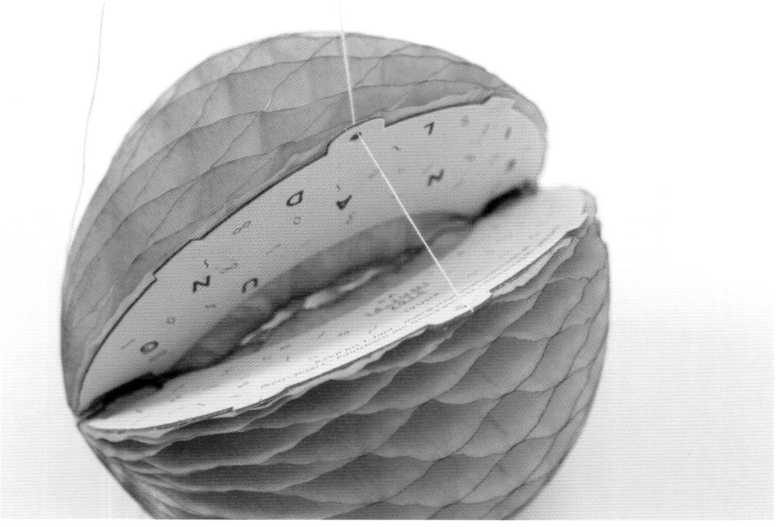

SA
14.JUNI
2014
19UHR
RSVP bis 1.Juni – mail@stephaniehundertmark.de
Dress: Smart – Paulsborn am Grunewaldsee – Hüttenweg 90 – 14193 Berlin

Serpent Card

The Serpent Card is a live greeting that can turn into a decorative garland of nearly two metres in length. Each of the 100 cards has its unique colour combination and is individually numbered. The greetings make for a tangible and interactive statement, as opposed to today's digital communication. Colour gradation on the Serpent Card reinforced the significance of creating authentically personal messages to show gratitude to those who support and care about us.

DE Graphic design studio by Yurko Gutsulyak

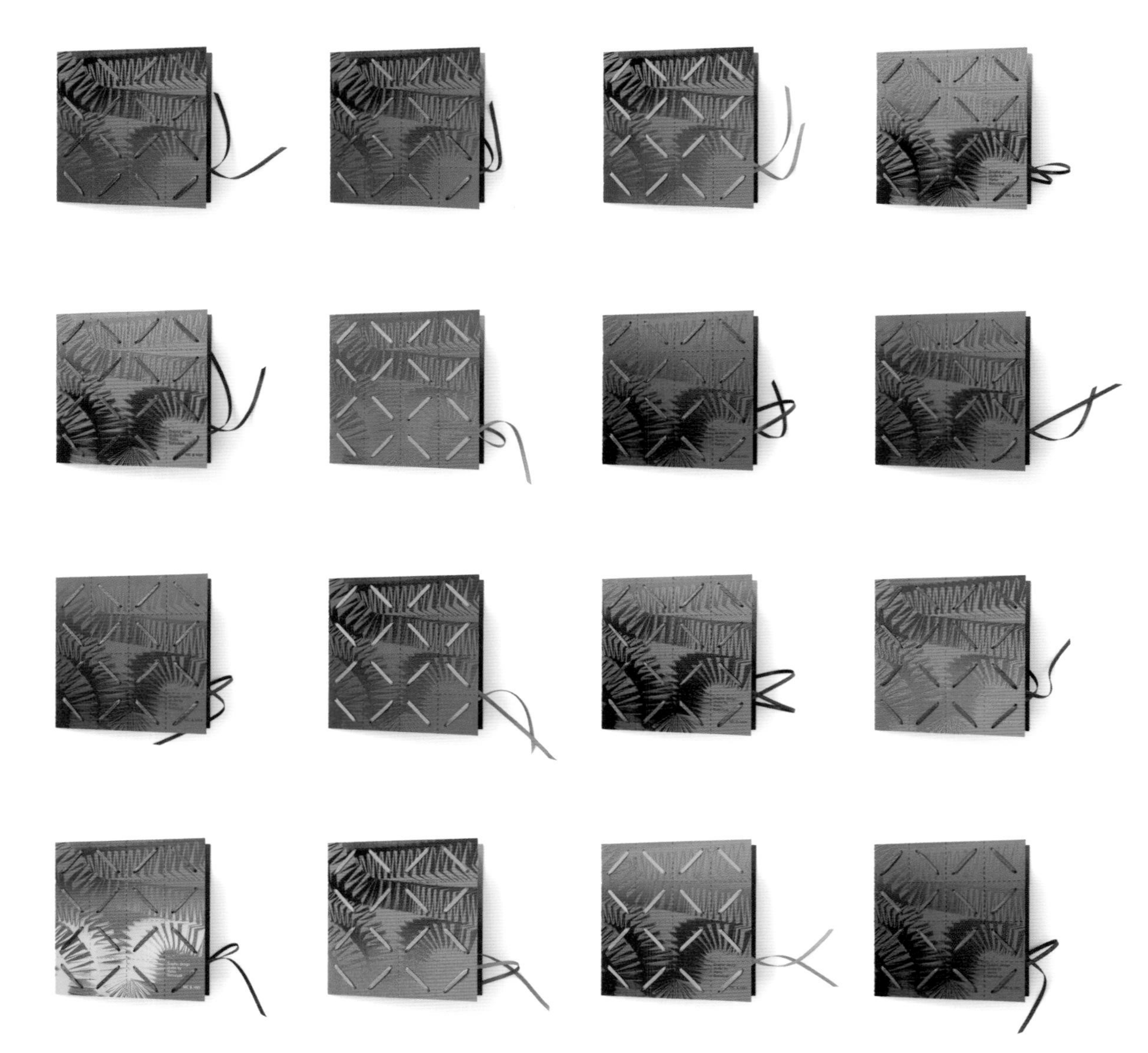

145 x 290mm
So...Silk Glamour Green, Fashion Purple, Beauty Pink, Fair Blue 350gsm
Spot colour
Perforation, screenprinting

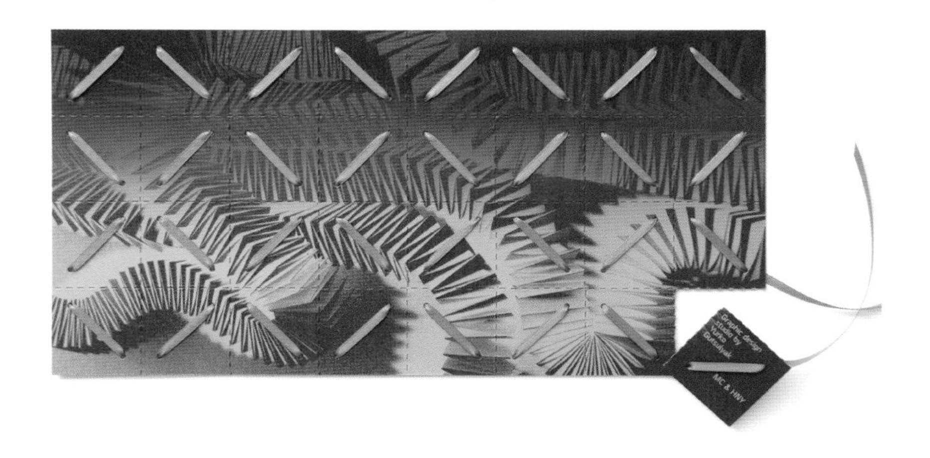

Adrian & Iris Wedding Invitation

In black sans serif and an explosion of golden confetti, Studio SP-GD created a simple and modern invitation that was the bride and groom-to-be's statement of celebration. Set in foil and polished finish, the single page invitation was chic, full of layers and beyond conventional.

DE Studio SP-GD **CL** Adrian & Iris

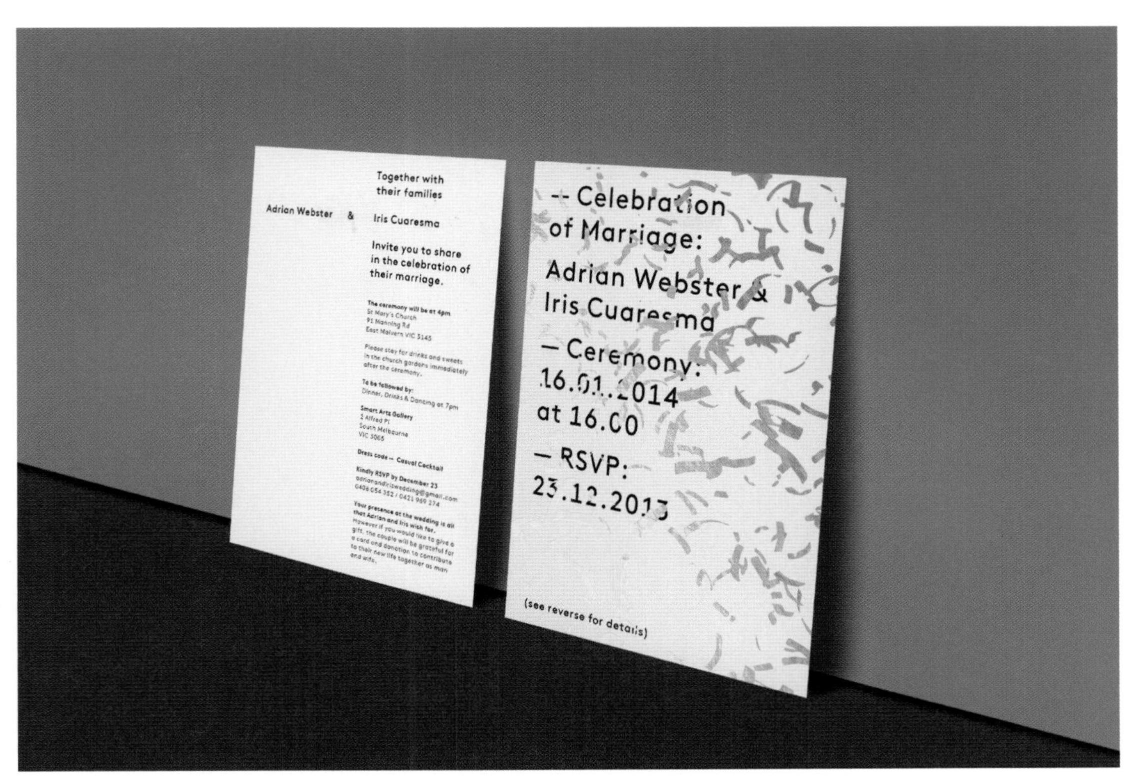

210 x 148mm
Cotton Stock 560gsm
Spot colour
Hot stamping

It's a Wrap! Invitation

Commissioned by The Bookstore Foundation from Amsterdam for their 2014 Christmas event, Marta Veludo collaborated with Sue Doeksen and Ricardo Leite to come up with a festive invitation that doubled as a wrapping paper. The concept was a literal translation from the event's theme, It's a Wrap!, which celebrated the end of a year. Riso-printed with a mash up of ten patterns, the A3 invitation was released in an edition of 150.

DE Marta Veludo, Sue Doeksen, Ricardo Leite
CL The Bookstore Foundation

420 x 290mm
White paper 90gsm
Riso printing

Invitations and greeting cards

Stan Smith Relaunch Invitation & Poster

Adidas relaunched their legendary sneakers, Stan Smith, at the beginning of 2014.
An opening party was held at The Gaîté Lyrique, Paris to celebrate the occasion with dance and video performances. Taking up the signature green and white of the original sneakers, studio My name is designed a typography-based invitation that plays with alignments and the legendary tennis player's signature. The studio also produced a set of typography-based posters as part of the set design, which aimed at evoking dance and rhythm while staying true to the minimalist codes of the sneakers.

DE My name is **CL** Adidas / Iconoclast

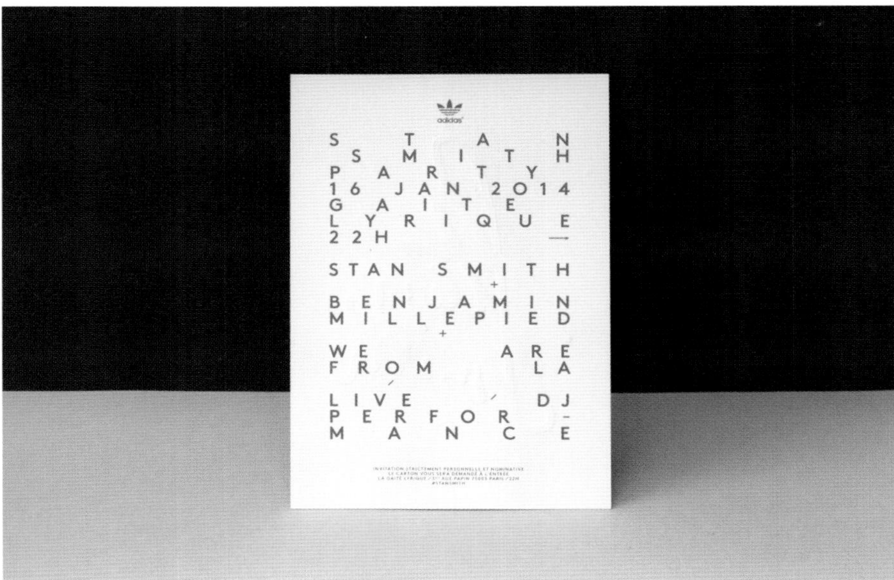

210 x 150mm
Fedrigoni Sirio White 400gsm
Spot colour
Debossing

A3 Studio Greeting Card

Hello Hello is a compliment card designed by A3 Studio and mailed to their friends and clients. The card featured two hellos oriented to opposite sides, with strokes fitted and faded into each other perfectly within the dimension. Simple, robust typography in clever composition constituted the beauty of this project.

DE A3 Studio

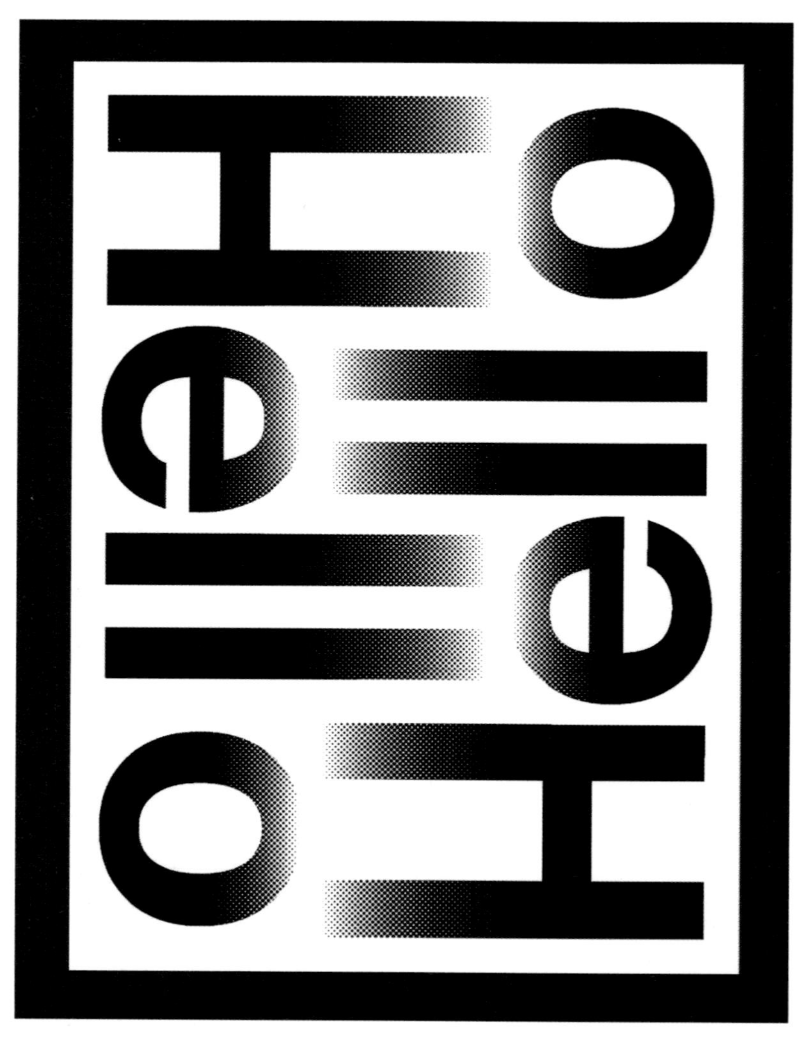

148.5 x 210mm Papyrus Munken Polar Extra White 400gsm Spot colour

Invitations and greeting cards

WHITE IMAGINATION inspired by GALAXY

More than just a plain white card, the paper mobile phone mock-up was the key to activate the 3D projection mapping installation at Tokyo Designers Week 2013. These paper models were made of HAPTIC paper, on which hot stamping could produce transparent graphics and enable the projection of stunning visuals on top. The projection was triggered by an IC tag embedded inside each card when placed on the palms of hand models at the booth.

DE Naonori Yago **CL** Samsung Electronics Co., Ltd.

70 x 135mm HAPTIC 180gsm

Lyndon & Nick Wedding Invitation

Wedding invitation and Save the Date for Lyndon & Nick was set to illustrate equality and difference. As near mirrored reflections of each other, the couple's initials 'V' and 'A' were interlocked like mountains and valleys. The highs and lows were an honest portrait of every relationship. The logo also resembled the outlines of a six-point star, a symbol that stood to mean perfection by the union of the two. From the logo to the contrasting palette, differences that complement each other were united, creating a moment of coming together.

DE Nick Adam

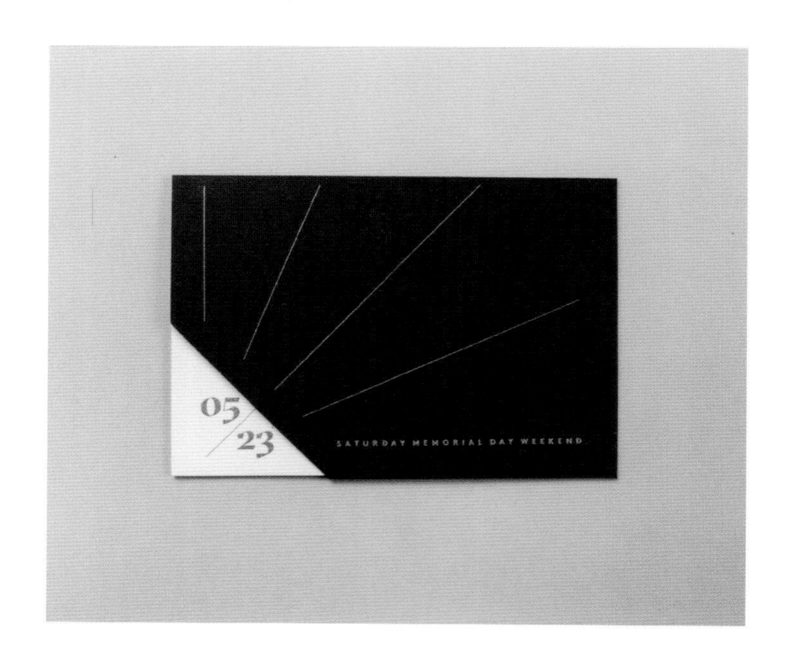

80 x 120mm

Neenah Classic Crest Epic Black Smooth 80lb Cover

Spot colour

Die cutting, engraving

AMBIDEX A/W 2013 Exhibition Invitation

Distributed as a stack of self-enveloped cards, AMBIDEX Co., Ltd.'s Autumn/Winter 2013 exhibition invitation unfolds a collection of snapshots. Captured by musician Itsuqi Doi, the shots represent a part of ordinary life in Japan in the eyes of a non-professional photographer. Since perforated, each picture could be detached and sent out separately as postcards, with exhibition details at the back.

DE Kamimura Typografie Gestaltung **CL** AMBIDEX Co., Ltd. **CR** NSSG Inc. (AG), Itsuqi Doi (PH), Sanwa Printing Co., Ltd. (PT)

367 x 150mm TAKEO Vent Nouveau V 215kg CMYK Perforation

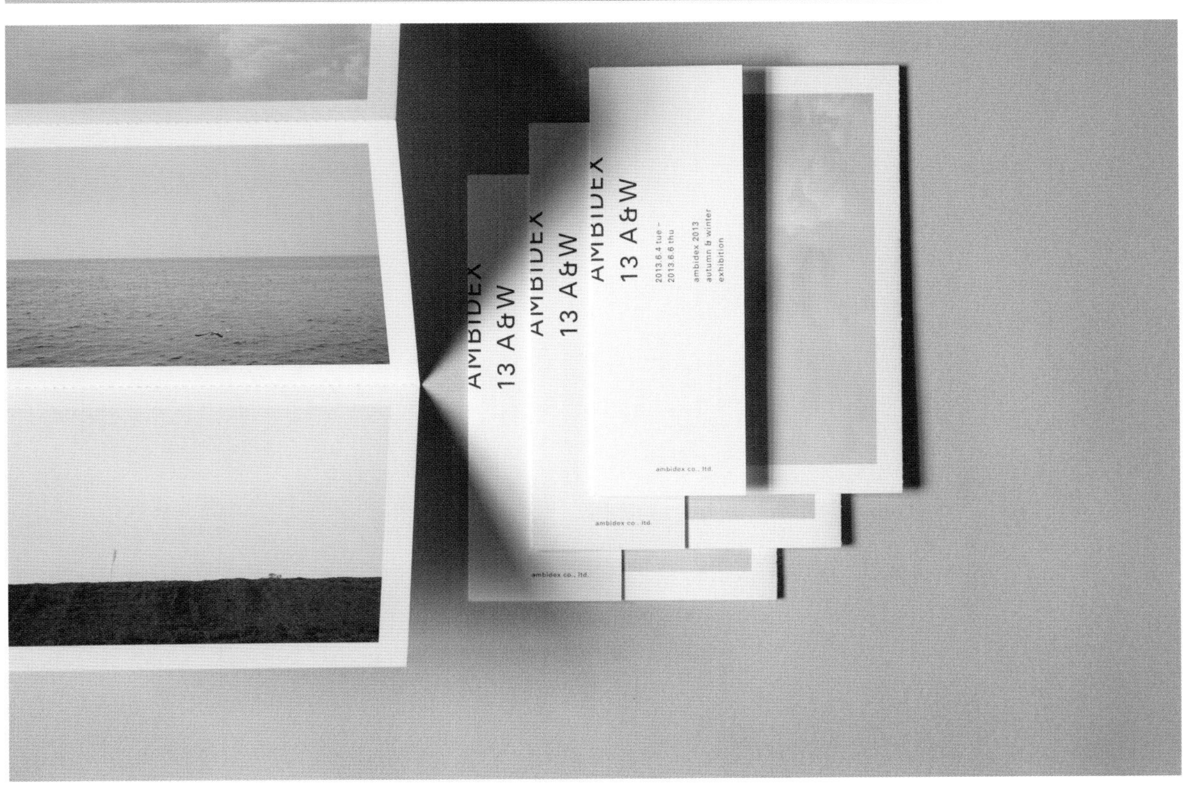

Oyamaten Exhibition Invitation

Oyamaten is a joint exhibition of Japanese illustrators Toshiyuki Hirano and danny. The exhibition's flyers came in as a rhombus. Folded in the middle, it fitted two mountains drawn by the two illustrators on the outside and event information on the inside. The drawings, as well as the earthy and green palette both resonated with the exhibition's theme of mountain.

DE UMA/design farm **CL** Toshiyuki Hirano, danny **CR** Yoshiro Masuda (PH)

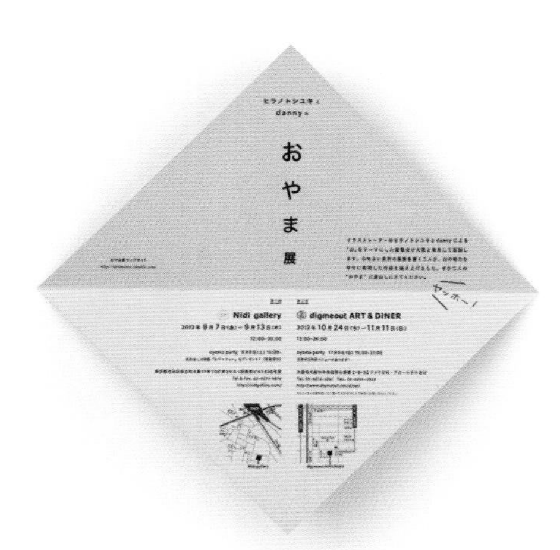

210 x 210mm
OK Gold 120gsm
CMYK

Moon & Sun Wedding Invitation

Moon & Sun is the invitation created by Indonesia based designer Wildan Ilham Mahibuddin for his sister's wedding. Based on dreamy pink, white and glamourous gold, he came up with a modern piece that exuded the heart-warming vibe when the moon meets the sun. Unique floral elements bore a subtle Art Deco reference, making the design stood out from traditional wedding invitations.

DE Wildan Ilham Mahibuddin **CL** Dena & Dhika

Info Jalan
10
01
20
15
PLEASE
SAVE THE DATE
20
15
MEETS
Turut mengundang
Keluarga besar kedua mempelai
Yth.
Resepsi
SABTU
10
01
20
15
11.00 wib – 13.00 wib
Dena & Dhika
10
01
20
15

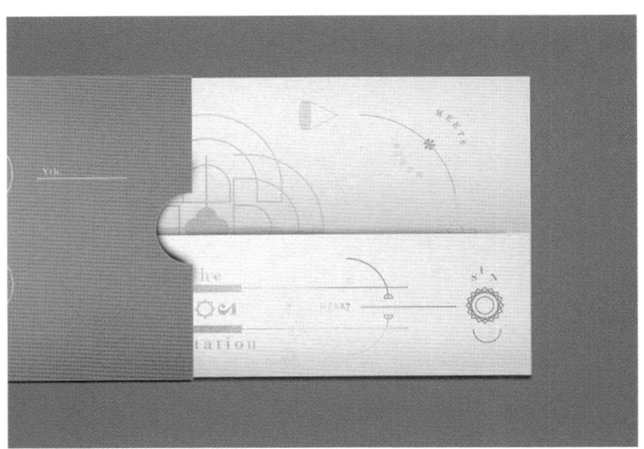
Yth.
MEETS
HEART

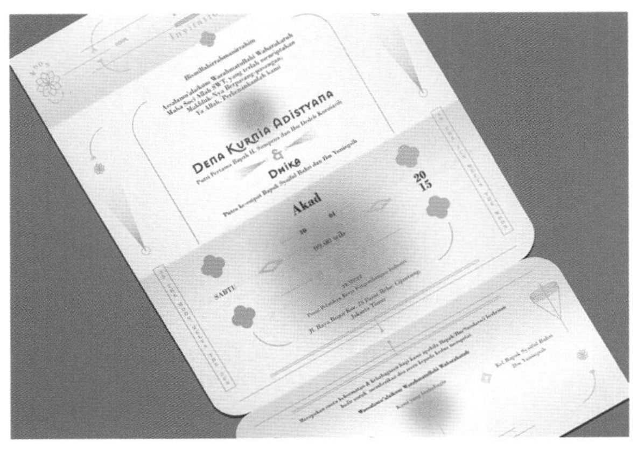
Dena Kurnia Adistyana
&
Dhika
20
15
Akad
SABTU

AMBIDEX Summer 2013 Exhibition Invitation

Invitation for Japanese women's fashion label AMBIDEX Co., Ltd.'s Summer exhibition 2013 honoured the ubiquitous paper stationery in Japan. For that reason, archetypes including a business card, a bookmark and an A4 letter paper, in their most popular formats were taken to compose a sincere request. All items were mailed out in a typical ready-made envelope with varied types adding the slightest personal touch.

DE Kamimura Typografie Gestaltung **CL** AMBIDEX Co., Ltd.
CR NSSG Inc. (AG), Sanwa Printing Co., Ltd. (PT)

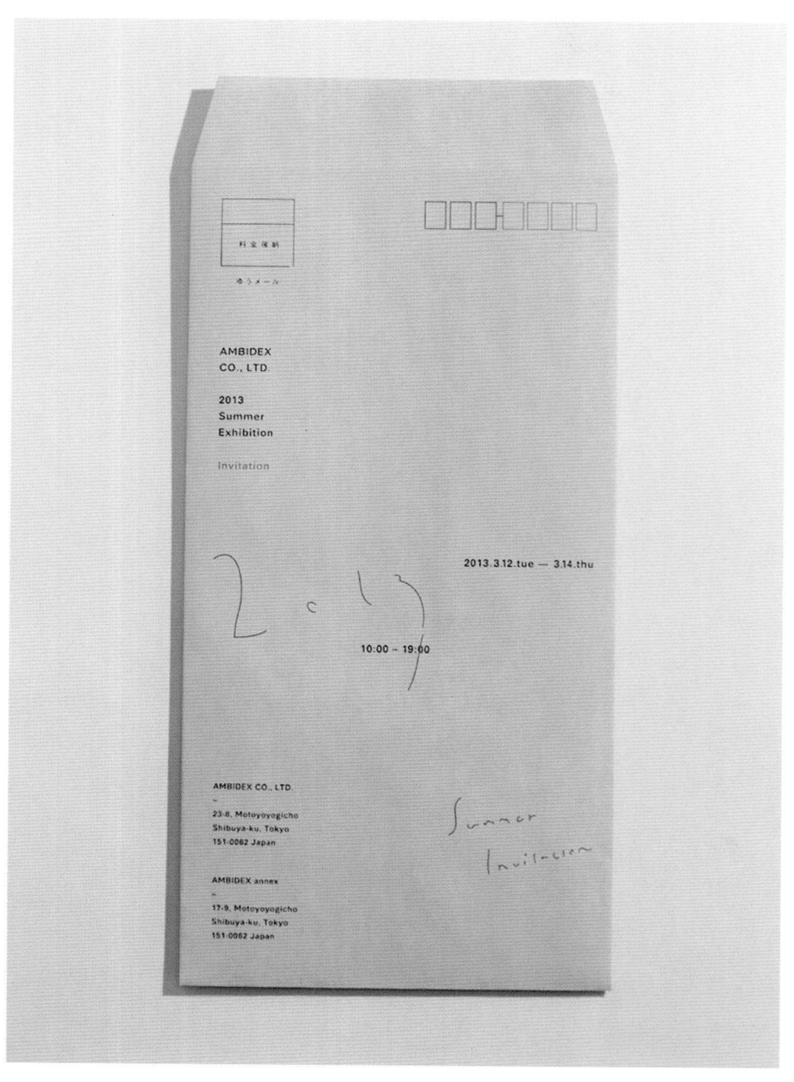

Exhibition

Invitation

2013
Summer
Exhibition

料金後納
ゆうメール

AMBIDEX
CO., LTD.

2013
Summer
Exhibition

Invitation

Summer
Invitation

AMBIDEX
CO., LTD.
-
2013
Summer
Exhibition
-
2013.
3.12.tue –
3.14.thu

2013

10:00 – 19:00

AMBIDEX CO., LTD.
-
23-8, Motoyoyogicho
Shibuya-ku, Tokyo
151-0062 Japan

332 x 240mm (envelope)
Matted & coated paper
CMYK, spot colour
Hot stamping

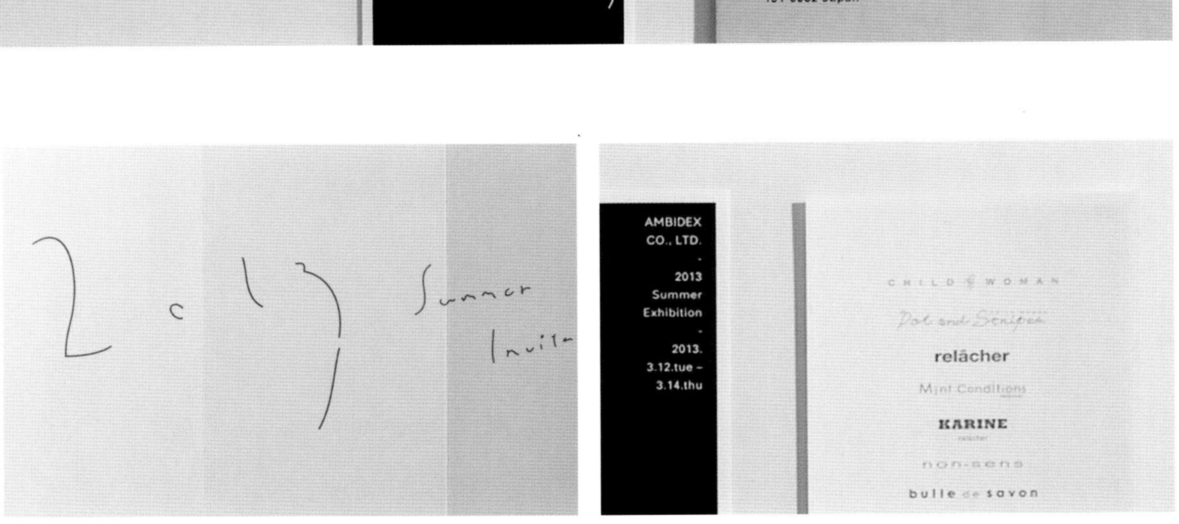

■ Invitations and greeting cards

Marina & David Wedding Invitation

Marina and David is a Swedes couple whose love bloomed during frequent travels to Tuscany and Sicily. Their wedding invitation was adorned with illustrated botanic elements for a natural vibe referencing the beautiful landscape they've seen together. Epitomised by the ornate frame and gold foil typography, subtle Art Deco elements fostered elegance of the set.

DE Menta. **CL** Marina & David

213 x 160mm
Sundance Felt Extra White 216gsm
CMYK
Hot stamping

Animal Paper Puppet

Animal Paper Puppet is a paper toy series produced by illustrator Furze Chan. She illustrated seven animals in ink pen, which were printed and packaged individually in a DIY assemblage kit. Releasing 1000 pieces for each animal, each kit included a prop, the animal's semi-die cut body parts and joints ready for making a puppet that stars in storytelling and drama play.

DE Furze Chan

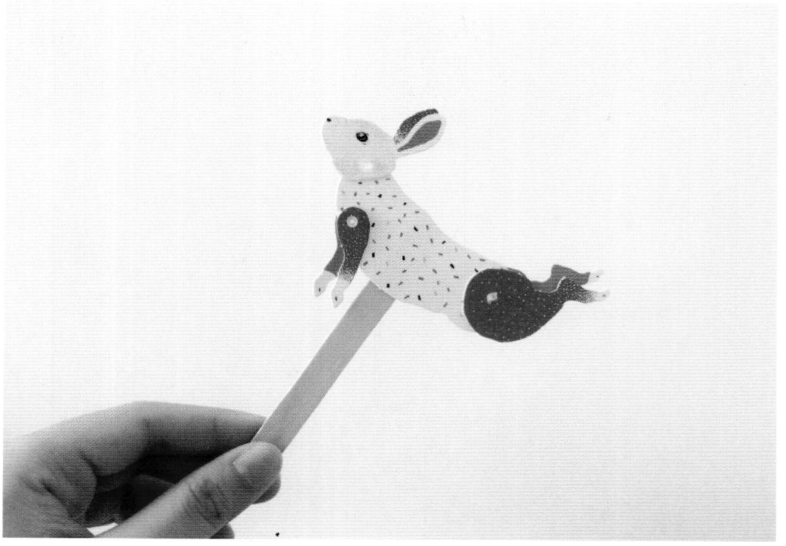

90 x 120mm White card 250gsm CMYK Die cutting

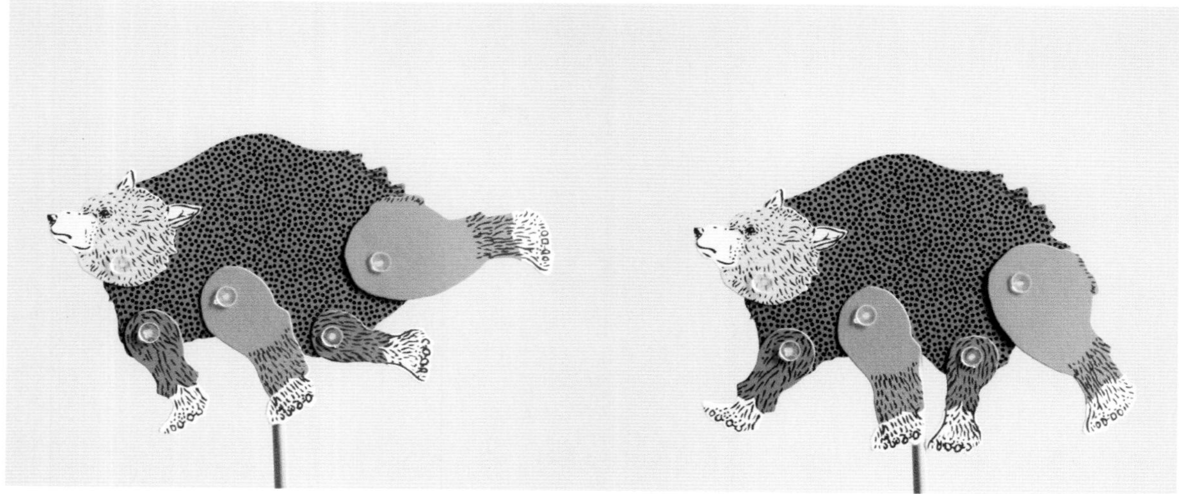

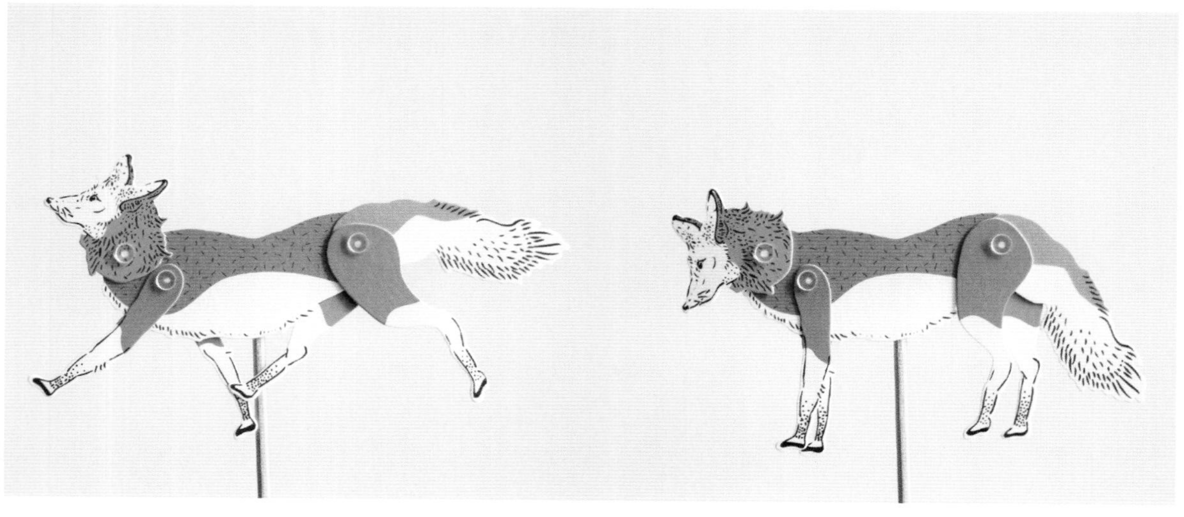

Teepee Wedding Invitation

Device Creative Collaborative was commissioned by event production studio Lisa Vorce Co. to create an invitation for a Native American-inspired wedding held in the Arizona desert. The result was a meticulously designed miniature teepee die-cut for DIY guest assembly. Letterpress printed, the design and typesetting of the 3D invitation incorporated traditional motifs and emblems, and could be supported by attaching bamboo skewers.

DE Device Creative Collaborative
CL Lisa Vorce Co.
CR Full Circle Press (PT)

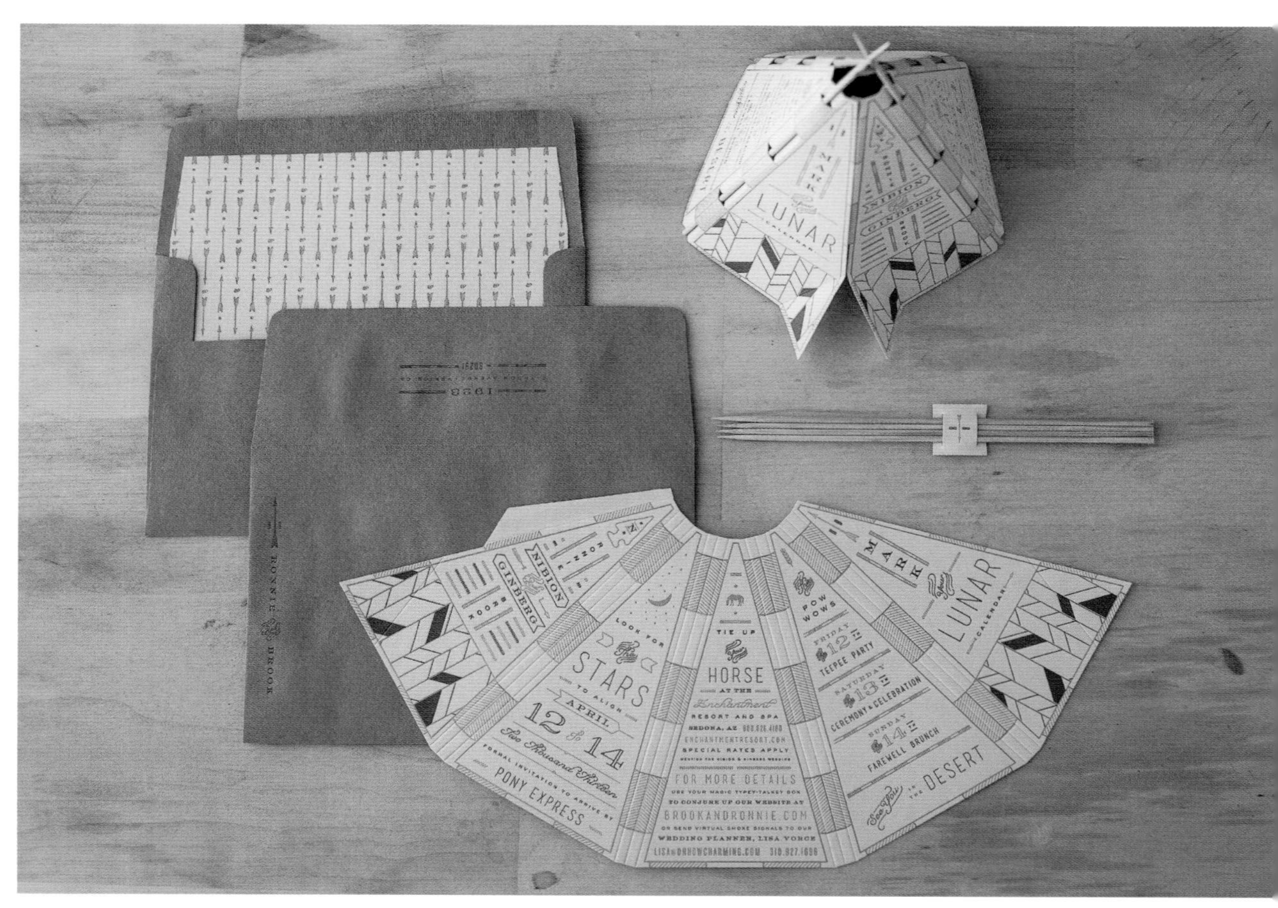

152.4 x 190.5mm

Gmund Cotton New Grey 110gsm

Spot colour

Die cutting, letterpress printing

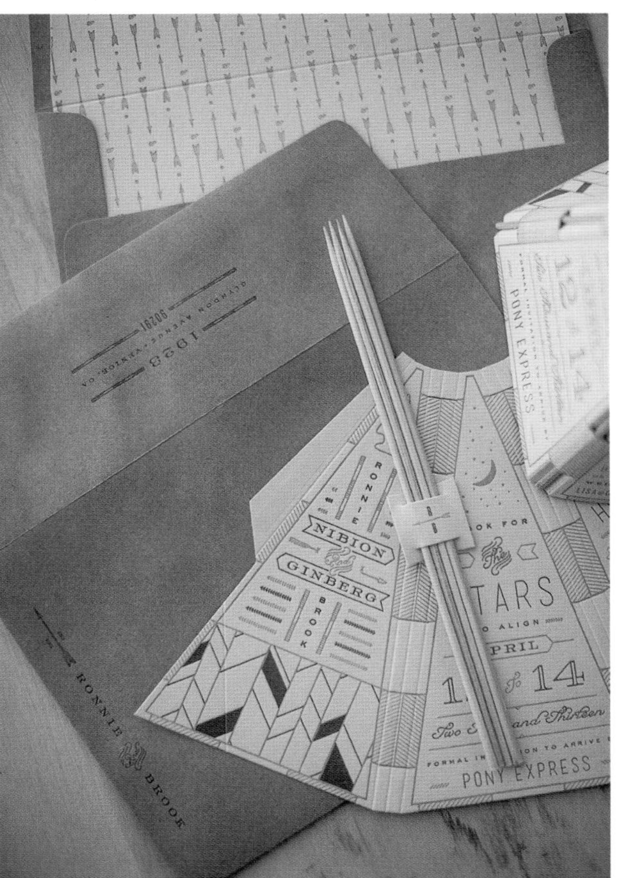

Hey, Listen — Works by Sandy Leong Sin-u Exhibition Invitation

Event identity for Macau born artist Sandy Leong's solo exhibition at the city's creative space Ox Warehouse incorporated some of her monochrome sketches, with a golden hue smeared on the edges of the collateral and occasionally on the text. The logotype seemed broken and doodled, relating to the artist's past and memories that led her to create the collection. The invitation's envelope was die-cut and made from the poster, a witty way to create a consistent visual identity.

DE SomethingMoon Design **CL** Ox Warehouse

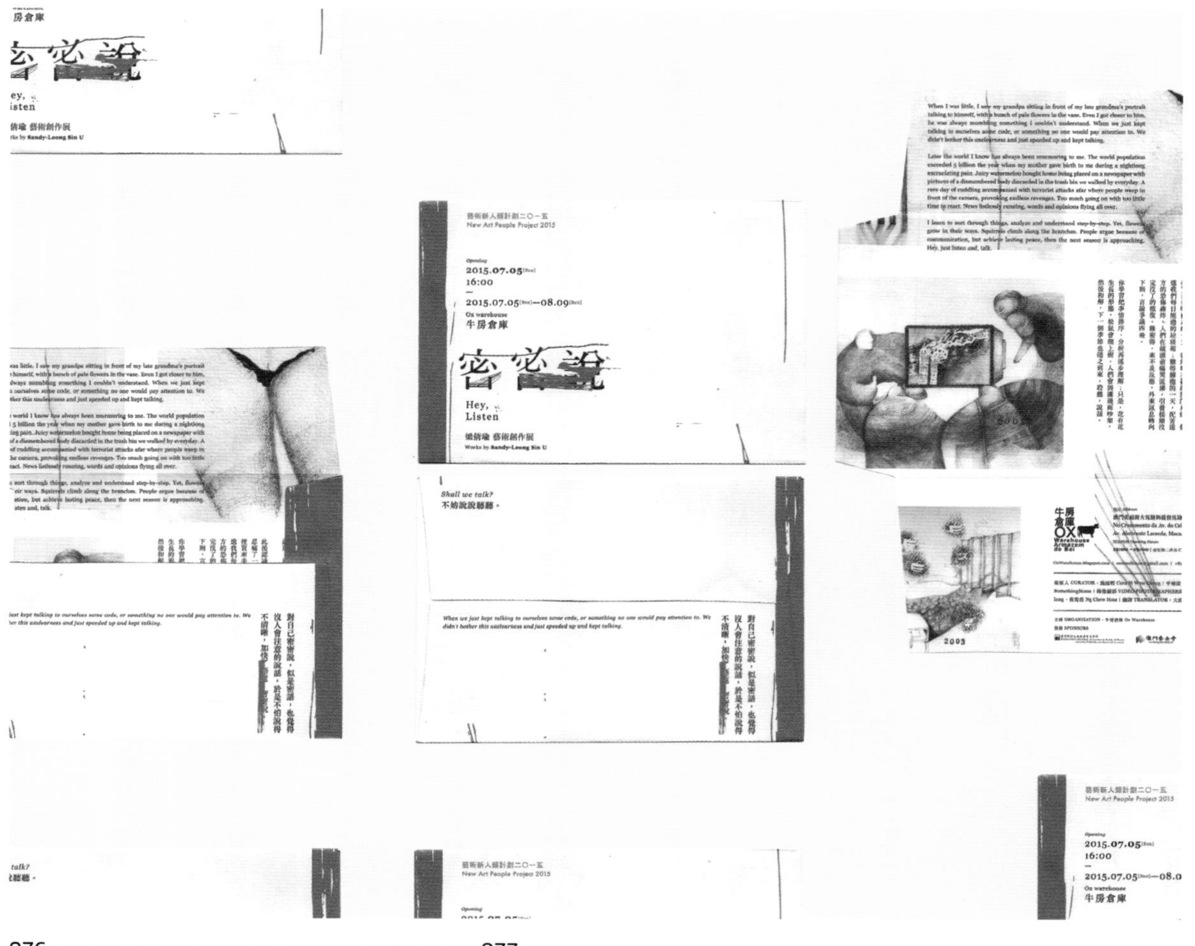

115 x 160mm
Polytrade Paper IMPACT Uncoated 80gsm
Spot colour

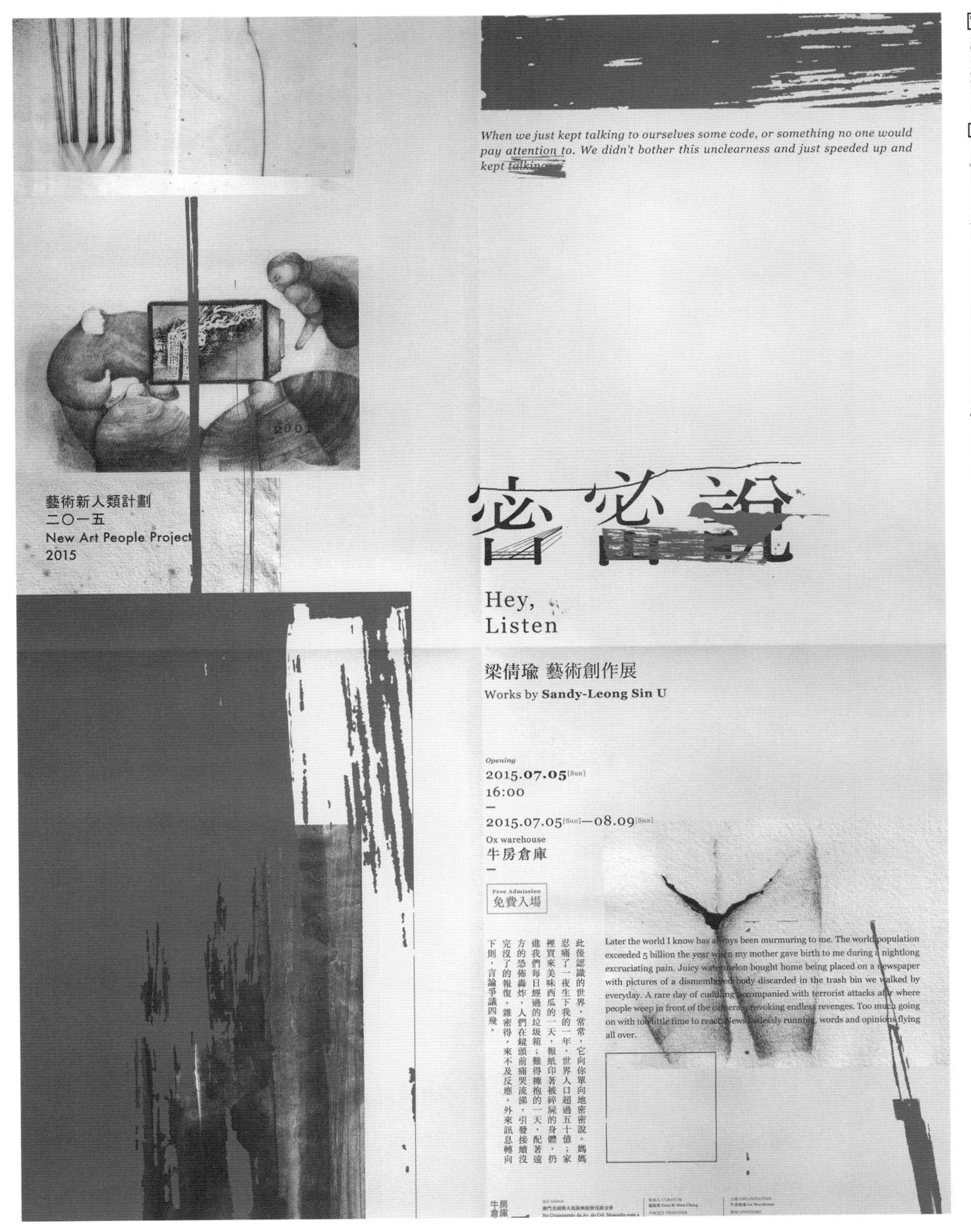
When we just kept talking to ourselves some code, or something no one would pay attention to. We didn't bother this unclearness and just speeded up and kept talking.
藝術新人類計劃
二〇一五
New Art People Project
2015
密密說
Hey,
Listen
梁倩瑜 藝術創作展
Works by Sandy-Leong Sin U
Opening
2015.07.05[Sun]
16:00
2015.07.05[Sun]—08.09[Sun]
Ox warehouse
牛房倉庫
Free Admission
免費入場
此後認識的世界，常常，它向你單向地密密說，媽媽忍痛了一夜生下我的一年，世界人口超過五十億；家裡買來美味西瓜的一天，報紙印著被碎屍的身體，扔進我們每日經過的垃圾箱；難得擁抱的一天，配著遠方的恐怖轟炸，人們在鏡頭前痛哭流涕，引發接續沒完沒了的報復。雜密得，來不及反應，外來訊息轉向下則，言論爭議四飛。
Later the world I know has always been murmuring to me. The world population exceeded 5 billion the year when my mother gave birth to me during a nightlong excruciating pain. Juicy watermelon bought home being placed on a newspaper with pictures of a dismembered body discarded in the trash bin we walked by everyday. A rare day of cuddling accompanied with terrorist attacks afar where people weep in front of the camera, provoking endless revenges. Too much going on with too little time to react. News restlessly running, words and opinions flying all over.
牛房倉庫

Aflo Mall New Year Card

Aflo is an online supplier of design related image and digital content, including illustrations, typefaces and greeting cards. In 2015, GRAPHITICA inc. created a set of New Year cards to add on to the designer's collection of the online resource. Available in digital formats, the typographic layout featured childlike Kanji design in the same line weight and bright simple icons that combined into an adorable card choice.

DE GRAPHITICA inc. **CL** Aflo

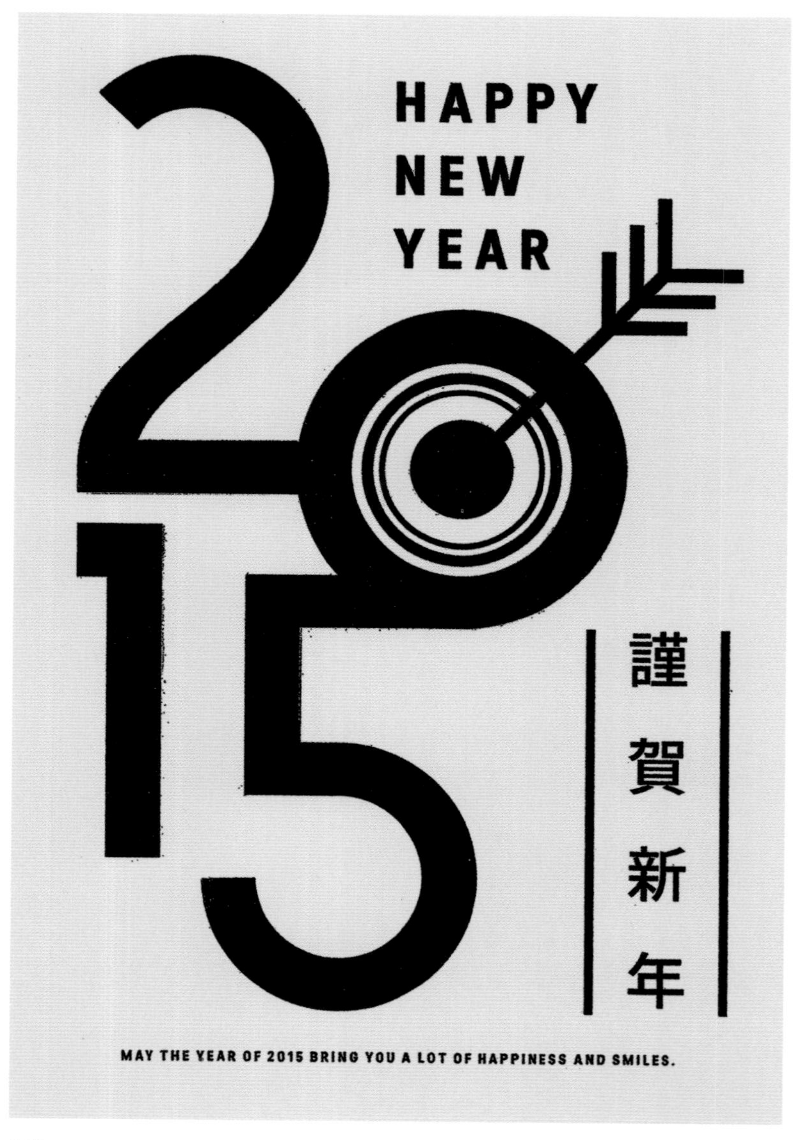

HAVE A GREAT NEW YEAR!

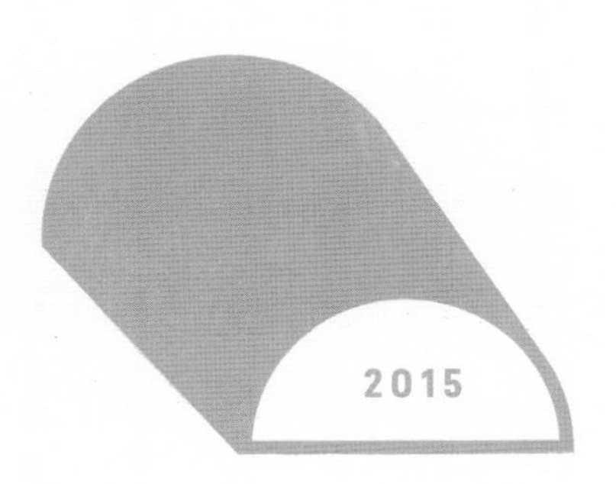

HAVE A GREAT NEW YEAR!

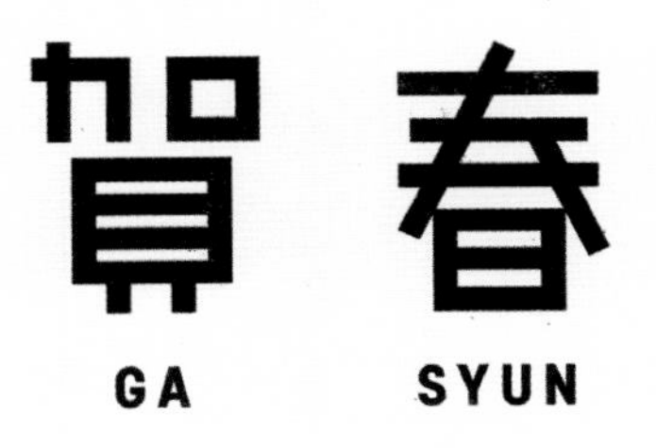

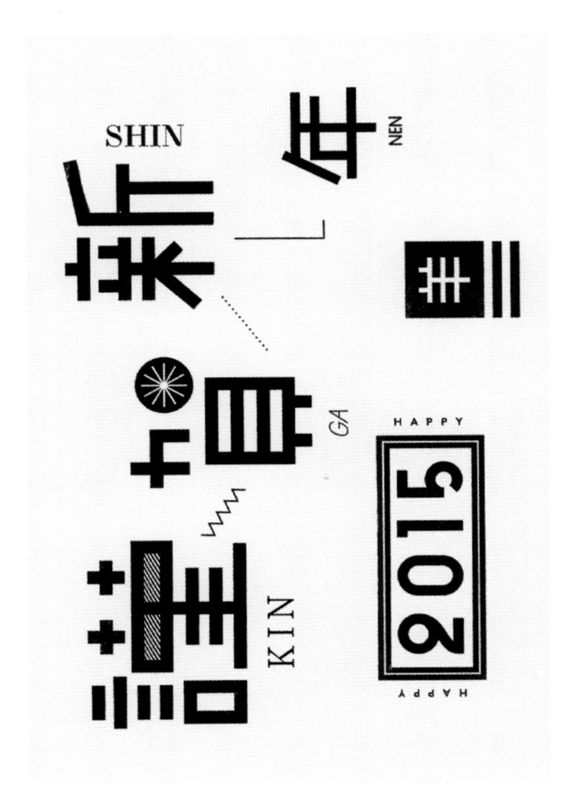

ADC Fall Paper Expo Invitation

This invitation was a student work produced by Max Kuwertz for Experimental Typography Class at Parsons School of Design in New York. Created for the Art Directors Club Fall Paper Expo, the monotone design aimed at visualising the peculiar physical qualities of paper — a medium that is considered 2D for its flat surface, yet is actually 3D as a physical object.

DE Max Kuwertz **CR** Kevin Brainard, Parsons School of Design

ADC FALL
PAPER EXPO
ADC GALLERY 106 WEST 29TH STREET,
NEW YORK
(JUST WEST OF 6TH CITY AVENUE)
THURSDAY, OCTOBER 27TH 5:30—8PM:
ADC MEMBERS FREE;
APC, SP TDC MEMBERS $5.00;
NON-MEMBERS $10.00
PARTICIPATING COMPANIES INCLUDE:
ABART INC., ALDINE INC., APPLE-
TON COATED, FINCH PRUYN AND CO INC.,
FOX RIVER GILBERT PAPER, GMUND
NORTH AMERICA, IGGESUND PAPER-
BOARD INC., MEADWESTVACO, MOHAWK
PAPER MILLS, MONADNOCK
PAPER MILLS, NEENAH PAPER, FRASER PAPERS,
SAPPI FINE PAPER, SCHEUFELEN NORTH
AMERICA, SMART PAPERS, STORA ENSO,
WAUSAU PAPERS, WEYERHAEUSER,
WILLIAMSON PRINTING, YUPO
CORPORATION AMERICA.
PROFESSIONALS ONLY. STUDENTS
WILL BE INVITED TO PICK UP REMAIN-
ING SAMPLES ON FRIDAY, OCTOBER 28TH,
FROM 11AM—2PM.

594 x 396mm
Uncoated paper 160gsm
Screenprinting

Rocking Card

The Rocking Card is a greeting card created by Yurko Gutsulyak to celebrate the year of the horse in 2014. The idea behind the design is a symbolic rocking mantra, in original minimalist design one can find maximum of symbolism. Made of natural cherry wood, every card features a unique texture, in rich wooden yellow and blue ink that sank deep to show the grain.

DE Graphic design studio by Yurko Gutsulyak

145 x 290mm
Double-sided Microwood Cherry
Spot colour
Die cutting, screenprinting, thermo folding

Viaduct Exhibition Invitation

London based furniture and lighting showroom Viaduct celebrated their 25th anniversary in 2014 by exhibiting their favourite pieces as well as upcoming designs. The invitation featured contrasting colours of blue and pink, accented by bold silver foil symbols. Incorporating the logo 'V', these symbols resonated with the mirrored surface used to mount the chairs at the exhibition.

DE Them Design Ltd. **CL** Viaduct

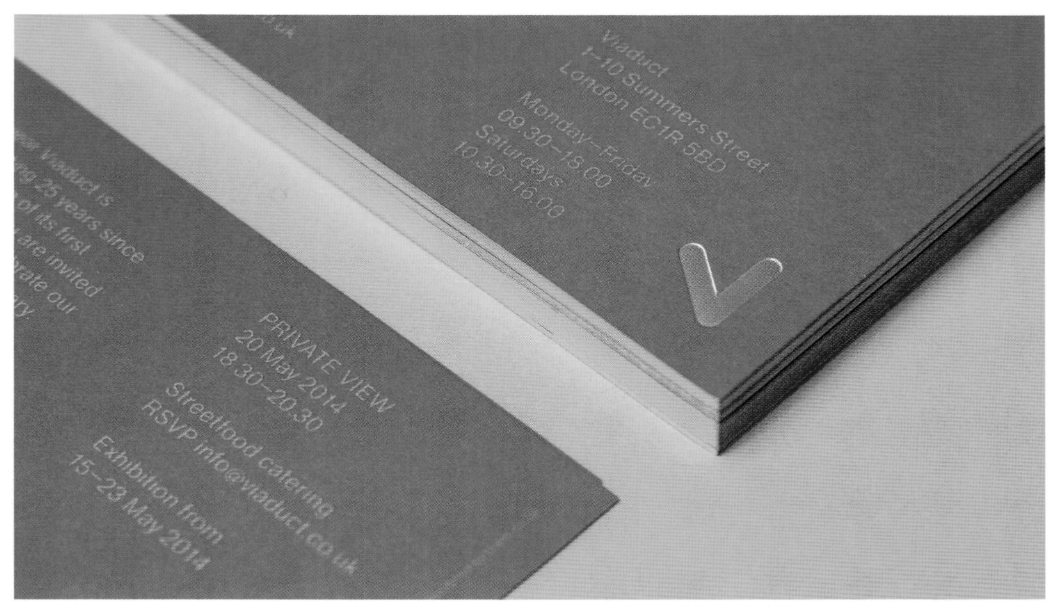

210 x 148mm

Advocate Rough 330gsm
Spot colour
Hot stamping

Chris & Leesa's Great Adventure!

Chris and Leesa's wedding was an intimate event set in cabins in the mountains of the Gold Coast Hinterland, with just twenty invitations going out to close friends and family. A small print run led The Hungry Workshop to focus on craft and detail. Going for a metaphoric theme that marriage is the couple's next great adventure, the studio letterpress printed the invitation in a hand-mixed red ink and tucked inside a rustic kraft envelope. A customised merit badge was hand-sewn onto each invitation as a memento for those who participated in the Great Adventure.

DE The Hungry Workshop **CL** Chris Currie & Leesa Wockner

Do I have to bring a tent or something? I'll have to start airing it out now...
Don't worry.
Please RSVP by 17.02.12
to
Chris
Leesa
currie.christopher@gmail.com
Mountains! Friends! Family! Wedding!
We've organised plenty of accommodation on site! Let us know if you'd like to stay over Saturday night.

Saturday
No really, where?
We can give you directions.
Don't worry.

148 x 105mm
Crane Lettra 300gsm
Spot colour
Letterpress printing

Great Adventure!
When?
Saturday March 17, 2012
Where?
Spring Creek Cottages
You are cordially invited to join in celebrating the marriage of
Christopher Currie
&
Leesa Wockner
No really, where?
We can give you directions.
Or you can Google it. Your choice.
Followed by dinner and drinks on the mountainside.
Don't worry.

Vogue Thailand Launch Party Invitation

Invitation Card design for the official launching party of Vogue Thailand plays with the beautiful contrast of what generally perceived as fashion and Bangkok's true identity. In glamorous gold foil, the fashion magazine's logo was stamped onto the chromatic patterns of waterproof canvas. The allusion to the city's vibrant street vending culture went parallel with Vogue's belief that real fashion happens on the street, not in department stores.

DE FARMGROUP **CL** Vogue Thailand (Serendipity Media Co.,Ltd.)

170 x 240mm | Favini Burano Black 700gsm, Arjowiggins Skin Curious Collection Black 380gsm, waterproof canvas, linoleum | CMYK | Debossing, duplex, hot stamping

International Ibsen Award Invitation

Held every two years, the International Ibsen Award honours an individual or organisation that has brought new artistic dimensions to the world of drama and theatre. Pairing fine typography with intricate graphics, visual elements of the award's print collateral were largely executed in gold foil throughout as a tribute to this great honour.

DE Bleed **CL** Ibsen Awards

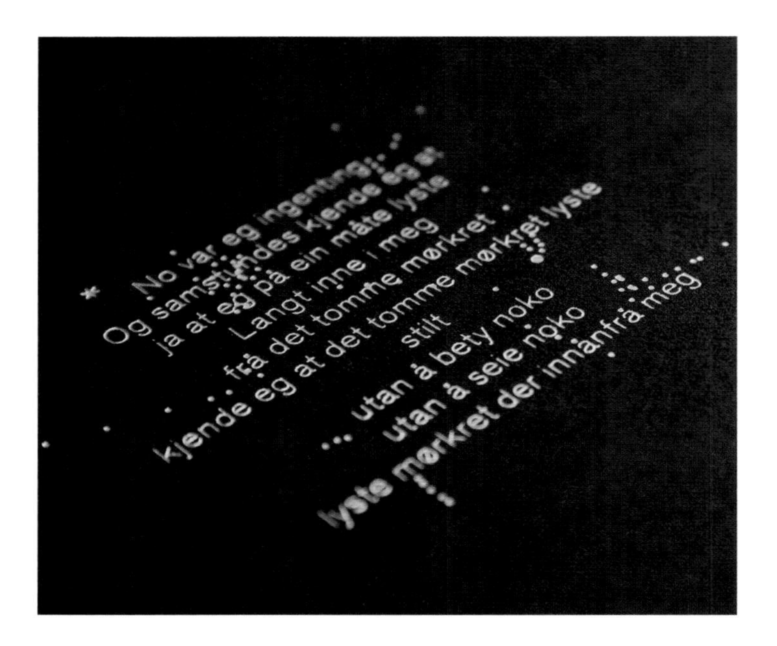

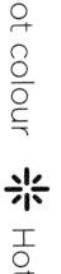

150 x 150mm Spot colour Hot stamping

Lisa Sanders Public Relations Mailer & Poster

Red Peak's mailer and poster designs for Lisa Sanders Public Relations underlined "word" being a PR's territory. To strengthen LSPR's image in potential clients' mind, the mailer serves as a vivid metaphor for how communication can be made right, with a chaotic message awaiting to be spun and sorted out by the recipient. The poster does the same by forming phrases out of LSPR's name. A deliberately limited palette mirrors the agency in correspondence with their corporate colours.

DE Red Peak Branding **CL** LSPR

HOPELESSLY
MISLED
JURIES
BLATANTLY
DISREGARD
ANOTHER
AMAZING
AND
UNEXPECTED
CREATIVE
SOLUTION.
PRAISE
REQUIRED.

LISA SANDERS
PUBLIC RELATIONS

GLOBAL
ACTIVIST
GROUPS
RALLY
AGAINST
CAMPAIGN
AND
ENRAGED
CLIENT
THREATENING
LAWSUIT.
RESPONSE
CRITICAL.

LISA SANDERS
PUBLIC RELATIONS

900 x 600mm (poster)
Mohawk Superfine Smooth Ultrawhite 270gsm
Spot colour
Screenprinting

Service de la Culture de la Ville de Lausanne Greeting Card

A3 Studio was commissioned by the City of Lausanne's Department of Culture to create a greeting card for year 2015. The card features the digits '1' and '5' assembled from minimal geometric shapes in assorted finishings. Juxtaposition of silver foil and natural paper stock was further enhanced by tactile embossing, which provided the card with a three-dimensional effect.

DE A3 Studio **CL** Ville de Lausanne

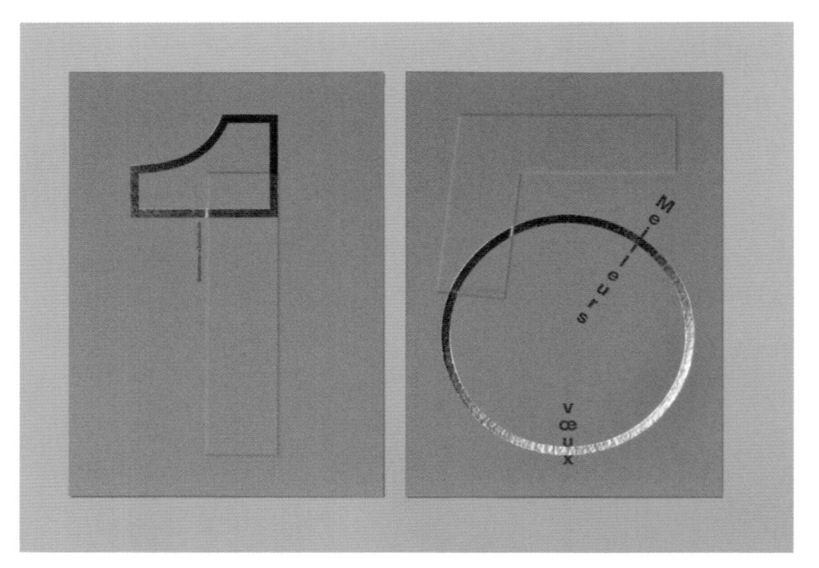

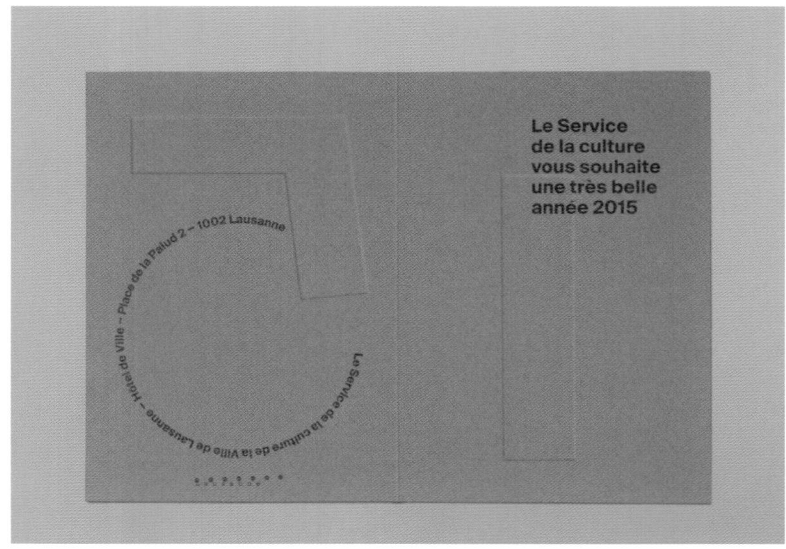

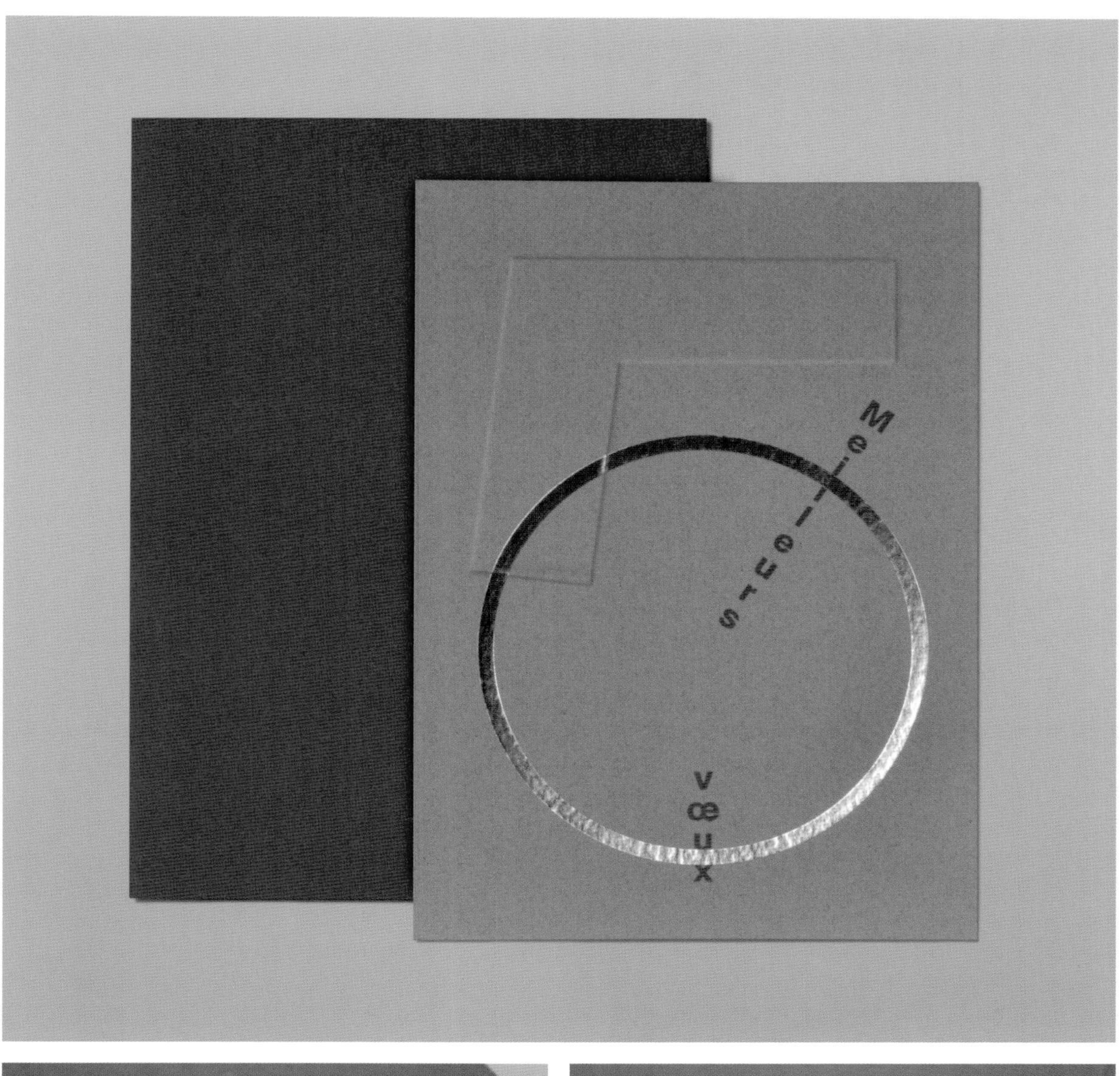

210 x 148.5mm Fischer Papier Tintoretto Melange Cumino 350gsm Spot colour Embossing, hot stamping, letterpress printing

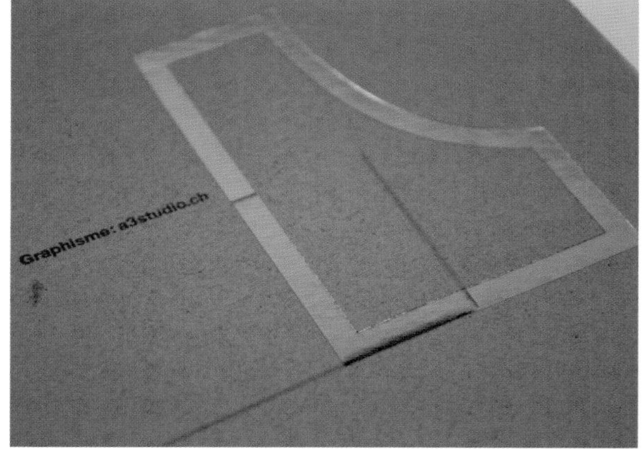

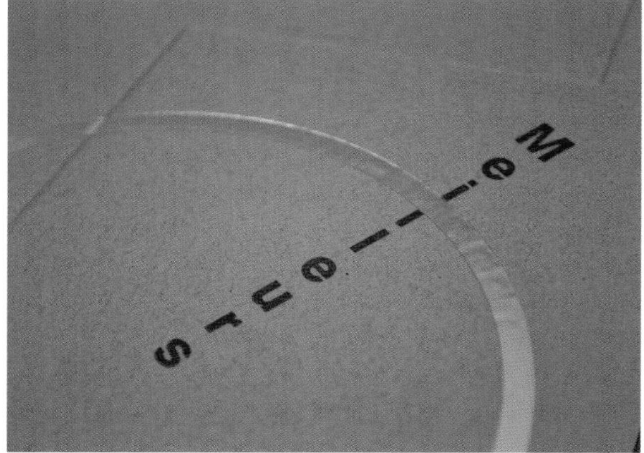

See you next time.

Biography

+ w o l f r a m g r a f i k

Founded in 2012 by visual artist Paschalis Zervas, + w o l f r a m g r a f i k is located in Athens, Greece meditating on images, objects, words with focuses on typography, editorial design, and package design.

page 142-143

3 Advertising

A full-service advertising and design firm based in Albuquerque with clients from around the U.S. With years of experience developing strategies and creating compelling, effective work for a variety of clients in just about every category, 3 is always up for a challenge helping companies succeed.

page 144-145

45gradi

Meaning 45degrees, the acute angle that stings more than others, that is not obtuse, and far sharper than the right and flat one. 45gradi is a graphic design studio based in Milan, Italy specialising in brand care. 45gradi believes that communication is all about choosing the right angle and coming up with striking ideas that are surprising.

page 082-083

A3 Studio

Consisting of graphic designer Yvo Hählen and visual communication designer Priscilla Balmer, A3 produces illustration, graphic design and typography with special attention to its prints quality, while also developing artistic production. Founded in 2011 in Lausanne, Switzerland, A3 is regularly rewarded in Switzerl and abroad.

page 254-255, 294-295

ACRE

Specialising in art direction, branding and advertising, ACRE is idea crafters, T Y Zheng and Jason Song. Likening themselves to "a plot of arable land", ACRE promises to offer a good ground where untapped potential and possibilities within the seed of every good idea flourish at its best.

page 186-189

AD&D

Focuses on graphic design and art direction for signs and logos, campaign shops, and restaurants, AD&D is founded in 2011 by Ren Takaya who has been receiving numerous awards including the One Show Award Merit Award in 2011, 2012, and 2014 and Grand Prix in 2014.

page 060-061

Adam, Nick

Proudly practices strategy and design with Chicago's Firebelly, Adam specialises in creating suggestive esoteric concepts and transforming them into tangible solutions audiences relate to and understand. His work is often collaborative in balancing disciplined form with meaning.

page 258-259

Agnes Herr & Nóra Demeczky

Two freelance designers from Hungary and now based in Budapest. Since 2014, Herr and Demeczky collaborate on experimental projects with special interests in graphic design, identity, typoghy, branding and so on.

page 104-105

Alexey Malina Studio

The studio of Alexey Malina providing services in branding and digital communucation. It is based in Moscow and cooperates with clients all over the world creating unique brand experiences for companies and products.

page 056-057

Anagrama

Specialises in brand development and positioning for any type of projects covering the entire branding spectrum from strategic consulting to fine tuning brand objectives for the company to logotype, peripherals and captivating illustration design, Anagrama is also expertised in the design and development of objects, spaces and multimedia projects.

page 014-017, 156-157

Angelidou, Andia

Working solo, Angelidou usually draws inspiration from unexpected messages hidden in images and words. She presented her installation "The StArt Concept" in a group exhibition and was a member of the animation judging committee at the International Film Festival NIFF in Naoussa, Greece in 2013-2014.

page 138-139

Another Collective

Another Collective is formed in late 2012 and based in Matosinhos, Portugal. The design studio believes in engaging work methodology and provides services in branding, web design and editorial design with a focus on experimentation and exploration of concepts.

page 088-089, 222-223

AURUM INC.

Specialises in logo design, advertisement design, editorial design, package design and web design, AURUM's clients include amana, Tokyo Institute of Art and Design, and Asahiya Publishing Co.,Ltd, etc. The studio is established in 2010 by Yoshiyuki Kaneska.

page 076-077

Bleed

A multidisciplinary design consultancy based in Oslo, Norway and Vienna, Austria. Representing a mix of cultures and disciplines to challenge today's conventions around art, visual language, interaction, media and identity, Bleed creates identities and experiences through concept development, art direction, graphic design and service design.

page 290-291

Brands, Jolien

A graphic designer and photographer currently living in Antwerp, Belgium. Brands is passionately curious about everything. He loves to go to museums, watch movies and travel by every chance he gets. Brand's main inspiration for his work is the nature and simplicity.

page 094-095

Bravo

Bravo Company is a creatively-led design studio based in Singapore. Specialising in identity, brand development, printed communications and art direction, the independent workshop works with a variety of individuals and organisations to deliver thoughtful and engaging design.

page 050-051

Brownfox Studio

An independent design studio based in Jakarta, Indonesia. Established in 2011 by Yusuf Asikin and Fergie Tan, Brownfox Studio's range of work features publication, branding, packaging and multimedia, with clients ranging from local to international.

page 048-049

BÜRO UFHO

BÜRO UFHO is a multidisciplinary design studio based in Singapore delivering beautifully crafted solutions for aspiring clients around the world. Crafting stories through the use of beautiful type, images, illustrations and layout, they believe design challenges status quo and improves life experiences.

page 110-111

Campbell Hay

A multidisciplinary creative agency that strives to create meaningful brands and digital experiences. Since its inception from 2003 by Elly Campbell and Charlie Hay, Campbell Hay has been creating original work for clients across a varied sectors from property and architecture, to fashion and beauty, to larger corporate institutions.

page 154-155

Chan, Furze

Graduated in visual communications at Hong Kong Polytechnic University in 2006, Chan is now a design freelancer who owns 2 brands, "With Her Animal Poetry" and "Ferse Verse". Her works include publication design, web design and illustration.

page 270-273

COMMUNE

A creative team based in Sapporo, Japan specialising in graphic design. Motivated by the will to make things better, COMMUNE works to encourage people and the society for a change. At times, their creations take people by surprise, awakening their emotions, or even moving them to tears.

page 062-063, 068-069

Confetti Studio

A Melbourne-based multidisciplinary design studio headed up by Tomas Shanahan and Kevin McDowell in 2012 offering services across a wide range of mediums, Confetti has also spoken at various design conferences and regularly conducts lectures and workshops at Melbourne universities.

page 080-081, 128-129

cosmos

cosmos is an award-winning studio, they received Silver and Bronze from D&AD LONDON, Silver from Pentawards Belgium, Bronze from One Show Design New York, the Reddot Design Award Germany, Merit Award from NY ADC, from and got into Shortlist of the CLIO Awards, and won the Gold award from JAPAN PACKAGE DESIGN AWARDS, etc.

page 214-215

Defort, Cindy, Kovac, Nicolas

Fashion designer and illustrator Cindy Defort worked for Harricanna and Les grand Ballet Canadiens before moving to Biarritz, France where she launched her own swimwear label - Bain. Being an art director for Bain, Kovac is also a freelance motion and graphic designer in Europe and Canada.

page 044-045

Device Creative Collaborative

Founded by Ross Clodfelter and Shane Cranford, Device is a tight-knit group of creators and collaborators who are dare to pitch attention-grabbing ideas, offering clients a range of heart-pounding design and production skills from art to ads, booze to books, and cuisine to couture.

page 146-147, 274-275

el estudio™

A graphic design studio based in Tenerife, Spain. Co-founded in 2012 by Mauro Sánchez and Fran Monroy, el estudio™ works closely with clients to ensure good design, clear communication and holistic brand projection. Whether they are digital or print, their design is long lasting and environmental, and economic and social sustainable.

page 132-133

Eskimo design studio

One of the leading design agencies in Russia, Eskimo's services cover various creative fields including logo design, brand identity and web design. Started from a small team of likeminded people, Eskimo now works worldwide elaborating subtle ideas with strong visual character for a diverse range of brands and clients.

page 030-033, 198-199

F61 Work Room

An independent design studio and print house based in St. Petersburg, Russia creating identity, packaging, signage, editorial, illustration and typography. F61 believes that design should evoke real emotions and dares to challenge the conservative world by create utterly unique visuals.

page 196-197

FARMGROUP

FARMGROUP is a Bangkok-based creative and design consultancy working across disciplines of art and design, such as branding, art direction, identity, environmental, print, wayfinding, exhibition and installation.

page 288-289

Farnworth, Nicholas

Farnworth is a creative freelancer who aesthetically improves quality and impact of design by exceeding expectations of functionality and purpose.

page 092-093

Fibra

Based in Lima, Peru, Fibra specialises in designing visual identity from the concept of a brand to the creation of a name, to packaging, editorial, and web design. The graphic design studio is also dedicated to the advertising and art direction of each unique project.

page 122-123

Figure
Founded by Jeremy Hall, a multidisciplinary designer living and working in Quebec City, Canada. Hall has won design awards from the Art Directors Club, Grafika, Eye magazine, Slanted, to name a few, and his work has been featured in numerous magazines and books.

page 148-149

Foreign Policy Design Group
Helmed by creative directors Yah-Leng Yu and Arthur Chin, the group works on projects ranging from creative/art direction and design, branding, brand strategy, digital strategy, strategic research and marketing campaign for luxury fashion and lifestyle brands, FCMG, arts and cultural institutions and think tank consultancies.

page 086-087

Fp7 Dxb
An all rounded ad agency under the McCann Worldgroup that has been leading the industry in advertising and design, in the MENA (Middle East & North Africa) region.

page 226-227

Franklyn
Founded in 2012 by partners Michael Freimuth and Patrick Richardson, the Brooklyn-based creative studio works to provide beautiful means to business objectives. Bringing a boutique approach to innovative global brands and startups alike, Franklyn strives to think before act, respond rather than react and stay trill.

page 168-171

Freydina, Maria
With an academic background in graphic design and management from the UK and Russia, Freydina specialises in corporate identity design, print and digital design. She is currently an art director at Proekt Agency in Moscow, Russia as well as Head of Visual Communications Department in Institute for Social Systems and Technologies in Novosibirsk, Russia.

page 100-101

gardens&co.
With specialties in brand identity, communication design and web design, the design studio is good at storytelling through design. Founded in 2005, gardens&co. is a small team of diversified talents and expertise, yet sharing the same belief and value - design is a creation of solution - solution to a better society, healthier planet and happier people.

page 074-075

Graphic design studio by Yurko Gutsulyak
Born in 1979 in Ukraine with an academic background in economics, Gutsulyak began his design career when he moved to Kiev in 2001. Founded his own studio in 2005, the winner of more than 30 international awards was elected as the first president of Art Directors Club Ukraine in 2010.

page 098-099, 246-247, 282-283

GRAPHITICA inc.
GRAPHITICA is a Tokyo-based studio founded by Kazunori Gamo in 2008 for graphic design and illustration.

page 278-279

Grosz Co.Lab
An interdisciplinary design consultancy possessing a diverse creative skill set tempered with strategic insight. Grosz Co.Lab excels in producing work that achieves a balance of analytical and inspiration led design, combining facts and feelings, empathy and commerce with a positive cultural impact.

page 022-023, 164-165

Hey
A multidisciplinary design studio based in Barcelona, Spain. Specialising in brand management and editorial design, packaging and interactive design, Hey shares the profound conviction that good design means combining content, functionality, graphical expression and strategy.

page 040-041

HOUTH
A playful studio based in Taipei which can flexibly integrate creativity, design, graphics, visual and resources. The two "H"s of "HOUTH" represents the two co-founders, Ho Wan-Chun and Huang Chi-Teng; while "OUT" translates their most important faith of pursuing every new thoughts and practices that can jump "OUT" from the established systems or frames.

page 184-185

Imagaki, Chisako
Born in 1989 and graduated in Editorial Design from KOBE DESIGN UNIVERSITY, Imagaki is an independent graphic designer specialises in book design.

page 210-211

Julia Kostreva Studio
California-based graphic designer and art director studied at Maryland Institute College of Arts before she founded her own creative studio and shop. Kostreva works closely with companies for their brand and product lines. For the shop she creates small run and limited edition home goods and accessories.

page 012-013, 034-035, 190-191

Kamimura Typografie Gestaltung
The studio of Makoto Kamimura with an approach based on "Dialogue", "Research", and "Gestalt", they do design as a culture in a broad sense. With a focus on typography, symbols and characters, the team specialises in the field of fashion, architecture, music, art, and academic.

page 150-151, 260-261, 266-267

Kong Studio
A Singapore-based communication design consultancy working to exceed client expectations and standard. Kong Studio's work is known for strength in conceptualisation and efficiency in execution through a wide range of mediums from extensive exhibitions to print collaterals, advertisements and websites.

page 202-205

Kuwertz, Max

Born in 1988 in Düsseldorf, Germany, Kuwertz studied integrated design in Köln, communication design in New York and industrial and product design in Hong Kong. He worked as an art director for Meiré und Meiré before he moved to Berlin to work independently. Together with Yanik Balzer Kuwertz realises design-related objects now.

page 280-281

La Tortillería

Originally founded in an old tortilla factory building in 2003, La Tortillería is a creative company with a passion for images and words with exceptional ability of turning them into an exquisite reflection of an idea. The Monterrey-based studio creates, brands, designs, publishes and advertises blending creativity and functionality to grant each project a unique personality.

page 038-039

La, Brigitte

A 2014 graduate from California State University, La is now working on print and packaging design at a boutique design studio, The Yellow Loft in Los Angeles while devoting herself to developing personal illustration and design projects in spare time.

page 130-131

Lakosi, Krisztián

Lakosi is currently studying graphic design at Hungarian University of Fine Arts in Budapest, Hungary.

page 176-177

Limonov, Lesha

Limonov is a graphic designer, illustrator, freelancer.

page 116-119

Lundgren+Lindqvist

Work to create efficient and interesting communication across various disciplines including identity design, web design and development, art direction and print design, Lundgren+Lindqvist has a wide base of national and international clients that include a variety of corporations, media and cultural institutions.

page 018-021

Mahibuddin, Wildan Ilham

Currently studying in Jakarta, Mahibuddin is an independent graphic designer from Indonesia whose focus is on explorative media and fundamental things. Keen to learn new things and collaborate with talented people, Mahibuddin provides an inconsistent style in every works.

page 264-265

Malin, Victor

Born in Kielce, Poland in 1988, Malin realised a strong passion for visual arts since his childhood. Spending the last three years working in advertising for companies like Ogilvy & Mather, Havas and Leo Burnett, Malin is now an independent art director and graphic designer based in London.

page 108-109

MANMANTEAM Design Office Inc.

Born in Qingdao but now working and living in Beijing, China, graphic designer Tianyang Liu graduated from China Central Academy of Fine Arts and worked in OgilvyOne Worldwide as artistic director before founding MANMANTEAM in 2012. Several of his work is collected by museums and published in Tokyo TDC. He also created the new brand 'TEUAN' in 2015.

page 228-229

Menta.

An independent branding and illustration studio founded in Guadalajara, Mexico by Laura Méndez in 2008. With a passion in carefully crafted and well executed print, Menta. works to deliver effective brand identities that balance classic and contemporary aesthetics, building meaningful human connections that stir up beautiful experiences.

page 052-053, 268-269

Murmure

Murmure, the creative communication agency overturns the limits between art, graphic design and communication via the awakening of the senses, poetry, and elegance of textures, creating original and efficient communications.

page 174-175

My name is

Run by Alexandre Bouichou and Thomas Ibars, the Paris-based art direction and graphic design studio creates print and digital graphics across various sectors, from cultural institutions to businesses. Founded in 2007, My name is designs logotypes, visual identities, books, magazines, record covers, posters, signages, typefaces and websites.

page 252-253

NECKTIE design office

NECKTIE is establish in 2014 by Takeo Chiboshi who designs graphics, web and products in a cross-sectoral manner. His practices also include photography and letter press.

page 070-071

Necon

Works to give clients the right environment to reach their goals, Necon is dedicated to battling irrelevance and creating value through simplicity. Their work is honest, aesthetically appealing and above all, true to its designated function.

page 200-201

not available design

Established in 2009 by kitcheuk, jerrychow and sungbilly, the multidisciplinary studio focuses on branding, art direction and space design that do not follow a set routine available in the market. Daring to be different, NA has received no less than 30 awards, serving the playful public who loves unexpected twists on everyday simplicity.

page 112-115

O'Shea, Michael

Originally from Sydney, O'Shea has created award-winning design for clients big and small for over 15 years. The experienced designer, art director and copywriter has worked extensively across the public, private and third sectors specialising in print, packaging, editorial and digital. The Scottish-based designer established Owen | O'Shea in 2013.

page 058-059

Oddds

Founded in 2013 by designers based in Penang and Singapore respectively, Oddds focuses on graphic design, branding, photography, publication design, and illustration. Their work reflects significantly on behaviours while the team believes in aesthetics and futurism.

page 046-047

Oggian, Marco

A young Italian creative director, graphic designer and photographer working on a wide range of projects such as logo creation, illustration, brand identity, font design and typography, photography, fair stand creation and many more. Oggian won the 2nd place of Behance Italian Portfolio Award while he was 22.

page 134-135

ONOGRIT

Founded by award-winning designers, Janina Braun and Daniela Kempkes, the creative consultancy and design studio based itself on the principle that design is not only an aesthetic style but ambitious problem-solving. The duo successfuly ran ARE WE DESIGNER for 10 years before the startup of ONOGRIT.

page 236-237

Papsuy, Olga

A graphic designer from Moscow, Russia with a professional symphonic musician background and studied art at British Higher School of Art and Design. Papsuy is experienced in doing UX research and designing sites, her focus on design include packaging, brand identity and conveying marketing message through art.

page 024-025

Passport

Informed and influenced by certain destinations and international design culture, Passport is an independent branding and print design studio based in Leeds, UK. creating thoughtful and effective identities with carefully crafted and well executed print through constant research and experimentation. The studio is founded by Jonathan Finch and Rosalind Stoughton in 2012.

page 054-055

Pinmo Design Studio

An all-rounded agency started from a small graphic design studio since 2002, Pinmo has also developed their own brand of retail store, selling their own goods, with a paper lab collected over 200 types of papers for sale. The Taipei based studio also initiates social projects cooperating with artists, designer and even children.

page 090-091

plat

plat, not plæt but pla:t, is established in 2014 by Eunji Lim, Hwayoung Lee, Hyungseuk Cho, and Sangjoon Hwang. Specialises in branding, exhibition, printing, packaging, and web design, the graphic design studio produces narratives from versatile perspective, offering solutions for a diverse range of projects for clients big and small.

page 240-241

PLEASANT by Hank and Maxwell Design Studio

PLEASANT is a Taiwanese design brand creating neat and elegant objects for the public, with a vision to deliver pleasure celebrating and commemorating meaningful days.

page 220-221

Portnova, Masha

Based in Saint-Petersburg and New York, Portnova received a master's degree in graphic design at Saint-Petersburg State University. Her main focuses of interests are branding and web design and she likes structural, simple and geometric style in particular.

page 078-079, 238-239

Porto, Leo

A 22-year-old Brazilian designer based in New York, USA, Porto is a BFA student at SVA and an Intern at Pentagram.

page 224-225

POST—

POST— is an independent, London-based design agency working to achieve clear and intelligent design solutions for identity, print, online and publishing applications collaboratively with clients across sectors from fashion labels and art galleries to bars and restaurants, global or local.

page 084-085

RE

A full service brand and design consultancy. RE's work is known for the courage to amaze and set benchmarks, creating value and success for clients.

page 102-103

Red Peak Branding

A place where creativity, design and strategy meet to transform brands, Red Peak assembles a cross-platform team of award-winning creatives and strategists. The studio's services include brand identity, brand strategy and marketing, naming, photography, packaging and innovation workshops.

page 292-293

Romanes, Ryan

A young graphic designer and art director from Rotorua, New Zealand. Romanes has worked in various places before relocating to Melbourne, Australia. His work has been celebrated in the New Zealand Best Awards and featured by numerous publishers like Domus, Ignant, and The Dieline.

page 120-121

Saint Bernadine Mission Communications Inc.

A communications firm based in Vancouver, Canada. Saint Bernadine Mission Communications strives for strategic solutions that are inspiring, innovative, relevant and authentic. They pride themselves on being media neutral and not being distracted by the shiniest object in the room.

page 026-027

Savvy Studio

A multidisciplinary studio dedicated to developing brand experiences that generate emotions between clients and target audienc. Composed of specialists in areas of marketing, communication, graphic design, industrial design, creative copywriting and architecture, Savvy Studio also collaborates with talented artists and designers worldwide.

page 042-043

Sekido, Kimiko

Born in San Francisco in 1988 and graduated in graphic design from Tama Art University in 2010, Kimiko Sekido is an art director and designer working for DENTSU INC in Tokyo, Japan.

page 064-065

Shito, Motoi

Shito is an art director and graphic designer based in Tokyo, Japan.

page 106-107

Shlygin, Vladimir

A graphic and interaction designer from Moscow, Russia. Since 2008, Shlygin works on various media using different production and execution techniques. In recent years his professional focus is brand identity.

page 024-025, 124-125

sionhsu

A graphic designer from Caotun Town, Taiwan, sionhsu is also a freethinker who works without specific plan.

page 160-161

SomethingMoon Design

The work place of Chi-wai Cheang who called himself a part-time graphic designer but a full-time idiot. Cheang participated in many big yet low profile projects. He likes graphics, literature, photography, music and traveling, in no particular order.

page 276-277

STIT™ Creative studio.

Cofounded by award designer and visual artist Angelos Botsis, the Athens-based studio specialises in branding, packaging, digital and Print media. Strong visual concepts, quality, functionality and innovation are the main characteristics of STIT™'s work.

page 036-037

Studio 10

A Hong Kong-based design house founded by Tak Cheung in 2012, Studio 10 specialises in branding, visual identity, packaging, promotional design, print and environmental graphics.

page 182-183

STUDIO 2×2

Both online and printed materials, STUDIO 2x2 creates coherent visual identity and wayfinding systems for brands and institutions. A small graphic design studio with knowledge from Poland and abroad, the studio is especially enthusiastic about challenging projects where they can take creativity and skills to a new level.

page 166-167

Studio Hausherr

A small graphic design agency based in Berlin, Germany that focuses on corporate, editorial and web design for clients in the field of art, fashion and culture. The studio provides a comprehensive design and visual communication tailored to suit their needs.

page 230-231, 244-245

Studio Mosgroen

Owned by Tyra van Mossevelde, an infographic designer with a 'green heart' based in Utrecht, The Netherlands, Studio Mosgroen works to make the world more understandable by translating complex information into infographics.

page 178-179

Studio Much

Work to bridge the gap between concept and practice, Studio Much generates sound ideas and transforms them into inspiring, well-crafted designs. Founded in 2010 and directed by Times Pang following his graduation in fine art from Academy of Art University, San Francisco, their work is recognised by Type Director's Club, New York and HKDA, Hong Kong.

page 194-195

Studio SP-GD

Founded in 2010 by Surya Prasetya, the graphic design and visual communication studio works with a diverse range of clients developing innovative solutions in print, digital and environmental media. Based in Melbourne, Australia, Studio SP-GD's work derives from a need to clarify and create relevant answers that will visually intrigue.

page 248-249

Studio Worldwide

Established by Dutch designer Thijs van Beijsterveldt and British designer Joel Priestland, Studio Worldwide is a multidisciplinary design practice specialising in crafted and considered graphic design and art direction. Their clients range from arts and culture, fashion and luxury to property development and education.

page 180-181

Taken By Storm

A Dutch design agency that believes in brands with an authentic and inspiring story. In close collaboration with its clients, Taken By Storm pinpoints the most effective strategy and translates content to a clear message. Throughout the process the team remains critical, taking a clear stance. And they always deliver on time.

page 152-153

The Counter Press

Sitting between a traditional private press and a contemporary graphic design studio, The Counter Press works exclusively with hand set wood and metal type on antique presses to create modern typographic design, artwork and limited edition prints. The letterpress workshop is based in an old chocolate factory in London's East End.

page 192-193

The Folks Studio

Working across all possible platforms, providing design and consultancy services in the fields of graphic, communication, branding, product, spatial and digital design, The Folks Studio is a design practice based in Singapore founded by Siewhui Soon and Zhengliang Yang in 2012.

page 072-073

The Hungry Workshop

Focusing on the craft of design with a creative approach to letterpress printing gives the work of The Hungry Workshop a unique aesthetic. A group of designers and printmakers with unwavering attention to detail and strategic thinking, the studio works with people who hunger to create great things, just as who they are.

page 286-287

Them Design Ltd.

Work to make people feel differently about brands through award-winning, strategic creatively-lead ideas, Them Design helps establishing and transforming clients as market leaders with measurable results to their business.

page 234-235, 284-285

Thomas Williams & Co.

Led by creative director Thomas Williams since 2005, the Los Angeles-based multidisciplinary design and development studio has completed more than 320 projects for over 80 clients, both locally and internationally, in a diverse range of sectors including architecture, professional services, publishing, retail, fashion, and hospitality.

page 096-097

Tofu

Native to Tiong Bahru's vibrant Yong Siak Street and Considered itself an institute for the incubation of ideas, Tofu is a young and ambitious creative studio consisting of designers, art directors, illustrators, thinkers, collaborators and dreamers, united in their unwavering quest for meaningful communication, and the perfection of their craft.

page 208-209, 212-213, 216-219

Together Design

Established in 2003, Together Design has a wealth of experience in retail, food and drink, beauty, licensing, arts and culture, and nonprofits through creating brand identity, packaging, POS, publications, style guides, campaigns and digital media. Together's current clients include Boots, Caffè Nero, Divine Chocolate, Royal Mail, Diageo, and The Prix Picket.

page 162-163

Tsai, Chia-hao

Born in 1986, Tsai is a graphic designer at The Eslite Spectrum Corporation who is recently finalised in Asia-Pacific Design No.10 with two of his work.

page 066-067

Tsto

A Helsinki-based graphic design agency focusing on visual concepts and art direction. Tsto was founded by Johannes Ekholm, Jonatan Eriksson, Inka Järvinen, Matti Kunttu, Jaakko Pietiläinen and Antti Uotila.

page 242-243

TU DESIGN OFFICE

Founder and lead designer of the studio, Ming-shang Tu is also a lecturer at Department of Industrial and Communication Design in National Taiwan University of Science and Technology. He has recently won the Good Design Award, IF Design Award and Taiwan International Animation Exhibition and got interviewed by IdN and Computer Arts.

page 126-127

UMA/design farm

Founded by art director and designer Yuma Harada in 2007, UMA/design farm works to provide book design, graphic design, exhibition design, space design, and also total art direction.

page 262-263

Veludo, Marta

Currently working in Amsterdam, The Netherlands, the graphic designer and art director designs and conceptualises for both cultural and commercial fields. Whether in the digital realm or on a three-dimensional scale, Veludo combines different disciplines and mediums to build engaging experiences.

page 250-251

Villarroel, Maggy

A freelance graphic designer living and working in Mallorca, Spain. Villarroel believes in design with strong ideas and simple executions. She also has a strong interest in illustration, hand crafted projects, cooking and travelling.

page 172-173

VOLTA Branding & Digital Studio

A design and digital studio based in Porto, Portugal, VOLTA works in the areas of branding, identity and visual design, graphic and web design, packaging, editorial and advertising. They are also part of WYgroup, the largest communication group in Portugal.

page 028-029

WAAITT™

Specialising in visual identities, typography, print design, websites, photography, video, art direction and creative consulting, WE ARE ALL IN THIS TOGETHER™ is a Copenhagen-based multidisciplinary design studio established by Anders Rimhoff, Jess Jensen, and Dennis Müller in 2011. The name indicates their approach and value of close relationship with clients.

page 140-141, 158-159

Wildhen Design

A full-service creative design studio based in Melbourne, Australia, Wildhen Design sees every aspect of businesses as a place to communicate values. Working to blur the line between art and design, they collaborate with a diverse range of clients from start-ups to established, both local and abroad, across various industries.

page 136-137

Work in Progress

A multidisciplinary design studio creating effective and captivating design solutions based on conceptual thinking and great attention to details with high levels of craft and finishing. Work in Progress' work and style is as varied as their clientele, covering all aspects from brand strategy, identity, art direction, digital media, through to packaging, signage and print.

page 232-233

Yago, Naonori

Yago joined Hakuhodo as a designer after graduated from Musashino Art University in 2009. He has received numerous awards including New York ADC Bronze, and D&AD inbook in 2014, Tokyo ADC pre-nominate, Silver prize from Young Lotus, and Silver prize in Spikes Asia Agency Shoutout in 2012.

page 256-257

Acknowledgements

We would like to thank all the designers and companies who have involved in the production of this book. This project would not have been accomplished without their significant contribution to the compilation of this book. We would also like to express our gratitude to all the producers for their invaluable opinions and assistance throughout this entire project. The successful completion also owes a great deal to many professionals in the creative industry who have given us precious insights and comments. And to the many others whose names are not credited but have made specific input in this book, we thank you for your continuous support the whole time.

Future Editions

If you wish to participate in viction:ary's future projects and publications, please send your website or portfolio to submit@victionary.com